IMAGES
of America

MICHIGAN'S DRIVE-IN THEATERS

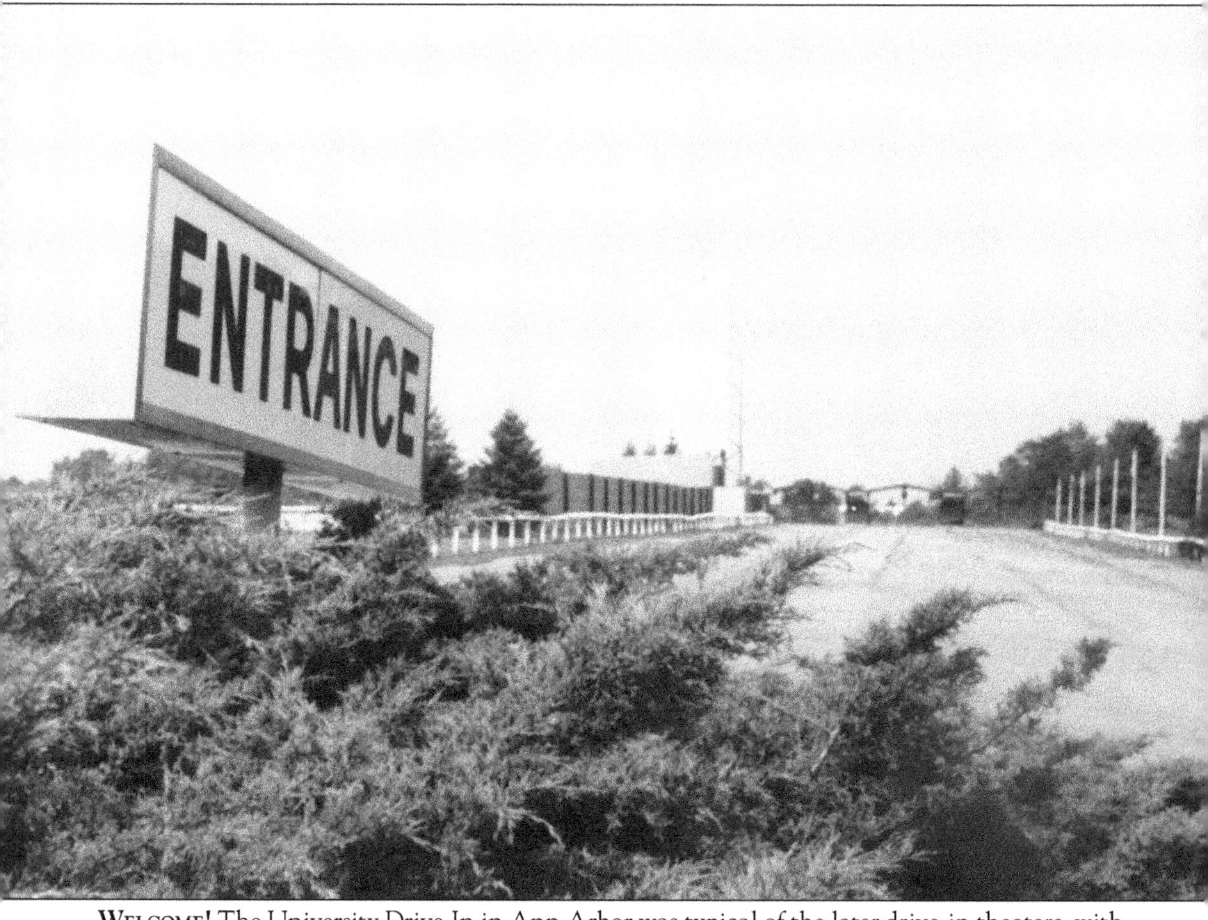

Welcome! The University Drive-In in Ann Arbor was typical of the later drive-in theaters, with a long, spacious drive provided to prevent traffic backups and an attractive appearance for the prospective moviegoer. The University was located on Carpenter Road adjacent to, and visible from, US Route 23. Drivers heading northward on the expressway could, however briefly, see the movie from their passing cars. (Courtesy of the author's collection.)

On the Cover: Fort Drive-In. Pictured is the Fort Drive-In, in all its neon-encrusted glory, shortly after its opening in August 1950. The Fort, later the Fort-George, was located on Fort Street near Eureka in Southgate. The Fort operated successfully until closing in 1990 (see page 28). (Courtesy of Rob Imes/Bacon Memorial Library.)

IMAGES
of America

Michigan's Drive-In Theaters

Harry Skrdla

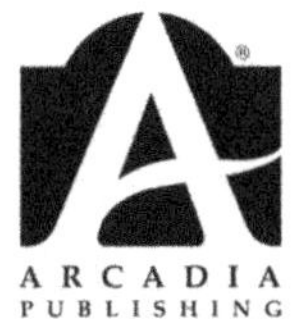

Copyright © 2014 by Harry Skrdla
ISBN 978-1-4671-1233-8

Published by Arcadia Publishing
Charleston, South Carolina

Library of Congress Control Number: 2014931297

For all general information, please contact Arcadia Publishing:
Telephone 843-853-2070
Fax 843-853-0044
E-mail sales@arcadiapublishing.com
For customer service and orders:
Toll-Free 1-888-313-2665

Visit us on the Internet at www.arcadiapublishing.com

To my mother, who first took us to the drive-in, to my friend Dave, who went with me to see many bad horror movies, and to Lily, in the hope that she too can enjoy drive-ins in the future

Contents

Acknowledgments

As with any endeavor of this kind, there are many people to thank. First and foremost among them is Ron Gross, the owner and operator of the michigandriveins.com website; without his many contributions of facts and photographs, this would have been a very different and no doubt lesser work. Thanks also go to his friend and coconspirator Gary Ritzenthaler, of waterwinterwonderland.com, whose magnificent website of all things cool and nostalgic in Michigan should be visited by anyone wishing to fondly revisit the recreations of his or her youth and our collective past. I also have to thank Desiree Anderson, for scanning photographs too numerous to count and that I did not want to deal with. As for the multitude of other photographic sources, I would like to thank Curt Peterson, for the many photographs of theaters he managed "back in the day"; Tosha Shenkenberg, of Goodrich Theaters; Steve Rossio, of the Portage Library; Karolee Tobey, of the Grand Rapids Library; Ron VanTimmeran, of Celebration Cinemas; Beryl Gabel, of the Lakeshore Museum Center; Ron Imes, for helping to recover the Fort picture from the Wyandotte library; Fred Goldberg, of Community Theatres; Karen Jania, of the Bentley Library; Jeff Raterink, for his beautiful Cascade photographs; Mike Veh, without whose original Toledo Drive-In photographs I probably would not have been inspired to continue these many years later; Bill Frisk, whose expertise could not be adequately cataloged in this limited space; and last but hardly least, Mike Hauser, the god of all things historic, for his many useful leads, encouragement, and general all-encompassing expertise regarding theaters. Unless otherwise noted, all images appear courtesy of the author's collection.

I would also like to thank my acquisitions editors at Arcadia, Jacel Egan and Maggie Bullwinkel, for their support, prodding, and general helpfulness in shepherding this project to fruition.

Introduction

Few things are more iconically American than the drive-in movie theater.

Oh, sure, you have your mom and apple pie, but neither of them holds a candle to the drive-in. Your mom could tuck you in at night, all warm and comfy in your pajamas, but then would she show you a movie? And would she bring you popcorn, a cheeseburger, and a Coke? That's loads better than an old piece of apple pie. And when you reached adolescence and started to long for the opposite sex, would mom offer a dark place for you and your sweetie to canoodle? Probably not.

No, there was nothing like the drive-in movies—not that the movies were particularly the point. It was always the drive-in moviegoing experience that was special. From the beginning, the picture was always a bit dim, and the sound, issuing from tiny three-inch speakers, was dubious at best. But at the drive-in, an entire family could go to the movies for one low price and not have to dress up, worry about rowdy or restless children, or make dinner. Moviegoers could snuggle with their honey, usually without fear of interruption; imbibe the beverage of their choice; and converse about the merits of the film, their partner's amorous inclinations, or whether little Susie and her boyfriend really did just "fall asleep."

At the drive-in, the old, obese, or infirm could attend a movie without worry about whether the accommodations were of sufficient comfort, the seats of sufficient breadth, or restrooms and snacks within sufficient proximity. You could park as close as you cared to the concession stand, and your comfort was as great as the interior of your car could provide. And in the 1950s and 1960s, cars could be pretty comfortable.

No, there was nothing quite like the drive-in. And for those of a certain age, the birth, maturation, and ultimate decline of the drive-ins mirrored their paths from childhood, through adolescence and adulthood, and ultimately into middle age. No wonder they are remembered so fondly and as such an integral part of so many lives.

But the drive-in did not always exist, not before 1933 anyway. It was the brainchild of Richard M. Hollingshead, who, in the early 1930s, wanted to branch out from his managerial position at his father's successful Camden, New Jersey, manufacturing company, Whiz Auto Products, makers of auto polishes, waxes, greases, and other supplies, and was looking for a Depression-proof way to do so. After much consideration, he decided that the last things that the public would abandon, even during the Depression, were cars and movies, and their combination wrought the miraculous alchemy that was the drive-in theater.

After consulting with engineers at Camden's RCA research laboratories to determine whether it was possible to broadcast sound from speakers clustered at a distant movie screen to cars parked before it (without deafening those patrons closest to the front), and experimenting with a 16-millimeter projector on the hood of his family's car (to project a movie onto a sheet stretched between trees in his yard), Hollingshead decided it was a viable idea.

Patent No. 1,909,537 for a drive-in theater was filed by Richard Hollingshead on August 6, 1932, and exactly 10 months later, on June 6, 1933, the world's first drive-in opened on Admiral Wilson Boulevard between Camden and Philadelphia.

Unfortunately for Hollingshead, even though technically patented and licensed to him alone, the drive-in was such an easily mimicked creation that the second one constructed was built without his participation or his license.

But despite the ease with which a person could construct and open his or her own drive-in, their advance was slow. In part because of the depressed economy, in part because of the technical difficulties inherent with giant, blaring screen-mounted speakers (and the unwelcome time delay to distant cars) and dim projection, and in part because of difficulty in obtaining current films at reasonable prices, the drive-ins remained a relative rarity for years.

Hollingshead himself was, from the beginning, busily suing drive-in operators across the country for patent infringement, with limited success. And even as drive-ins in general slowly gained momentum, by 1936 after only a few years of operation, the world's first drive-in was sold;

a victim of high film-rental costs. The buyer "moved" it to Union, New Jersey, where he could secure better rental terms, with apparent success.

Drive-in construction continued until the beginning of World War II, when it came to a standstill. But afterward, driven by postwar recovery and the baby boom, it began to accelerate. What had been a mere 100 drive-ins before the war, soared to 300 by 1947 and an astonishing 1,700 by 1950. By 1958, the United States had reached its peak with around 3,700 drive-ins.

The first drive-in in Michigan, the Eastside, opened north of Detroit in 1938 and was only the 10th drive-in in the country. The second drive-in in Michigan, the Westside, opened in 1940.

Michigan's drive-in growth generally paralleled that of the rest of the country, with numbers remaining low until after the war and then rising. Although all drive-in statistics should be taken with a grain of salt, since even reliable sources such as the *New York Times*'s and *Motion Picture Herald*'s numbers often vary widely, it appears that by 1947 Michigan had about 13. Compare that with the reported 120 in 1955 and 132 in 1964. Although there were probably a total of about 160 different drive-ins in the state over the years, they did not all exist simultaneously. The total at any one time was, according to best estimates, about 134.

At their peak, drive-ins were, in the best examples, part movie theater and part theme park.

Because the biggest profit center for a drive-in was always the concession stand, the longer patrons could be induced to stay on the property the better profits were likely to be. So in an effort to attract as many families as possible and get them to stay as long as possible, drive-ins began to employ methods unavailable to the indoor theaters.

Playgrounds were installed. Although in most drive-ins these might just consist of the usual slides, swings, teeter-totters, and monkey bars, in the more deluxe establishments, elaborate installations proliferated. Small-scale railroads were introduced, as were boat rides where tiny watercraft sailed around a water-filled tank in an endless regatta. In 1943, the Westside drive-in installed the nation's first drive-in-theater merry-go-round. Pony rides and petting zoos appeared. Picnic areas were provided, as were indoor viewing areas for walk-up customers. The Gratiot offered, among other services, an attendant who walked the lot cleaning windshields for free. Young mothers could take advantage of bottle-warmers and diaper services.

In order to further improve food sales, some drive-ins had portable concession carts roaming the lots and additional activities were scheduled, often in advance of dusk and the actual start of the movies. Beauty contests, car rallies, dance competitions, and celebrity personal appearances were held. Drive-in going was an event unequalled by even the fanciest indoor theater.

But nothing lasts forever. The golden era of the drive-in was during the decades of the 1950s and 1960s. Although still popular, by the 1970s, their economics and demographics had begun to change.

With the increasing popularity of television, first in black and white, then in the mid-1960s, in color, families could find entertainment without even leaving home. It was the era of TV dinners, and even drive-in going became less attractive. In the 1970s, the oil crisis made driving less financially desirable, and the drive-ins again suffered. Also, the drive-ins had never had much luck in securing first-run films. Indoor theater operators had continued to pressure distributors to stonewall the drive-ins' attempts to obtain newer movies, and as a consequence the outdoor theaters were forced to show second- or even third-run films. Although during their peak years, the drive-ins probably would have had enough clout to force the distributors to provide them with better product, they never used it. Consequently, moviegoers who wanted to see the latest films usually gave their business to the indoors.

In some cases, this did not matter. A mother taking her children to the movies might not mind that the Disney film was not the most recent one. And teens out on a date with amorous intentions might not worry about the film either. In fact, an entire industry had grown up within the larger motion picture industry of smaller studios producing low-cost films specifically for drive-in consumption. Science fictions and horror films were popular staples, as were adventure and action movies. Films like *The Blob*, in 1958, and *Night of the Living Dead*, in 1968, were specifically tailored for the drive-in audience. And unlike the early days, when drive-ins only offered one film per showing, double (and even triple) features had become the norm, and even dateless teenagers could fill a car, drink the ill-gotten beverage of their choosing, and while away an otherwise boring Saturday night with perhaps five hours' worth of what drive-in icon Joe Bob Briggs characterized as "Blood, Breasts and Beasts." The young drive-in audience that had begun going as pajama-clad children in the 1950s or 1960s was now navigating the perils of adolescence in the 1970s, and found that the drive-in product had changed to suit their needs. Meanwhile, family viewing had tapered off with the convenience of the television and the better product and presentation quality of indoor theaters. But even this evolution was to be short-lived.

In the early 1980s, several events outside of the drive-in operators' ability to control conspired to all but doom them.

First, the rule of thumb when building drive-ins had always been to construct them on major roads close enough to towns to be easily accessible, but far enough away so that the acreage required could be had at an affordable price. About 30 years later, the cities and suburbs had spread outward and all but engulfed them. The owners of the still-profitable Gratiot Drive-In, on Gratiot Avenue near 13 Mile Road in Roseville, a northern suburb of Detroit, sold the property for a reported $10 million in 1984; the property was vacant farmland in 1948 but was surrounded by strip malls by 1984.

Second, in the early 1980s, the first commercially available videotapes appeared, and with them came video rental stores. Much of the teen-oriented product, the horror and science fiction and soft-core porn that had been unavailable except at the drive-ins, became available on video and was now viewable in the privacy of one's home.

Additional factors contributed in varying degrees to the demise of the drive-ins at this time. First-run product was still unavailable in most cases. Movies like *Return of the Jedi* would not be distributed to drive-ins, as a matter of studio policy, until a year after their initial releases. Drive-in infrastructure—the miles of buried cables connecting the speakers, the condition of the screen surface (a typical screen had to be repainted every few years or serious brightness problems ensued), the aging screen superstructure—either required regular maintenance or, after some 30 years, needed to be replaced. Both were costly investments that a struggling drive-in could hardly afford.

In 1958, Michigan was ranked 15th in the number of drive-ins by state; in 1972, it was ranked 9th; in 1982, it was 4th. But rather than signifying a healthy growth in its numbers, as in years past, this ascent in the rankings highlighted the woeful decline in the total numbers of drive-ins across the country. By 1987, Michigan was tied with New York for fourth place, each possessing only 48 drive-ins, while the temperate states of California and Texas fared better with 113 and 56, respectively. The only Midwestern state that manage to retain a sizable drive-in population over the years was Ohio—possibly because so many were located in rural locations unscathed by increasing property values.

The early years of the 1980s were the last years of the drive-ins as a pervasive cultural entity. They began to fall like dominos. Often, drive-ins that were carefully winterized and closed for the season—their stainless steel counters and grilles covered in plastic and their speakers meticulously inventoried and stored—never reopened.

In 1984 alone, at least a dozen Michigan drive-ins were torn down, including the once great Gratiot, Algiers, Dearborn, and Westside. In 1985, probably another 10 vanished. Some were dismantled. Usually, their screens were relocated to other, more viable theaters and were used to convert them to twins or triplexes. Screens salvaged from the Wayne and Algiers were used in this way to further enlarge the already ravenous five-screen Ford-Wyoming. In other cases, strip malls or big-box stores, such as Target and Meier, replaced them almost immediately. And in still other cases, economics drove them under. But since their locations were of no value as retail property, they were left as ghost drive-ins at the mercy of vandals and the elements.

And such is the story of the drive-ins.

As of this writing, the newest threat to the existence of the few remaining is digital projection. As indoor theaters convert to digital (mostly because of the lower cost inherent in not having to ship around weighty and cumbersome film reels), the drive-ins are again being left behind. The cost of converting from analog to digital can be on the order of $60,000 per screen—an investment out of reach for the often cash-strapped drive-in owners.

As of this writing, there are eight drive-ins still operating in Michigan and fewer than 350 in the entire country. Almost certainly by the time you read this there will be fewer.

But the drive-in is not dead yet, far from it. Some, such as the Capri, in Coldwater, and the Getty 4, in Muskegon, have made the digital investment with the intention of remaining in operation for the foreseeable future. And a renewed interest in the drive-in, by those baby boomers who remember them fondly and by a newer generation only now discovering the pleasures of this all-but-vanished icon of our moviegoing past, seems to suggest that they might not be doomed after all. Some may always be with us, as a living memento of a simpler, more innocent time. We can only hope.

Note: In addition to recounting their history, this book attempts to list all known Michigan drive-in theaters, excepting those that were portable or temporary installations. Facts and statistics contained herein are the best available but will no doubt contain some errors. Sorry. Whenever possible, the drive-ins are pictured, but it is not possible to illustrate every single one since some, especially in rural areas, may never have been photographed at all. Despite this, I hope you find your favorite here and are reminded, if only for a moment, of those warm, popcorn-scented summer nights long ago.

One

Dawn of the Drive-In

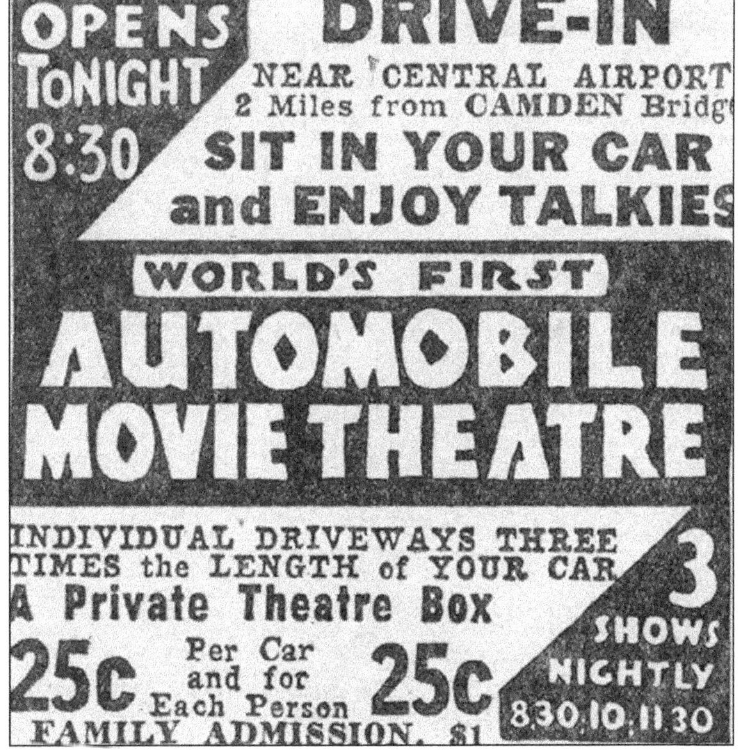

An Opening Night Ad. This newspaper ad is fairly succinct. On June 6, 1933, the world's first open-air theater, located just outside of Camden, New Jersey, was opened for business. The ad does not even mention what movie is to be shown; the fact that this was the world's first drive-in trumped that detail.

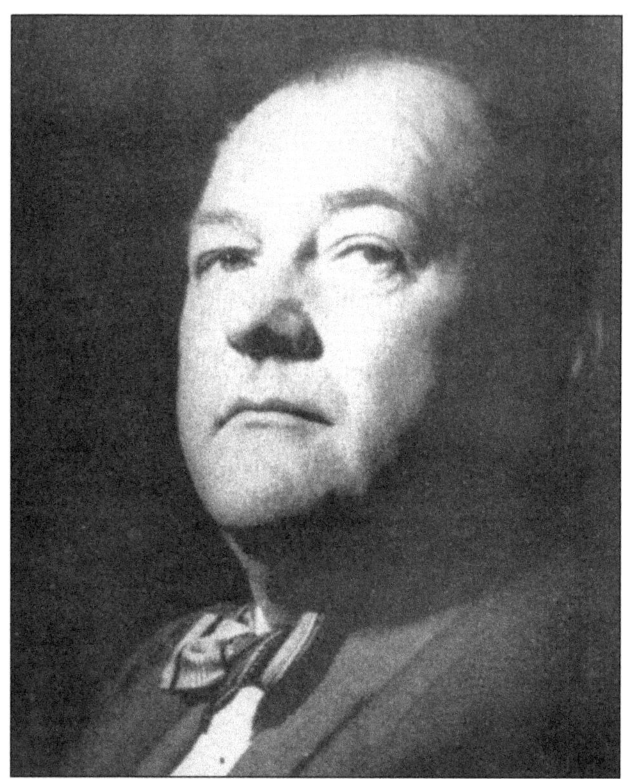

Richard M. Hollingshead. The father of the drive-in was looking for a Depression-proof business. He reasoned that the last things American's would relinquish, even during economic hardship, were their cars and their moviegoing habit. After experimenting with his family car, a 16-millimeter projector on its hood, and a sheet nailed between trees near his driveway, he decided it was a practical idea. He partnered with his cousin W.W. Smith, and together they transformed his driveway experiment into a practical scheme.

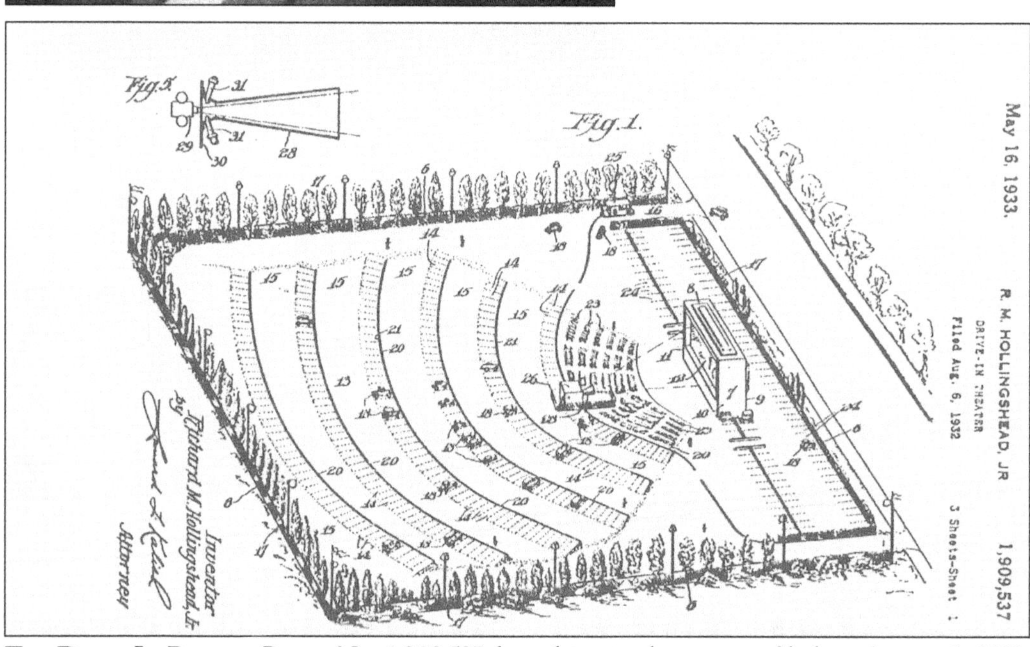

The Drive-In Patent. Patent No. 1,909,537 for a drive-in theater was filed on August 6, 1932, exactly 10 months before the opening of Hollingshead's first drive-in. It includes, along with the "arcuate arrangement" of parking spaces, the possibility of a seating area for walk-up patrons, and a device to blow compressed air on the projection window to prevent bugs from accumulating in the projector beam.

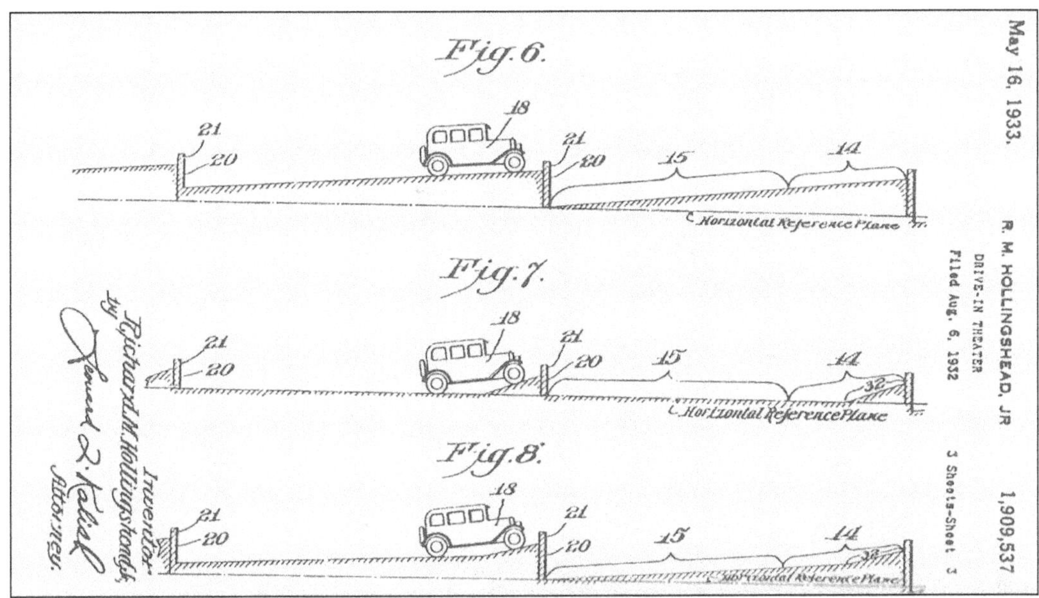

HOLLINGSHEAD'S RAMP SCHEME. The heart of the drive-in patent was the idea of individual sloping parking spaces, originally with a stop board for the front tires, which allowed the occupants to view the picture without their view being obstructed by the cars in the next row. Ultimately, this would be at the core of the Supreme Court case contending that the drive-in idea was inherently unpatentable.

DRIVE-IN CONSTRUCTION. Construction of the first drive-in commenced on May 16, 1933, when the patent was officially granted. Laborers were hired from the township relief rolls with pay ranging from 20¢ to 40¢ per hour, but almost immediately, union construction workers appeared demanding the employment of their members at a rate of $1 per hour. Fistfights ensued, but an eventual compromise allowed the theater to be completed in only three weeks.

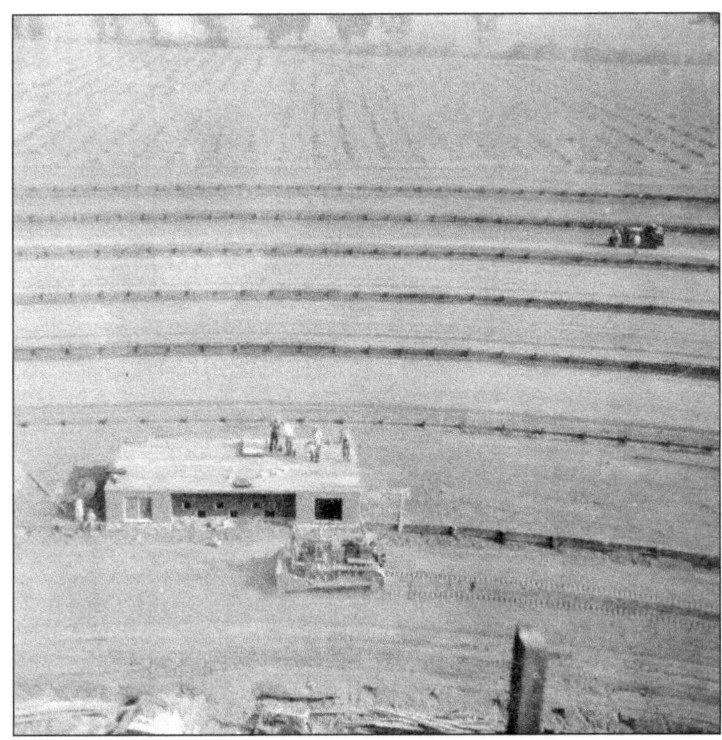

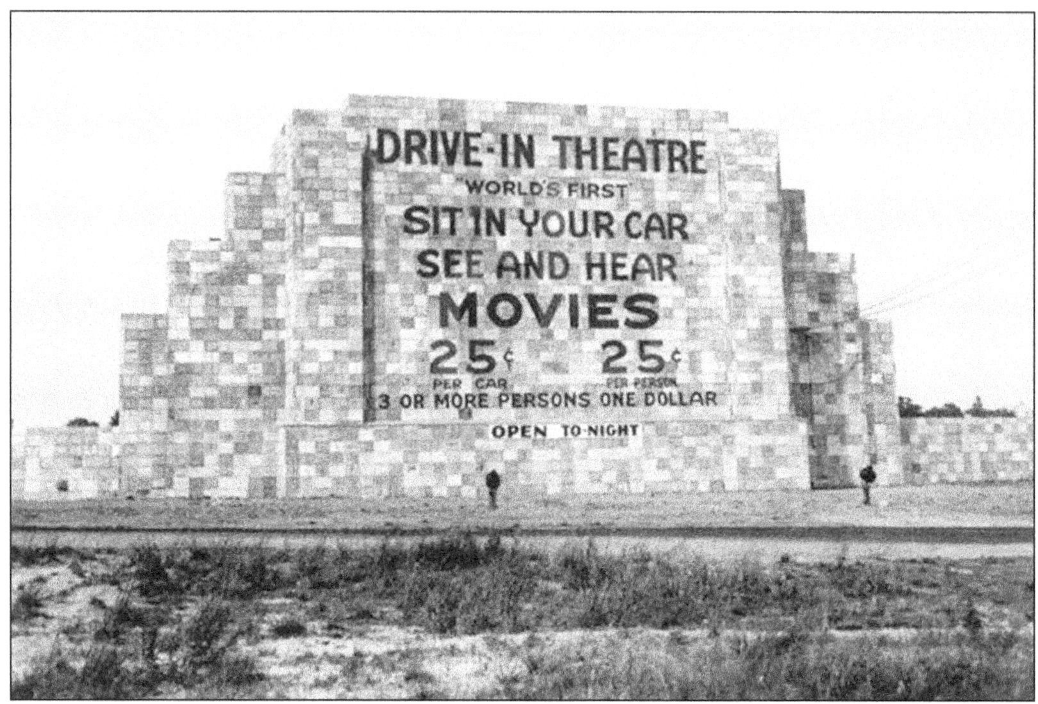

The World's First Drive-In Theater. The screen tower of Hollingshead and architect Howard E. Hall's drive-in resembled a Mayan temple. There was no question as to the rate structure for potential patrons; although, the initial plan of showing three films a night proved impractical after only a couple of days, and a two-films-a-night policy was adopted thereafter.

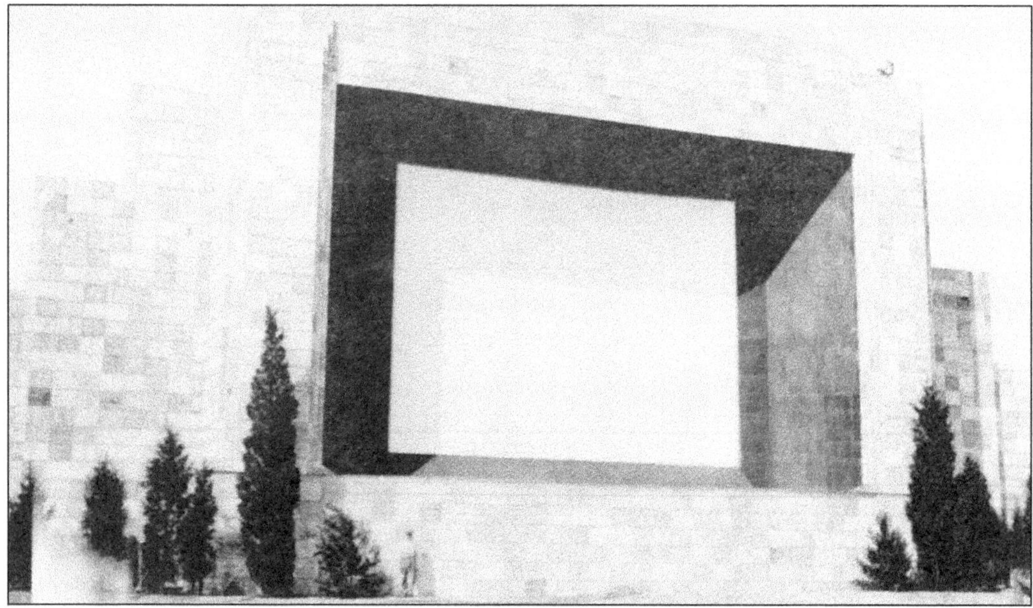

The Screen House. The original drive-in, along with all other early drive-ins, had the screen tower constructed as a sort of shadow box; the thinking was that it would shield the screen from extraneous light. Later, designers concluded that this was unnecessary. Although not visible in this photograph, the speakers were also contained within the screen house.

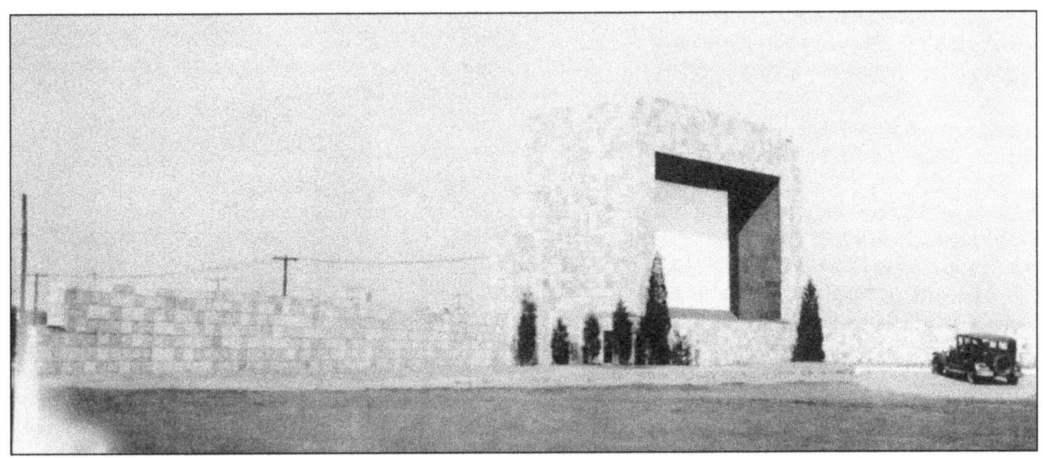

The Finished Lot. Although the lot was sparsely decorated at first, ultimately over 200 trees, ranging in height from 12 to 20 feet tall, were located around the perimeter. A fence was also constructed to restrict free viewing from outside the property. The 60-foot-high screen house contained a 30-by-60-foot screen situated 12 feet above the ground.

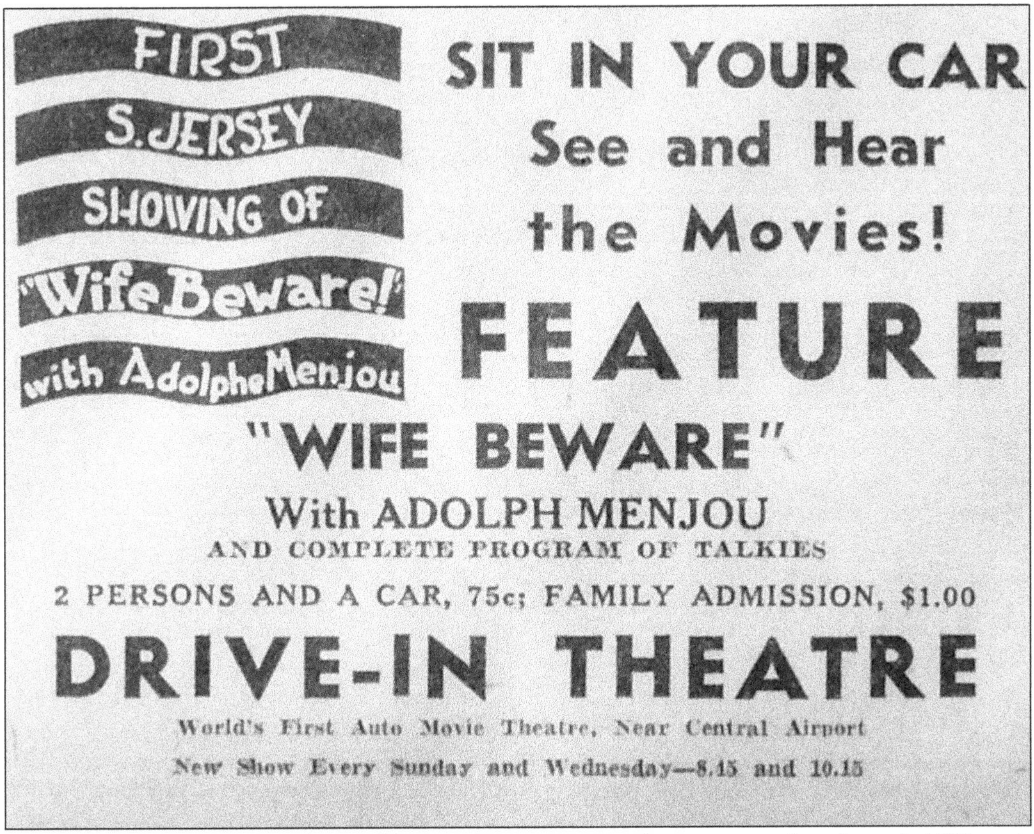

FIRST S. JERSEY SHOWING OF "Wife Beware!" with Adolphe Menjou

SIT IN YOUR CAR
See and Hear the Movies!

FEATURE
"WIFE BEWARE"
With ADOLPH MENJOU
AND COMPLETE PROGRAM OF TALKIES

2 PERSONS AND A CAR, 75c; FAMILY ADMISSION, $1.00

DRIVE-IN THEATRE

World's First Auto Movie Theatre, Near Central Airport
New Show Every Sunday and Wednesday—8.15 and 10.15

An Opening Night Ad. The world's first drive-in movie theater opened on June 6, 1933, with Adolph Menjou's three-year-old film *Wife Beware*. From the very beginning, it was difficult for the drive-in to get recent films to show, due to the unwillingness of the distributors to supply them. When the most-recent previous showing at a small local indoor theater had cost that theater $20 per week, the rental of *Wife Beware* cost $100 a day

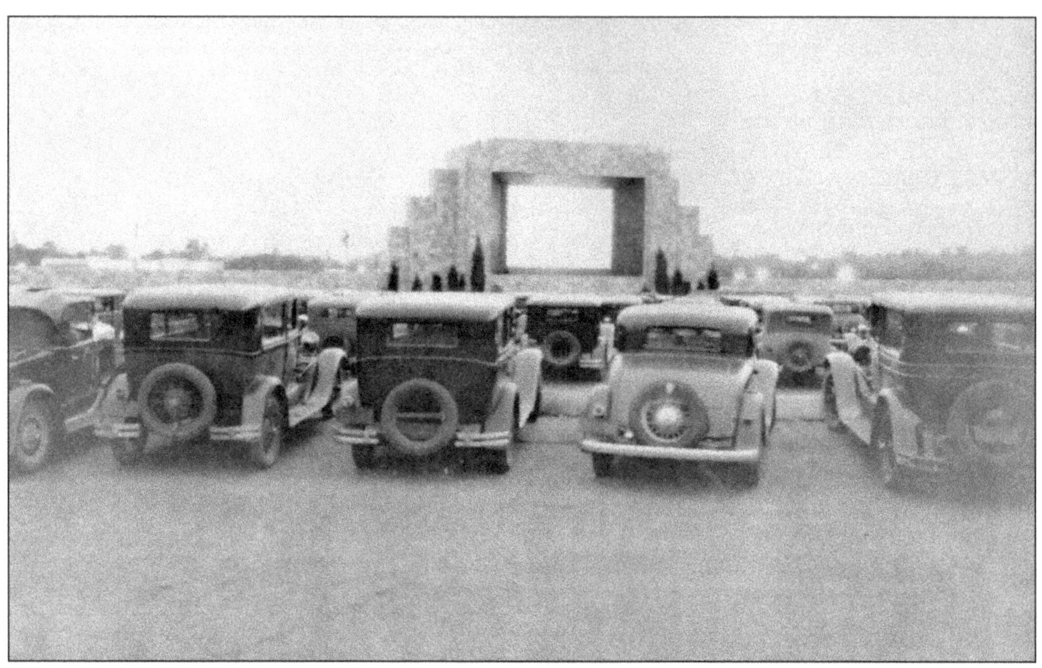

Opening Night. The night of June 6 was clear and warm—ideal drive-in weather—and the first show was well attended. Reviews the next day were generally favorable and predicted a future for this new and novel entertainment. The cost of the drive-in was probably around $20,000–$30,000. After the first week, beer and lunches were available for purchase.

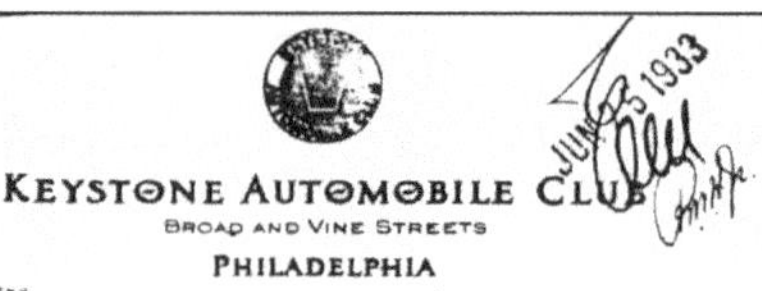

KEYSTONE AUTOMOBILE CLUB
BROAD AND VINE STREETS
PHILADELPHIA

J. BORTON WEEKS
PRESIDENT

June 23, 1933

Mr. R. M. Hollingshead, Jr.,
Park-In Theaters Corporation,
330 North Seventh Street,
Camden, New Jersey.

My dear Mr. Hollingshead:

It was my privilege to be among those attending the opening performance at your Theater

The principal impressions that I took away with me from this first of America's Automobile Movie Theaters were first, the wonderful convenience of being able to attend such an entertainment without hunting for a place to park and without alighting from the car. What a wonderful accommodation this must be for aged persons, invalids and others who could not well mingle with the crowds in the indoor theaters. My second impression was the great comfort of being able to sit in your own car, smoke or talk as and when you wanted, knowing that you would not disturb anyone else, and enjoy at the same time the cool evening air.

I was asked to give critical attention to the arrangements and to the performance, and to offer constructive criticism. I had nothing to offer but words of praise. The project has been finely conceived and splendidly executed for the convenience, comfort, and entertainment of the motiring public.

The Camden Drive-In Theater, brought into being by W. W. Smith and yourself, is destined to be copied throughout the country, and very probably throughout the world. I congratulate you both on your vision and courage, and the City of Camden on being the fortunate locality which can proudly claim credit for the world's first Automobile Movie Theater.

Cordially yours,

President.

Opening Night Reviews. Mindful of the value of good publicity, Hollingshead and Smith invited several local dignitaries to the opening night show for the purpose of eliciting their impressions of the drive-in. J. Borton Weeks, of the Keystone Auto Club, in Philadelphia, was one such luminary. Judging by his remarks, he was likely to be an ardent future enthusiast.

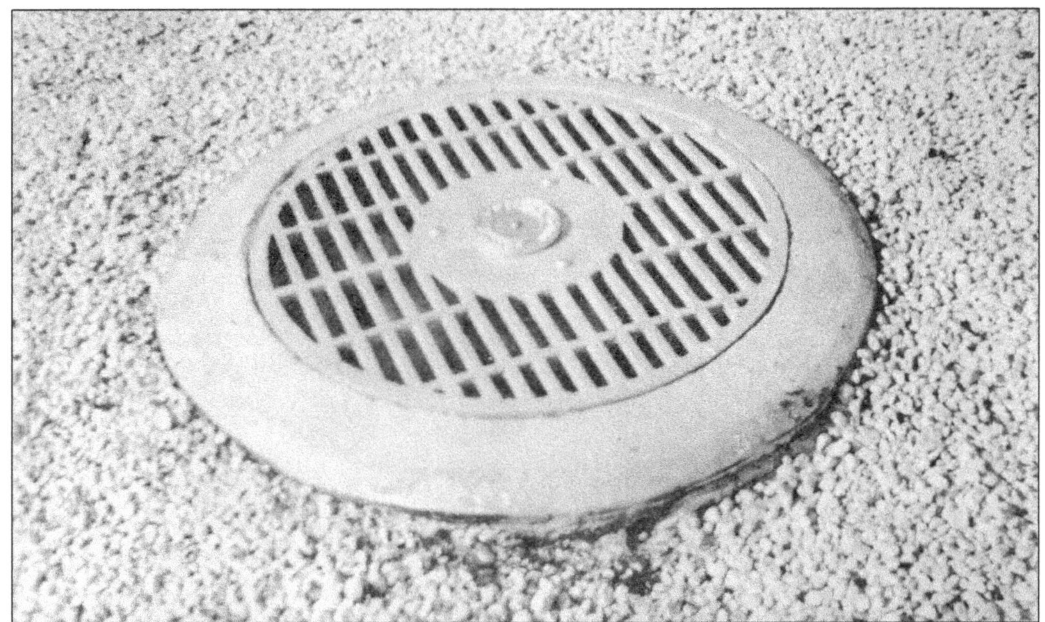

INGROUND SPEAKER. The speakers housed in the screen tower were a problem from the beginning. Hollingshead's son recalled that a gunshot fired in a Western movie would not be heard in the back rows until about the time the cowboy was hitting the ground. The neighbors were also far from enthusiastic about the incessant noise disturbing their nightly slumber. In an early attempt to fix these problems, inground speakers beneath the cars were tried, but they were a dismal failure.

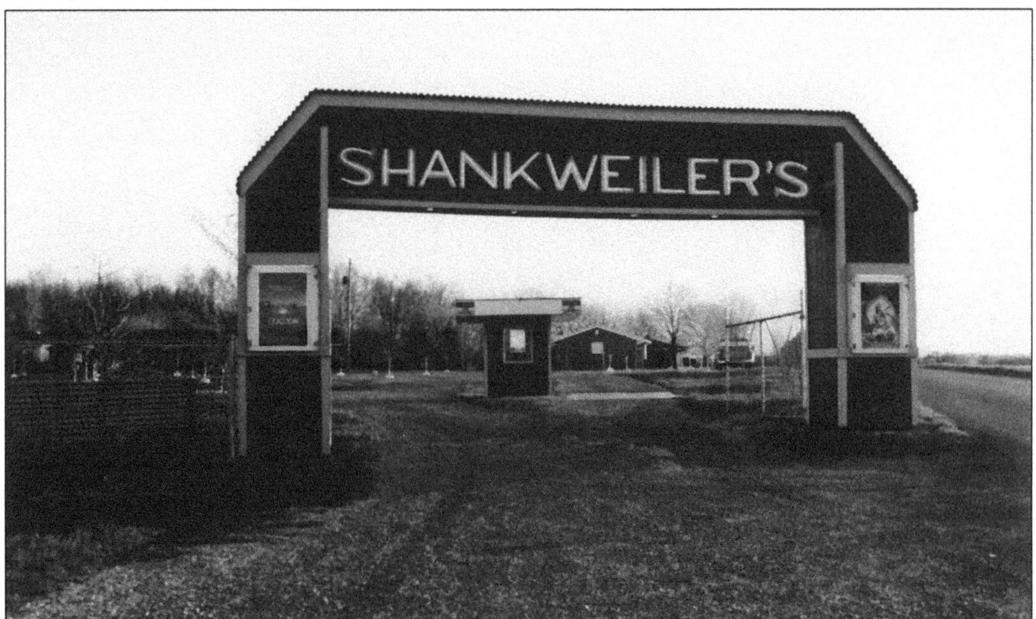

THE SECOND DRIVE-IN. Despite Hollingshead's intent and attempt to sell licenses for the construction of subsequent drive-ins, the second drive-in was built without his permission or knowledge. Wilson Shankweiler, who owned a hotel in the tiny town of Orefield, Pennsylvania, attended one of the early shows at the Camden drive-in and saw no reason that he could not build such a thing back home. (Courtesy of Susan Geisinger.)

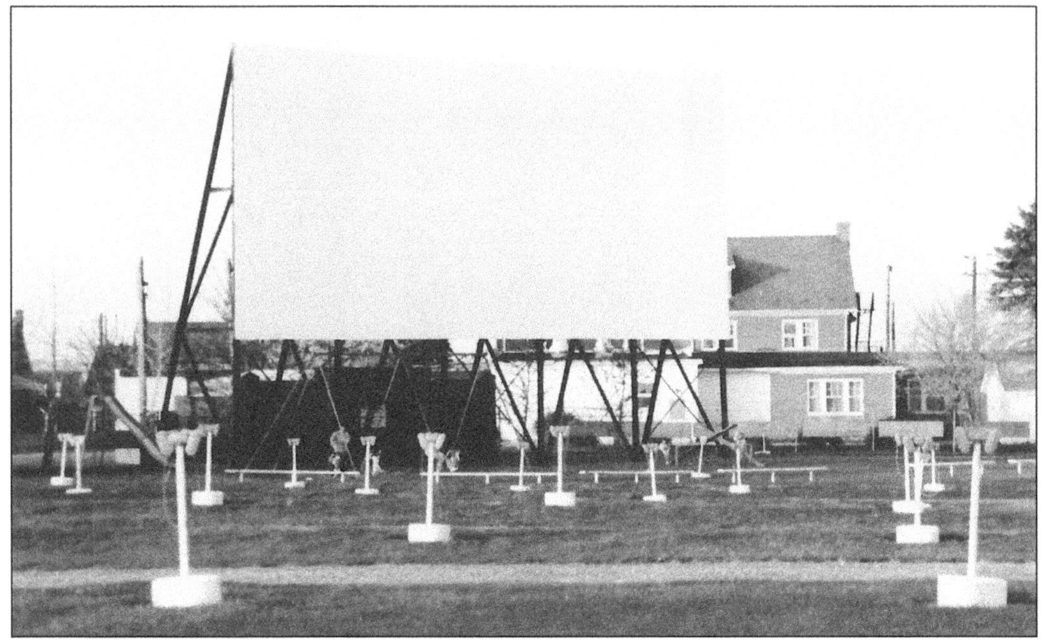

Shankweiler's Drive-In. Despite the fact that excessive film rental costs resulted in the closing of the original drive-in only two or three years after it opened, Shankweiler's still survives and prospers. Many changes have been made over the years, including this more recent, modern screen tower. In the mid-1980s, when these photographs were taken, in-car speakers were still used exclusively. (Courtesy of Susan Geisinger.)

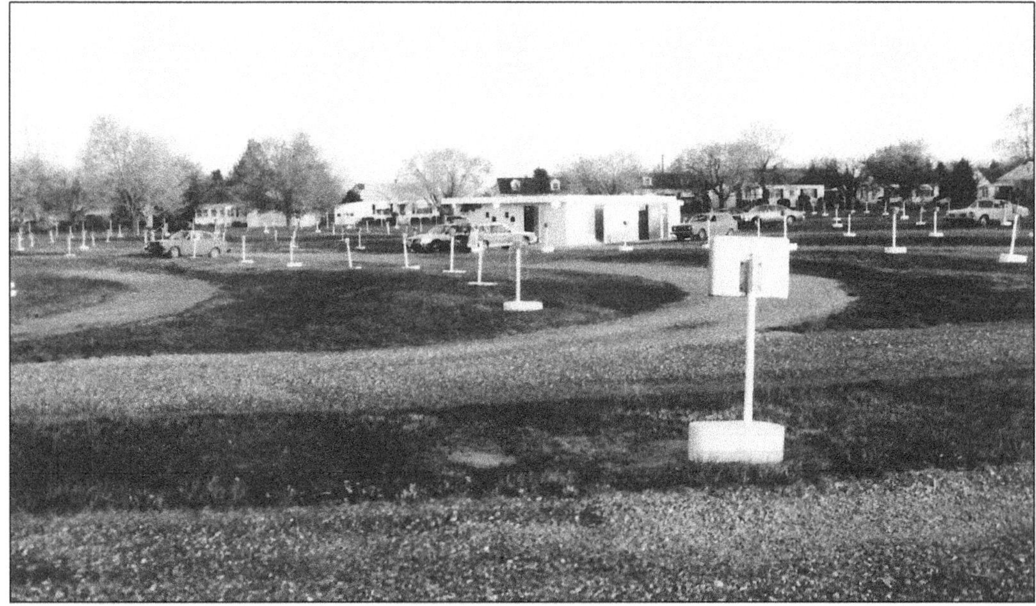

Shankweiler's Lot. The relative intimacy of Shankweiler's is evident from the small size of the lot and the proximity of neighboring homes. In an effort to accommodate the neighbors, speaker wires were run to porches allowing them to view the film with accompanying sound. Today, Shankweiler's still attracts both locals and supplicants at the altar of the drive-in from around the world. (Courtesy of Susan Geisinger.)

Two

Detroit and Environs

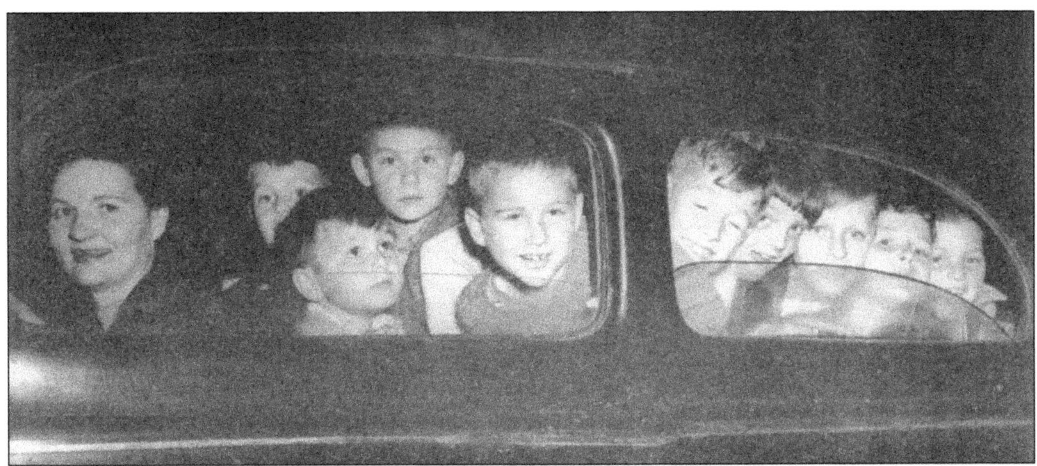

Her "Nine Little Appetites" at the Drive-In. This car full of cuties was photographed at the Gratiot Drive-In in the early 1950s; the image was used in a trade publication to illustrate how a car with only two paid adult admissions could still rake in profits by way of concession sales. Concession sales were often several times more profitable than ticket sales.

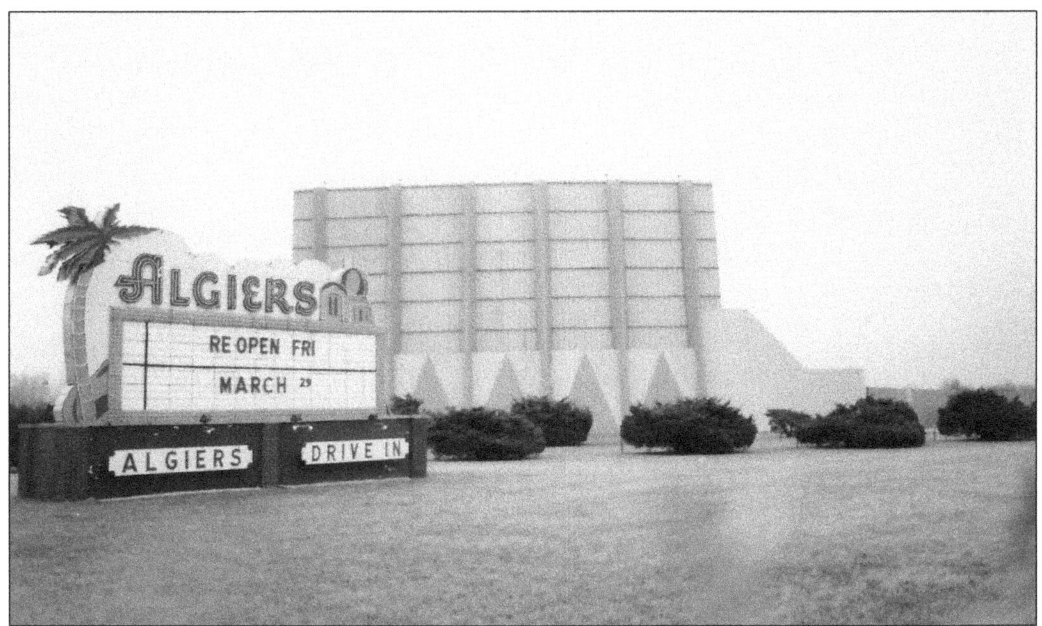

Impressive by Day. The Algiers Drive-In, seen here in 1985, was located at Wayne and Warren Roads in Wayne. Constructed in 1956, it boasted, as did many others, the "largest screen installed in the U.S." at 216 feet wide. Later theaters, such as this, usually reserved the decoration for their marquees and opted for a simply lit screen with well-groomed landscaping.

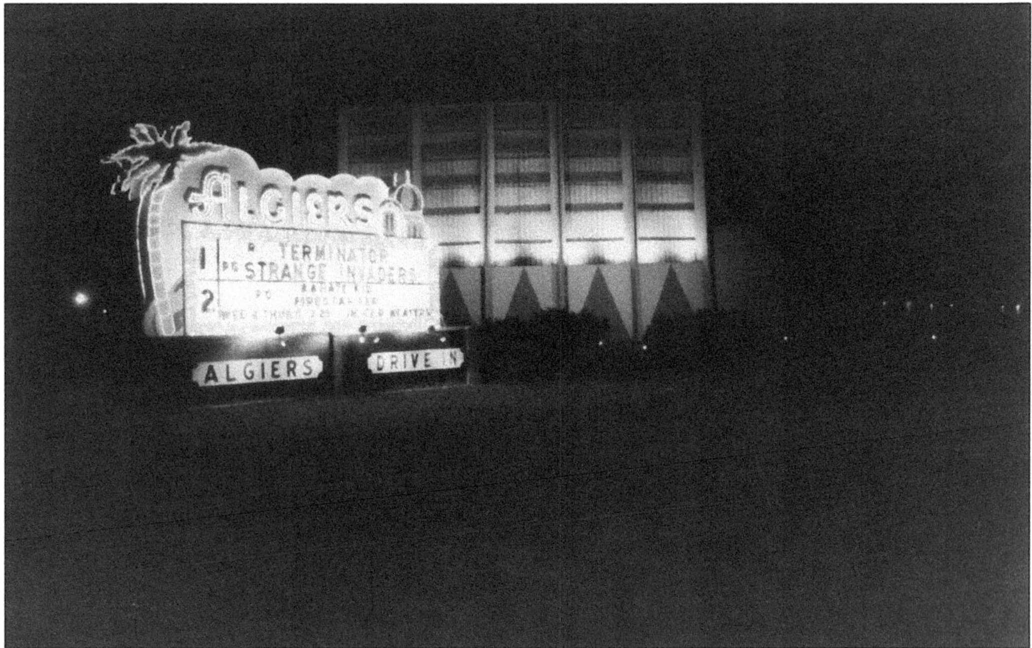

Luminous at Night. Although a spacious and modern drive-in boasting a 1,200-car capacity, the Algiers is most remembered for its minaret and palm tree–encrusted marquee. Like many others, the Algiers started life as a huge single-screen theater, but as times changed, a second screen was added to boost revenues. The Algiers property was sold, and the theater was demolished in 1985. It was situated next to the Quo-Vadis indoor theater, which outlasted it by several years.

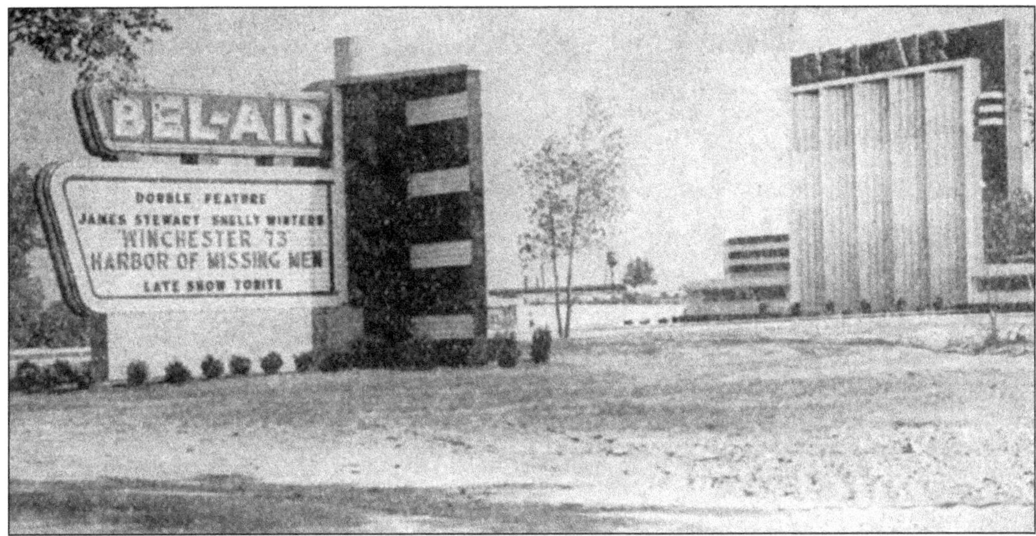

Impressive in Size. The Bel-Air, located at 8500 East 8 Mile Road, opened in 1950 and was one of the nation's largest outdoor theaters, boasting a 1,750-car capacity. Being of an earlier design, the screen retained some decorative elements when viewed from the street. The pre-Cinemascope screen tower retained roughly the same proportions as a television screen.

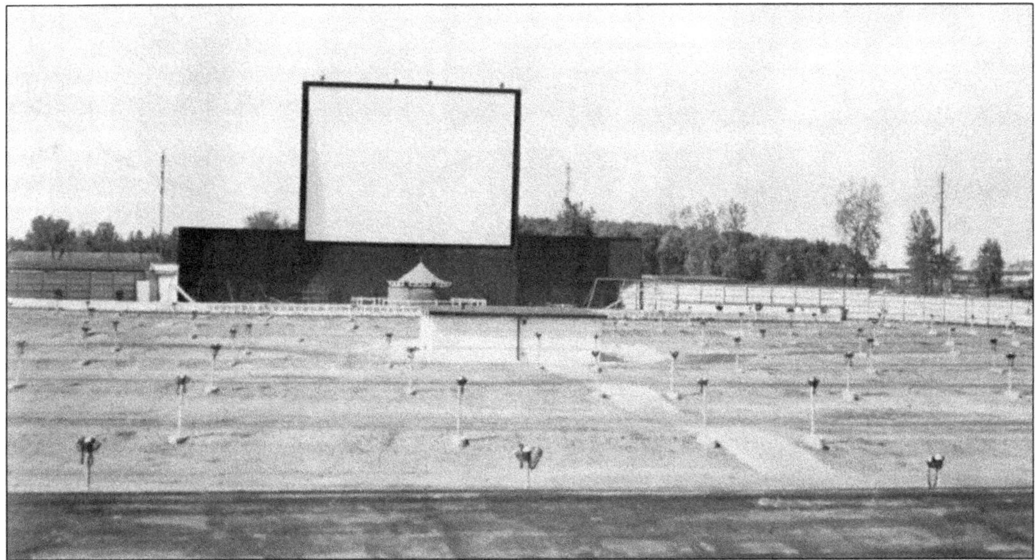

Lots of Room. The vast lot required that the projection and concession buildings be located apart; the concession building was best located at the center for ease of access, while the projection booth had to be closer to minimize the length of the projector's "throw" so as to maximize screen brightness.

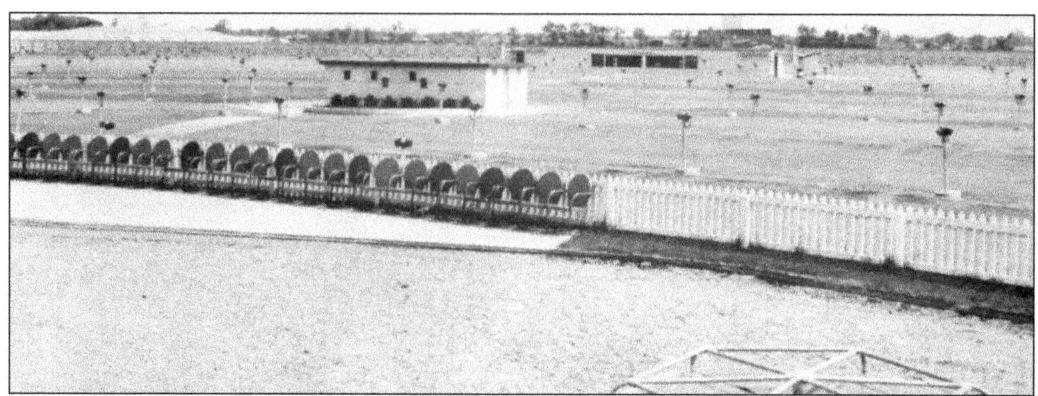

Youthful Enthusiasm Corralled. The spacious playground at the Bel-Air was circumscribed by a cheerful white picket fence and plentiful seating for those adults tending to their enthusiastic youngsters. Unlike the many unenclosed drive-in playgrounds, the Bel-Air's was designed to eliminate the possibility of an energetic child running out into the area where vehicles were in motion.

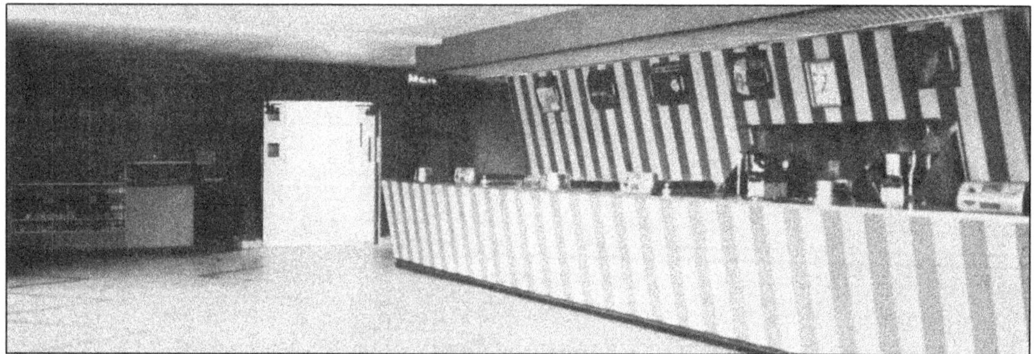

Refreshments Aplenty. The spacious concession counter, although designed to service over 1,000 patrons at once, was still of the early counter design, where customers stood in line to be waited on as in a modern fast-food establishment. In later years, a facility of this size would have availed itself of the higher-volume cafeteria arrangement.

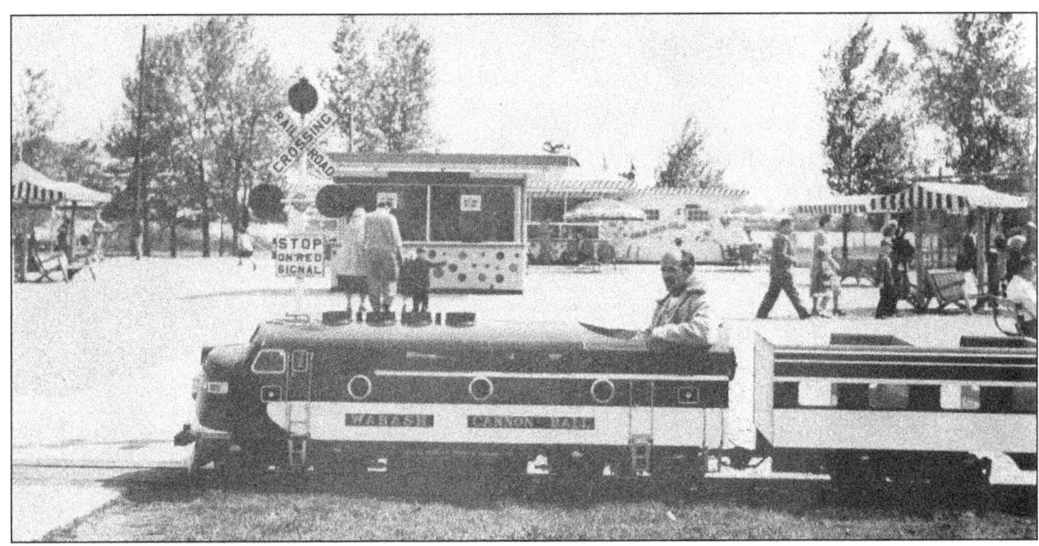

Escape into Fantasyland. Being a first-rate facility, the Bel-Air, or Belair, as some listings have it, boasted an elaborate playground for the kids. Perhaps elaborate does not adequately convey the borderline carnival nature of the facility, which, as the picture shows, included a passenger-carrying small-scale railroad and other amusement park attractions.

Multiple Screens on the Horizon. In 1972, the Goldberg family decided to add a second screen to the Bel-Air, thereby increasing the capacity and the variety of films being shown. Advertised as having a capacity of 2,200 cars, much was made of the twin screens being constructed for the twin Goldberg brothers. It can be seen from the photograph that they stole from the original lot in addition to commandeering new land for the somewhat irregular second theater. (Courtesy of Historicaerials.com.)

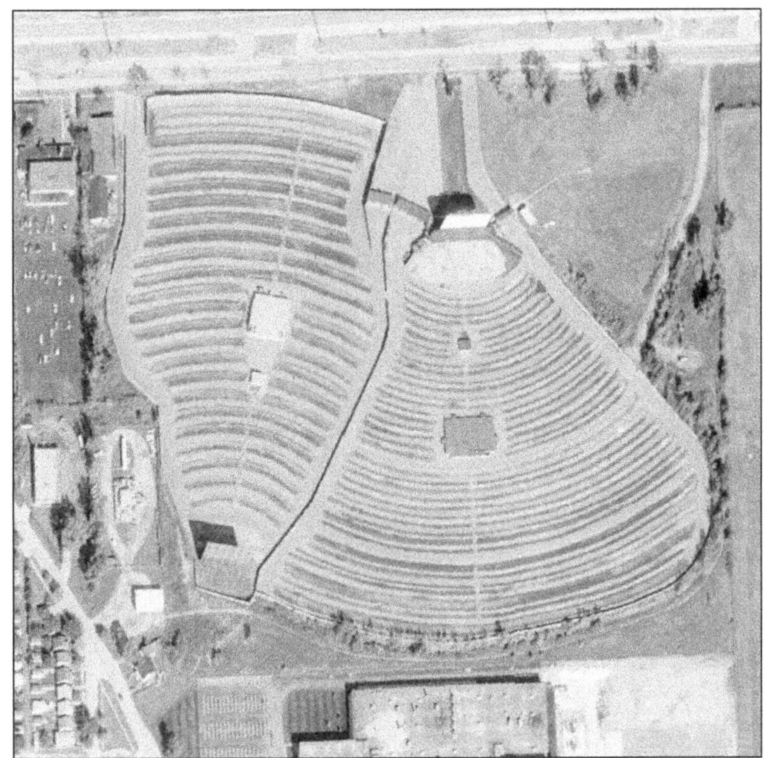

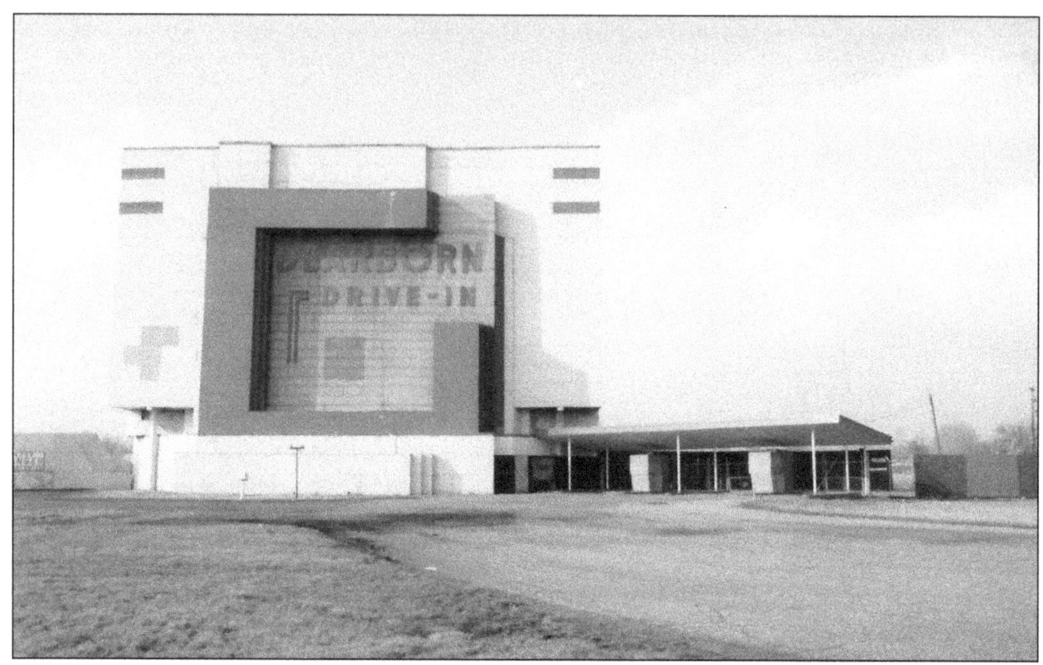

ECONOMY IN DESIGN. The Dearborn, located at 26500 Ford Road, was one of many utilizing the same screen design. The Beltline (see page 79) and the Portage Drive-In, near Bowling Green, Ohio, were virtually identical to it. Constructed in 1948, the Dearborn held 1,040 cars and, like the other large drive-ins, advertised a train in its playground. When the days of movies capable of drawing 1,000 cars had passed, it too was twinned and remained that way until its closing in 1984.

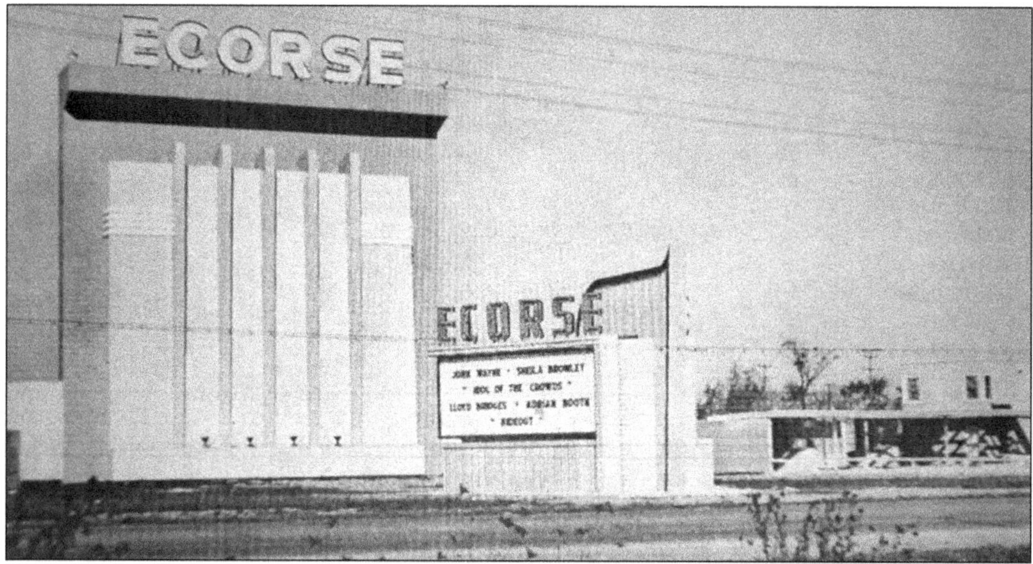

MORE OF THE SAME. The Ecorse, in addition to movies, also sported the now requisite scale-model railroad in conjunction with its more mundane playground fare. Built in 1951 and located at 21366 Ecorse Road, the Ecorse, like the Dearborn, held a reported 1,050 cars and, like the Dearborn, eventually sprouted a second screen. (Courtesy of Ron Gross.)

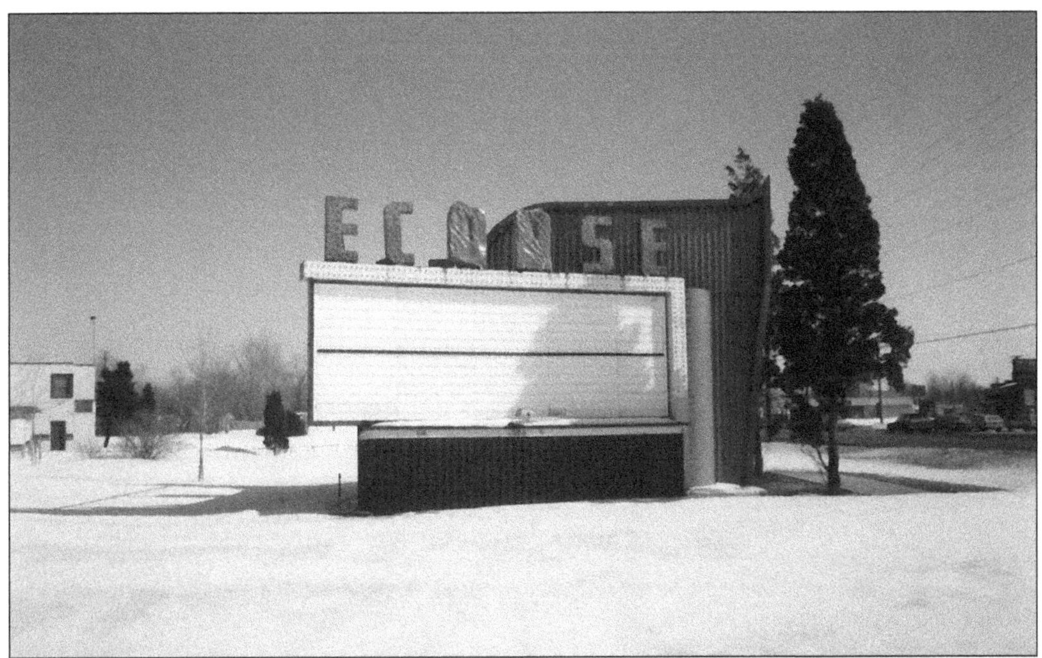

Braving the Winter. As with most drive-ins, the Ecorse closed during the inclement months, battening down its hatches until spring. In this case, the trash bags intended to protect the marquee letters from snow and sleet have almost all blown off. By this time, the theater has been twinned, thus the horizontal divider on the attraction board.

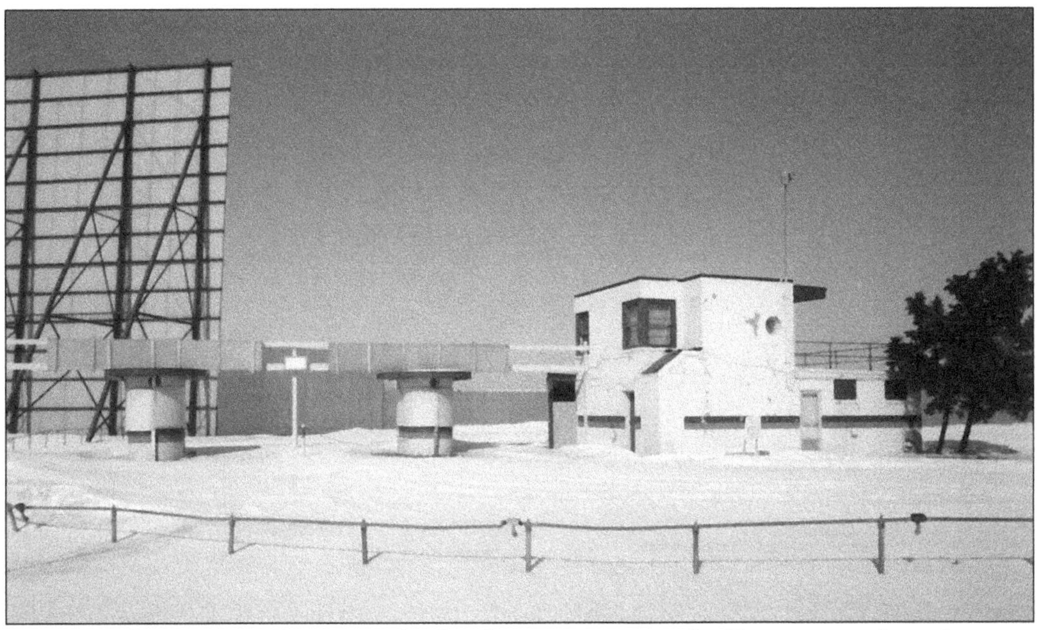

Everyone Remembers. Everyone who lived in proximity to the Ecorse remembers the great windstorm of 1980, in which the sky turned green, railroad cars were blown from their tracks, and the screen of the Ecorse was blown down. Damaged but still alive, the Ecorse replaced the demolished structure with a smaller screen, visible in this photograph, and continued in operation until 1985.

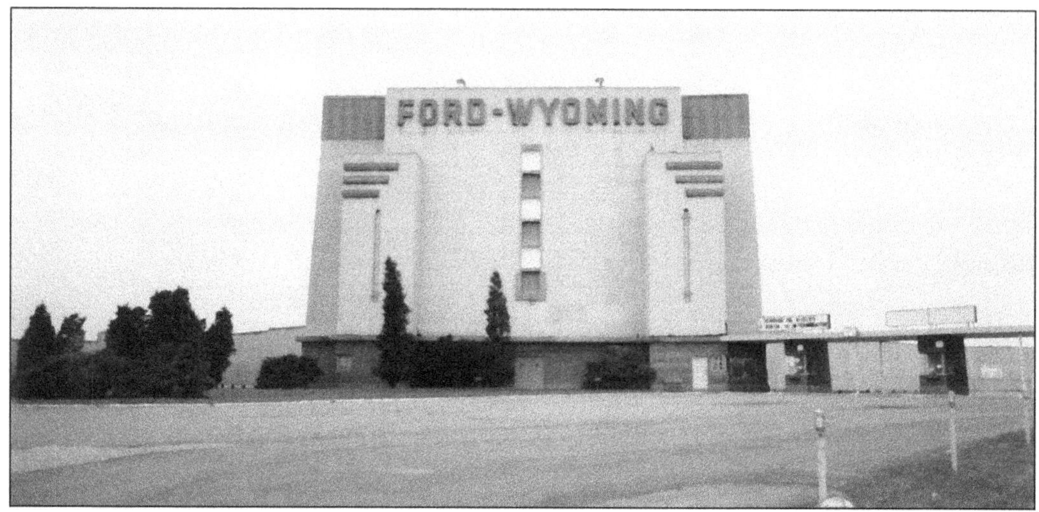

Rain or Shine. The Ford-Wyoming, so named because of its location at the intersection of Ford and Wyoming Roads, was, and still is, one of the few regional drive-ins to operate year-round, with in-car heaters available during the winter months. Built in 1950, it had a somewhat more modest 750-car capacity but still advertised a boat ride for the kids. As with other pre-1952 theaters, its screen was later widened to Cinemascope proportions, as can be seen by the vertical wings flanking the central screen structure.

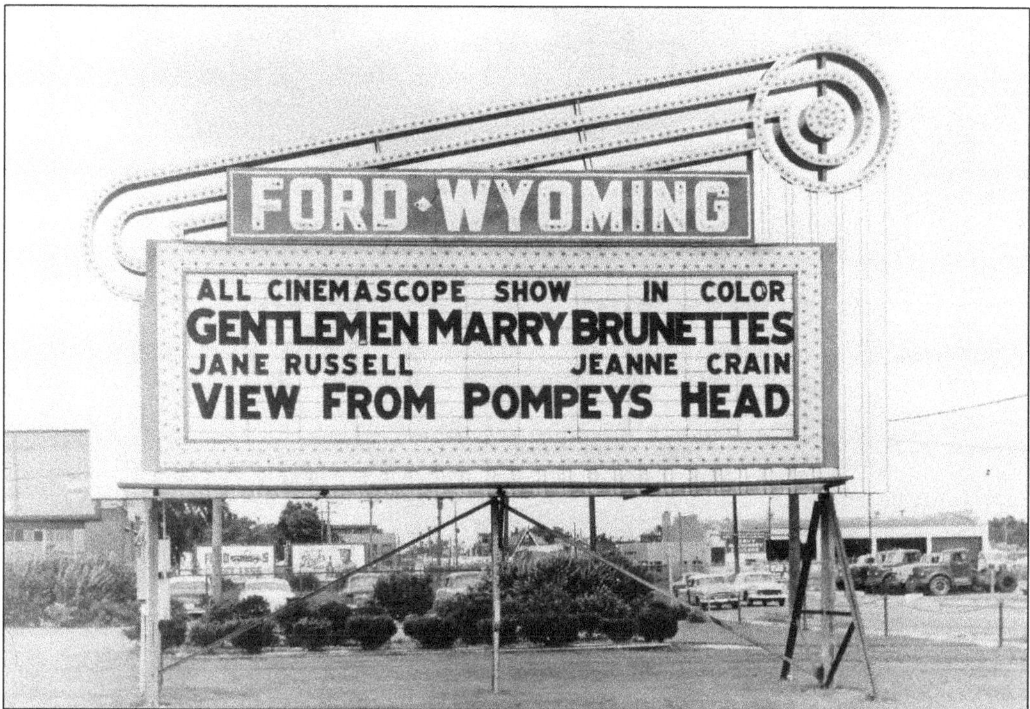

Gentlemen Marry Brunettes. The original marquee was a typically elaborate affair, with chasing lights around the attraction sign and the ornamental portion at the top and neon-filled letters and borders. Frequently, the originally ornate signs succumbed to Michigan winters and were either marred by burned-out bulbs and neon or replaced with much more spartan affairs. (Courtesy of Ron Gross.)

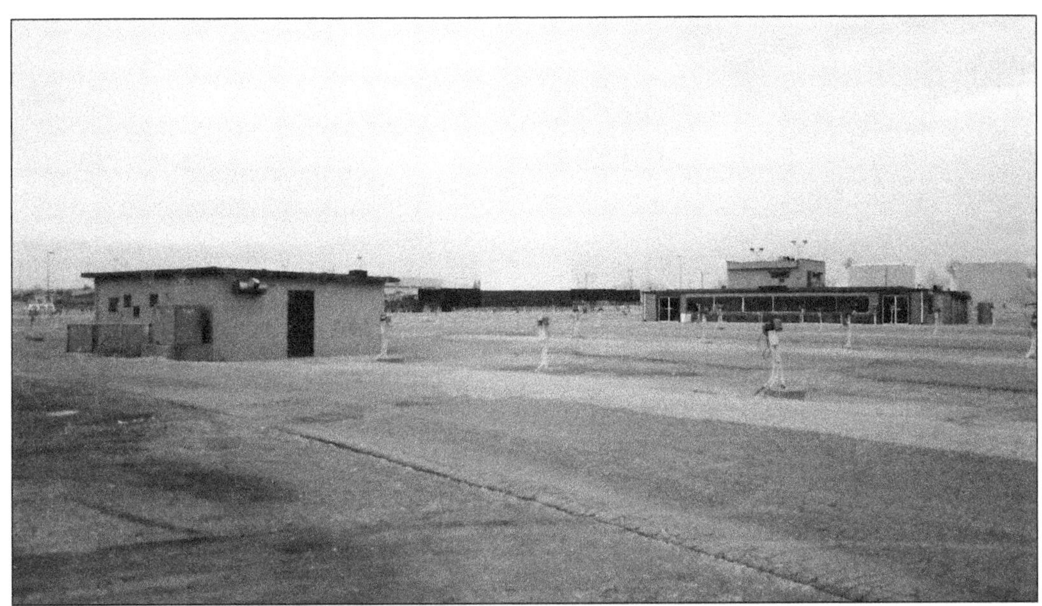

Refinery in the Rear. Not so much an oil refinery as tank farm, the Ford-Wyoming was constructed in a hardly picturesque location, being surrounded by chemical storage tanks. In this 1984 photograph, the theater, despite its industrial location, retains much of its original charm and most of its original layout. In later years, its location would be largely responsible for its survival.

Aerial Perspective. This aerial photograph, taken in 1973, shows the Ford-Wyoming in its original configuration as a 750-car single-screen theater. Although not nearly as large as some others, the design still employed separate concession and projection buildings. In later years, the layout was radically modified to allow for additional screens. (Courtesy of Historicaerials.com.)

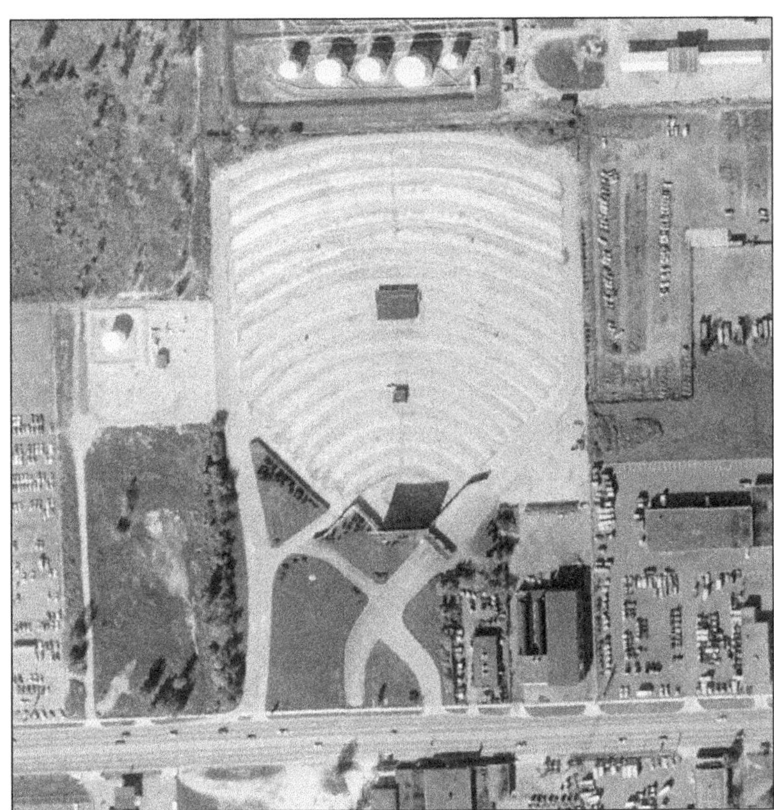

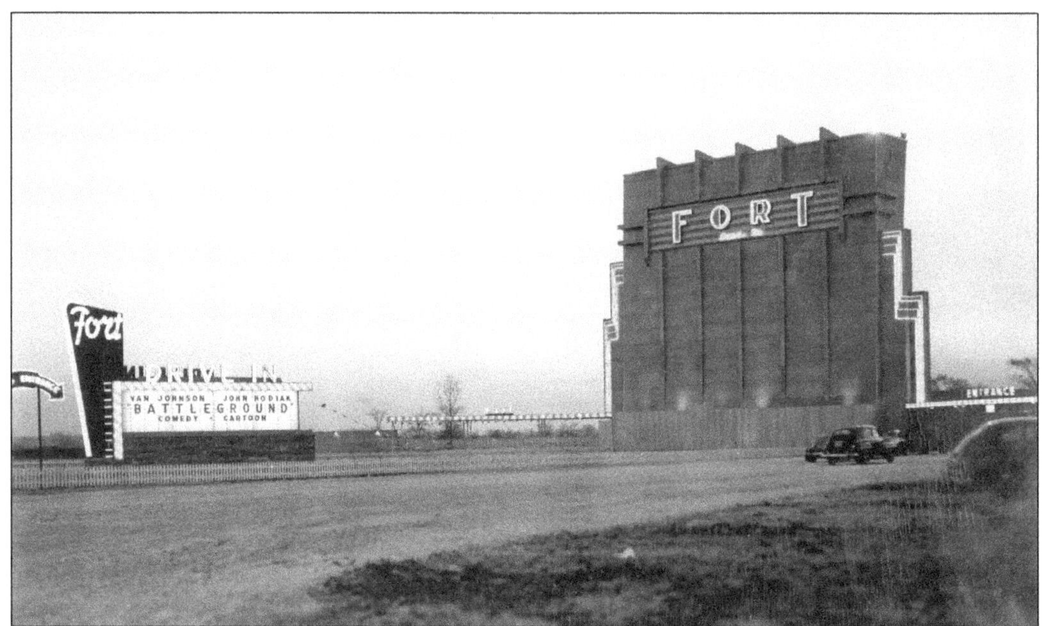

MASSIVE AND MODERNE. The Fort Drive-In was located at 16300 Fort Street (south of Eureka) and was another large urban drive-in. Constructed in 1950, it held 1,000 cars and is seen here as it originally appeared, around 1950. The screen tower design incorporated various Art Moderne elements, such as streamlined fins and neon accents. (Courtesy of Rob Imes/Bacon Memorial Library.)

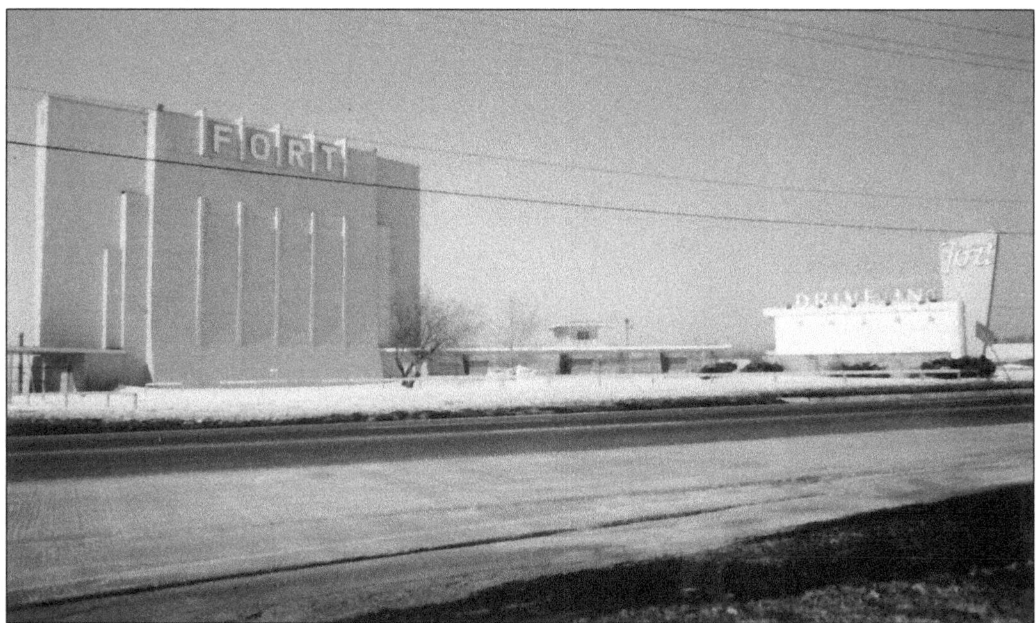

PROGRESS AND A WIDER SCREEN. Nicholas George Theaters took over operation of the Fort in 1955, and for most of its life it was known as the Fort-George. By this time, it had already seen the need to accommodate wide-screen movies and had modified the screen tower accordingly. As with other large theaters (such as the Ford-Wyoming), the modification was done in an architecturally sensitive manner and blended with the original design so as to be barely noticeable.

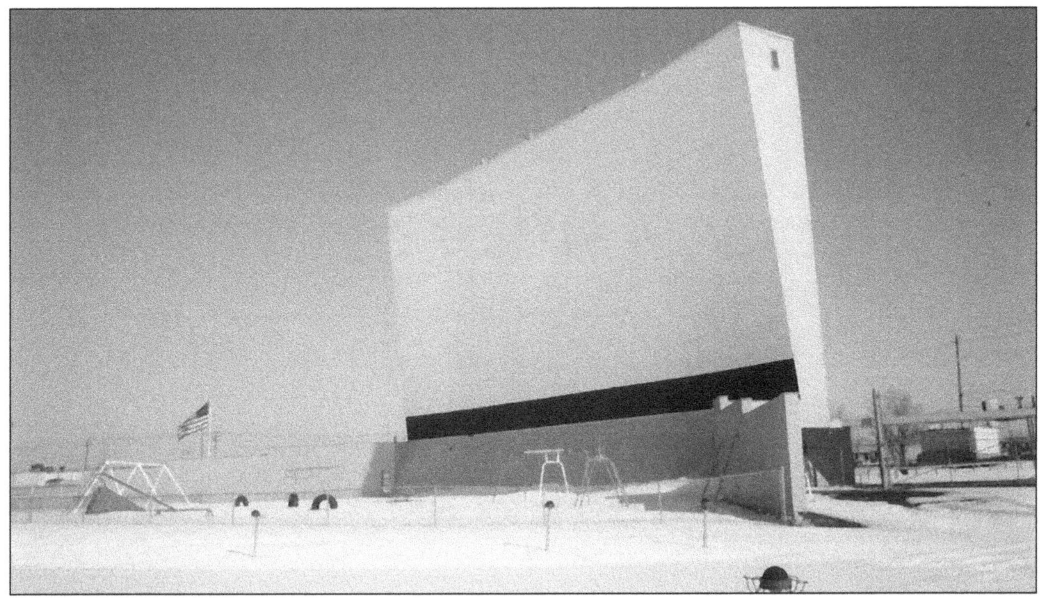

A Word about Aspect Ratio. Until the early 1950s, the proportions of a movie screen were 1.33:1, meaning that the picture was 1.33 times wider than high (the same as a television screen). But in 1953, in an attempt to combat the increasing competition of television, wide-screen movies were introduced. Screen proportions were quickly modified to the new 2.35:1 aspect ratio, creating a screen roughly 86 percent wider and requiring the rebuilding of all older movie screens. The screen of the Fort is one such example.

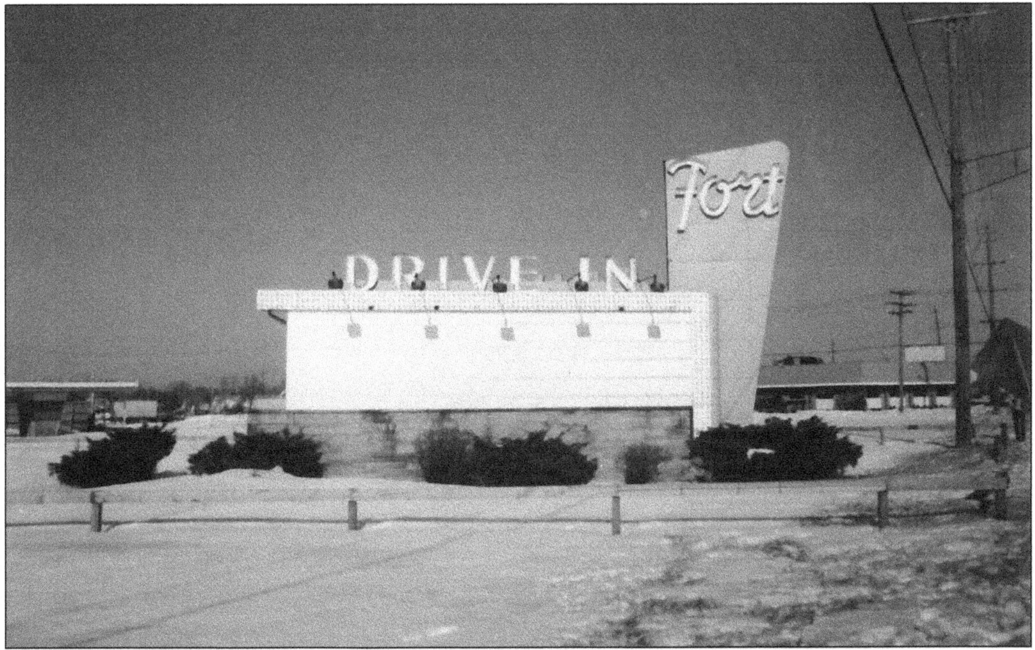

Looking Much the Same. The marquee of the Fort, although seen here in the snowy spring of 1985, is essentially unchanged from its appearance in 1950. The Fort (or Fort-George) continued in operation until a windstorm in 1990 inflicted severe damage to the screen. It was demolished in the spring of 1991.

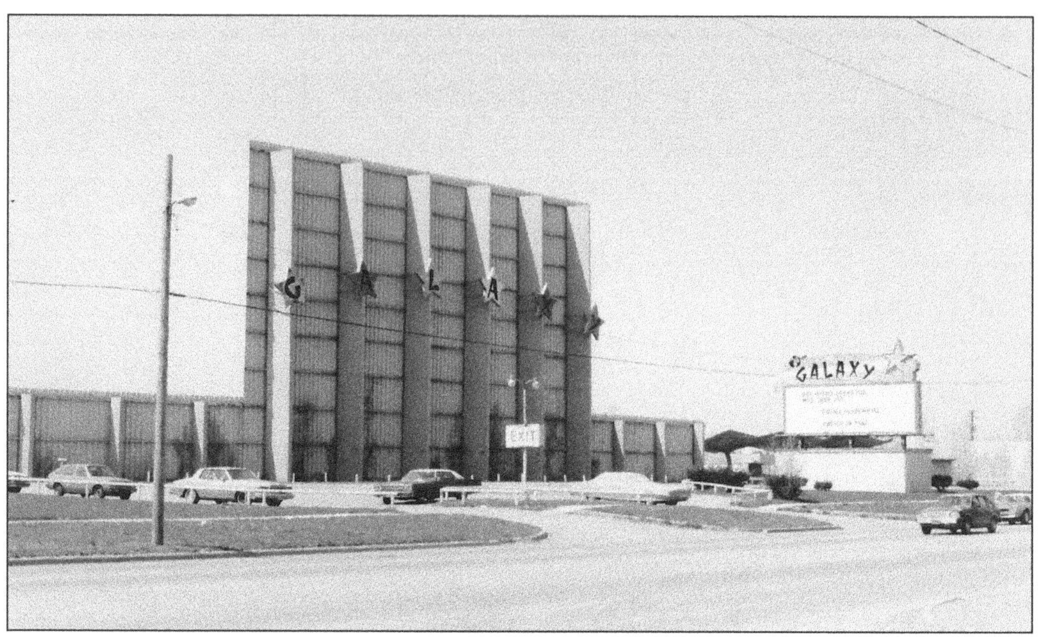

Open for Business. The Galaxy, located on Dequindre Road near 10 Mile Road, was one of the later drive-ins, having opened in the summer of 1963. It was also one of the largest, with a 1,400-car capacity. This screen was obviously designed for wide-screen features from the beginning. After the construction of Interstate 696, passing motorists could see the movie for a tantalizing few seconds as they sped by.

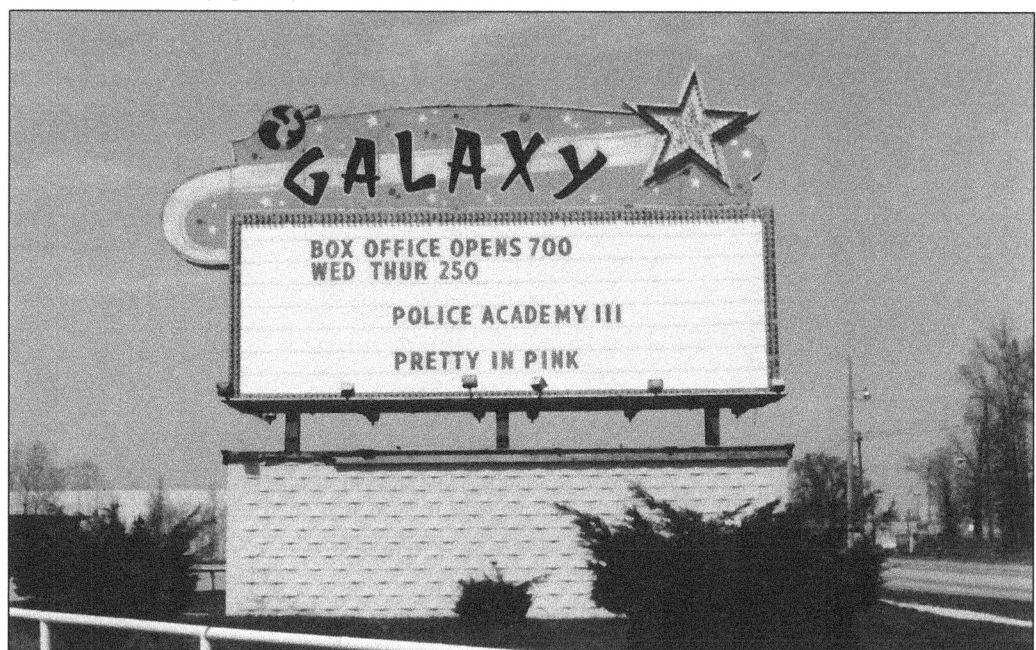

Visions of Space. The 1960s were the space age, and the star-spangled marquee of the Galaxy was obviously part of it. The name Galaxy was also emblazoned across the screen, leaving no doubt as to which theater patrons were approaching. This photograph, taken in 1986, displays typical first-run drive-in fare, with *Police Academy 3* and *Pretty in Pink* as its double feature.

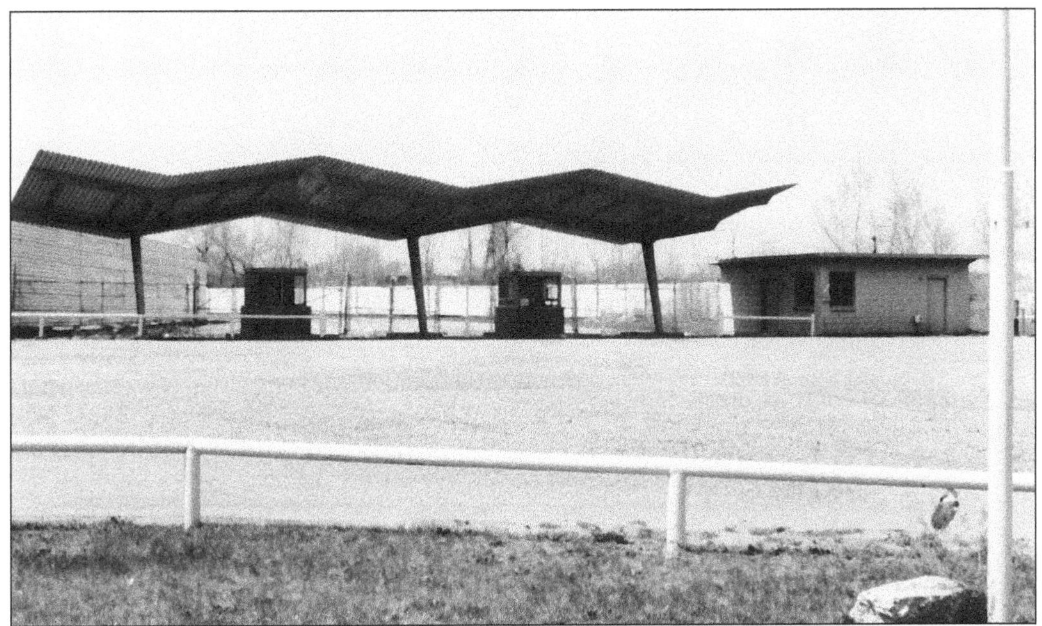

Entry Drive. The wide and capacious approach to the box office of the Galaxy is seen here. The zigzag configuration of the roof above the ticket windows is another normal feature of 1960s recreational architecture and was seen on everything from gas stations to motels and shopping centers constructed at the time.

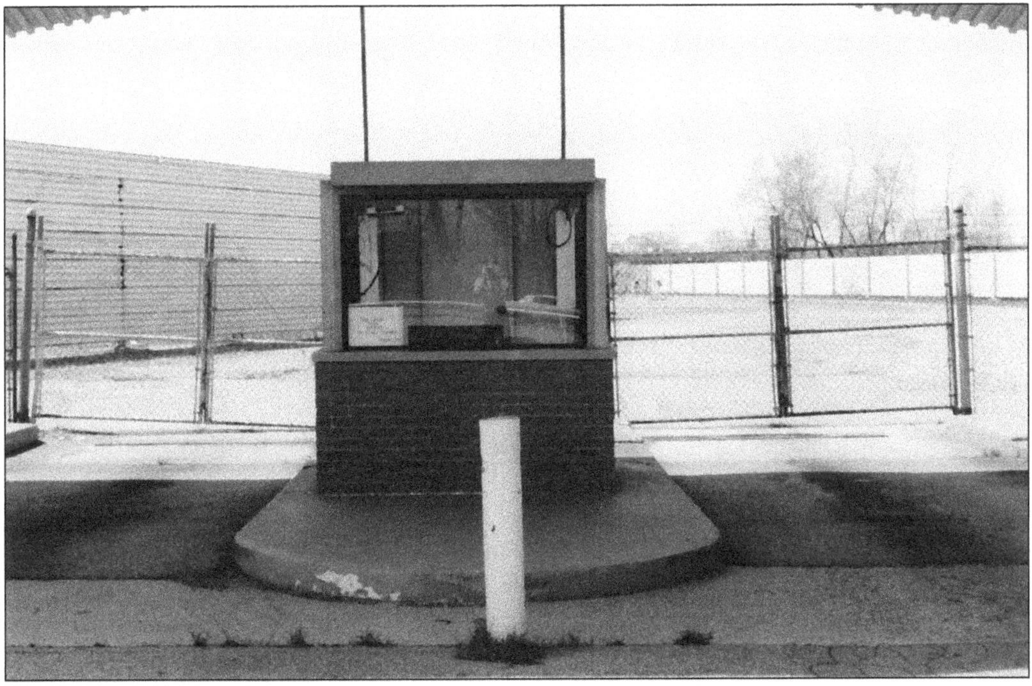

Summer's End. Seen just after its closing in the fall of 1986, the Galaxy would not reopen for the 1987 season. As with most of the Nick George drive-ins, and drive-ins in general, the Galaxy did not make it to the 1990s, as property values, home video, and other factors conspired against it. Note the photographer reflected in the box office window.

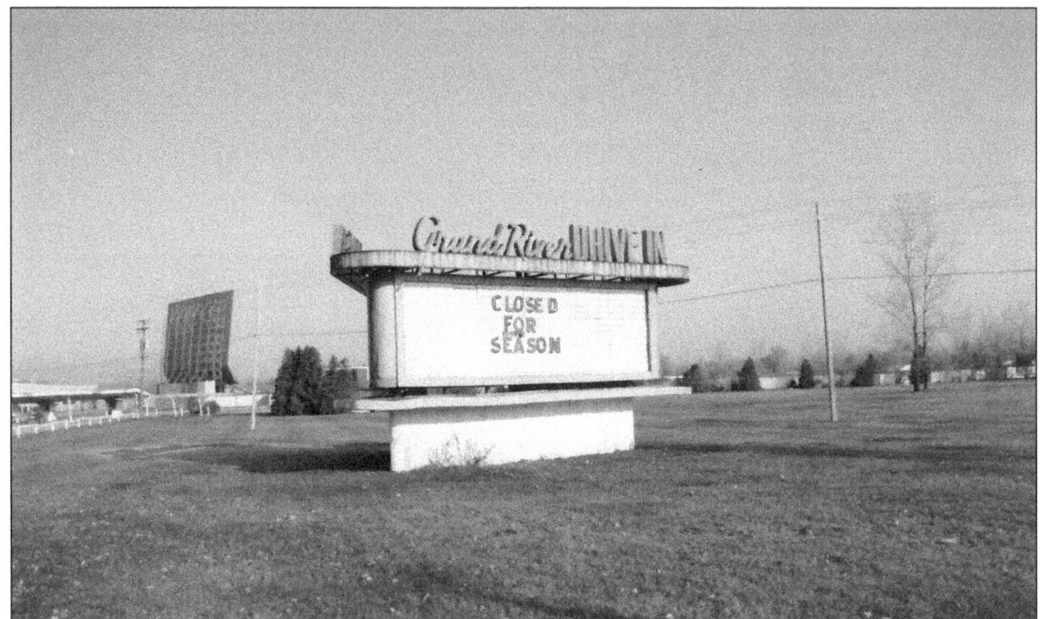

Yellow, Red, and Green. This 1984 black-and-white photograph hardly does justice to what was the glorious vista of the bright yellow and red marquee of the Grand River Drive-In, adrift in its sea of green grass. Located at 30200 Grand River Avenue, between 8 Mile and 9 Mile Roads, the Grand River originally boasted a modest capacity of 750 cars, but at the time of its closing had sprouted an additional two screens and had grown to a capacity of 1,100 cars.

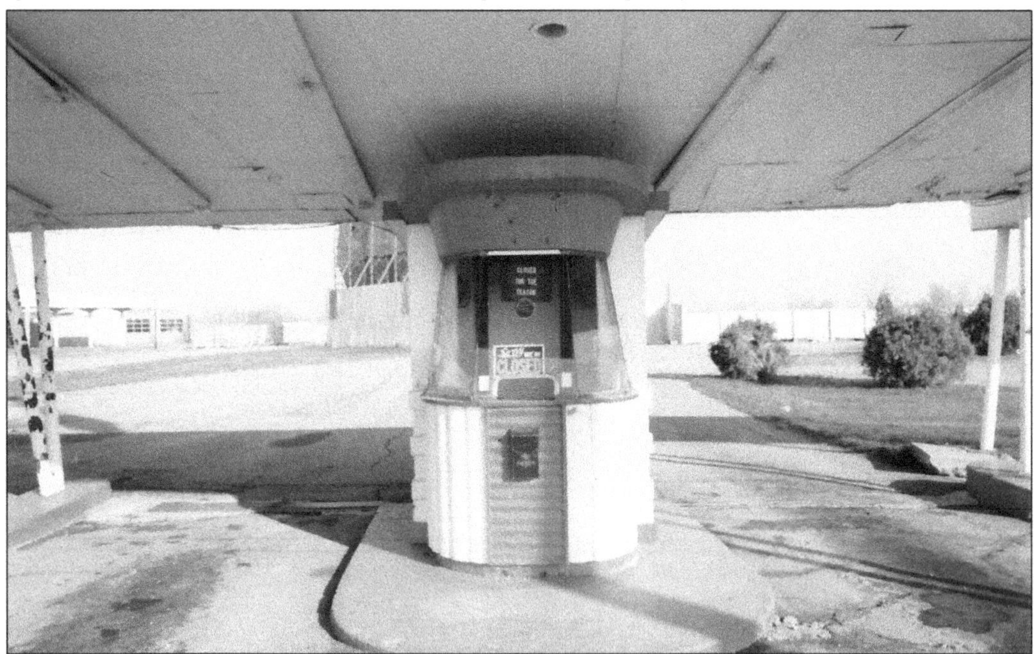

Outing in Deco. Probably the best example of the use of Art Deco in box office design, the appearance of the Grand River's curved and fluted original 1949 box office is perhaps spoiled slightly by the modern residential mailbox affixed to its front. Despite this, it is still far more interesting than others, such as the Galaxy's uninspired rectangular boxes.

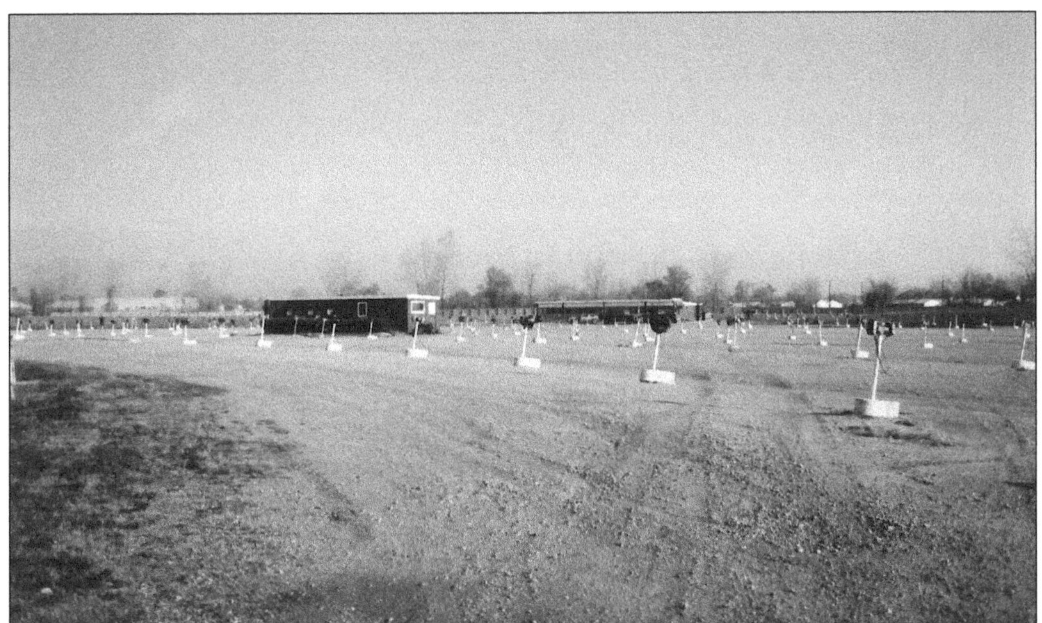

Undulating Waves. The rise and fall of the ramps in the Grand River's lot is broken by the ranks of speaker posts and the distant projection and concession buildings. Like many of the urban drive-ins, the Grand River was quite well maintained up until the day demolition began. The Grand River's last show was in 1988, four years after this photograph was taken.

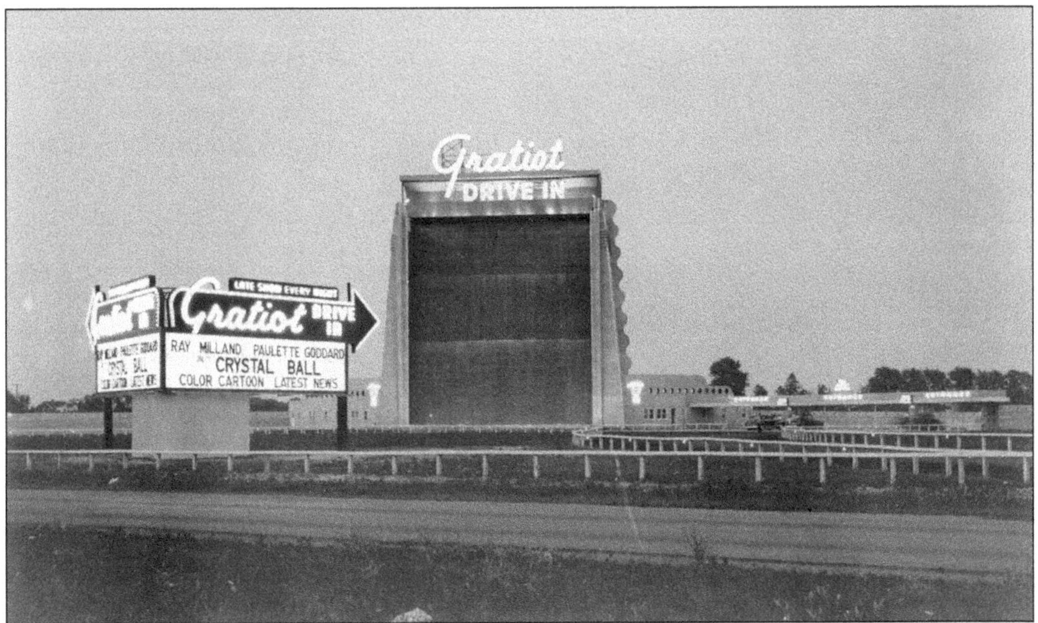

The Gratiot. Detroit's most spectacular drive-in was undoubtedly the Gratiot. Located on Gratiot Avenue near 13 Mile Road, it was one of only two drive-ins in the world to have an actual waterfall cascading down its screen face. Seen here shortly after its opening in 1948, the Gratiot was designed by Detroit architect Theodore Rogvoy, who quite likely patterned it after the Kallet Drive-In, which was constructed in Camillus, New York, two years earlier and also sported a water feature on its face.

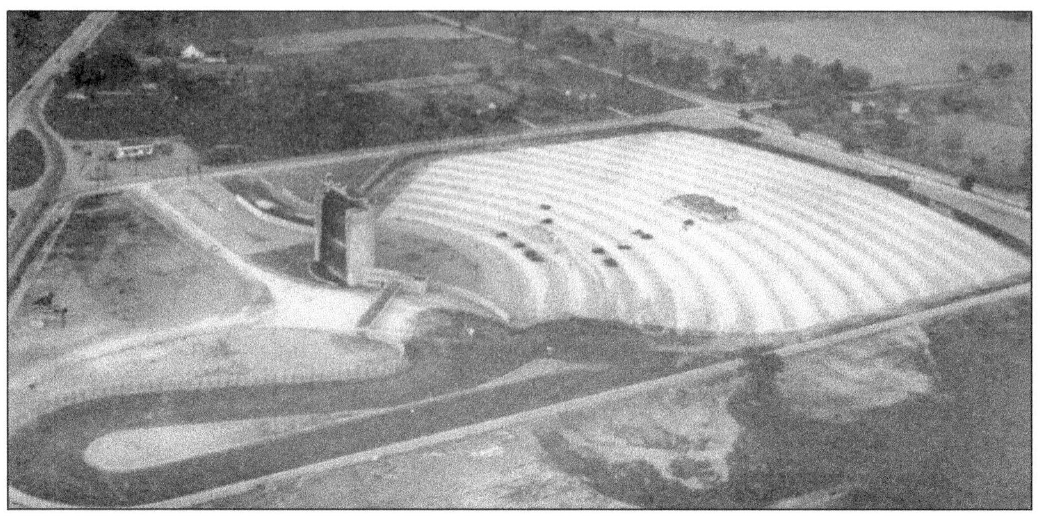

Aerial View. The most noteworthy feature of this aerial view is, in retrospect, the vast expanse of vacant land. In later years, all of the area around the Gratiot would be consumed by shopping centers and strip malls. In 1948, there was very little commercial architecture along Gratiot this far north, and the property was cheap. Period accounts claim the Gratiot's construction cost was anywhere from $400,000 to $1,000,000.

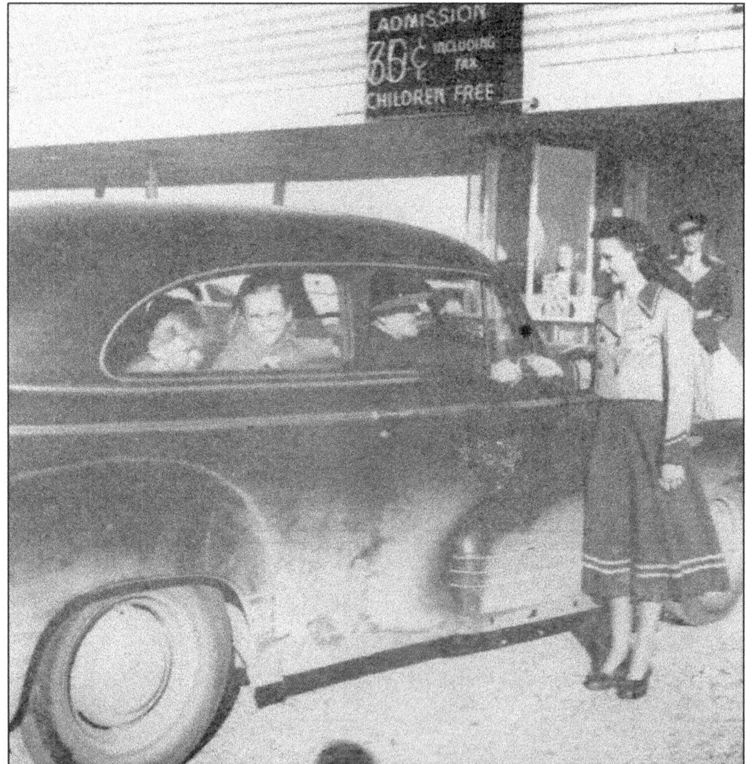

Two Box Offices Await. Unlike in the more familiar system where patrons purchased tickets from one of the girls who reported to the box offices, attendants greeted cars and sold tickets in all six lanes entering the theater, thus it was possible to service all the lanes from only two box offices. The Gratiot had a capacity of 1,056 cars on 17 ramps. The screen tower contained an apartment, storage space, and the 60-horsepower pump that powered the waterfall.

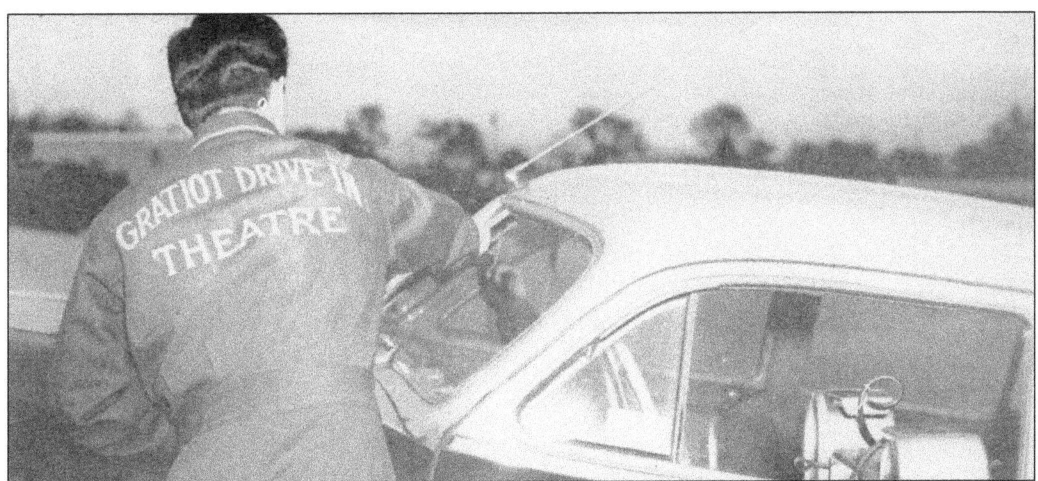

Attendants Await. Service did not stop at the box offices, as coverall-clad attendants roved the lot cleaning windshields for free to further enhance the viewing experience. Ushers equipped with flashlights directed cars in and out of the lot and patrolled during the film to render any needed assistance and to watch for troublemakers.

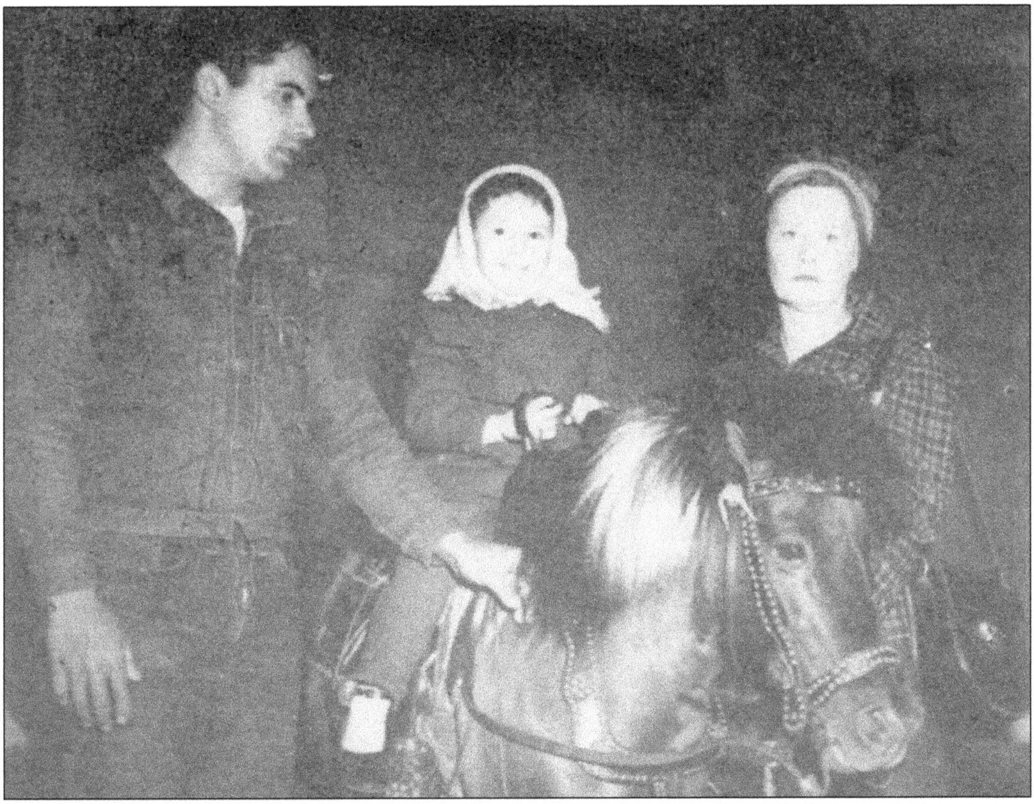

Although Not as Elaborate as Some. The Gratiot's playground was fully equipped and even offered pony rides to the kiddies. It was said that the pony ride "paid for itself in return admissions." The confection stand staff wore mushroom-shaped chef's hats to lend an air of professionalism to their duties. The waterfall was shut off in the late 1950s, and the Gratiot was later twinned and was demolished in 1984.

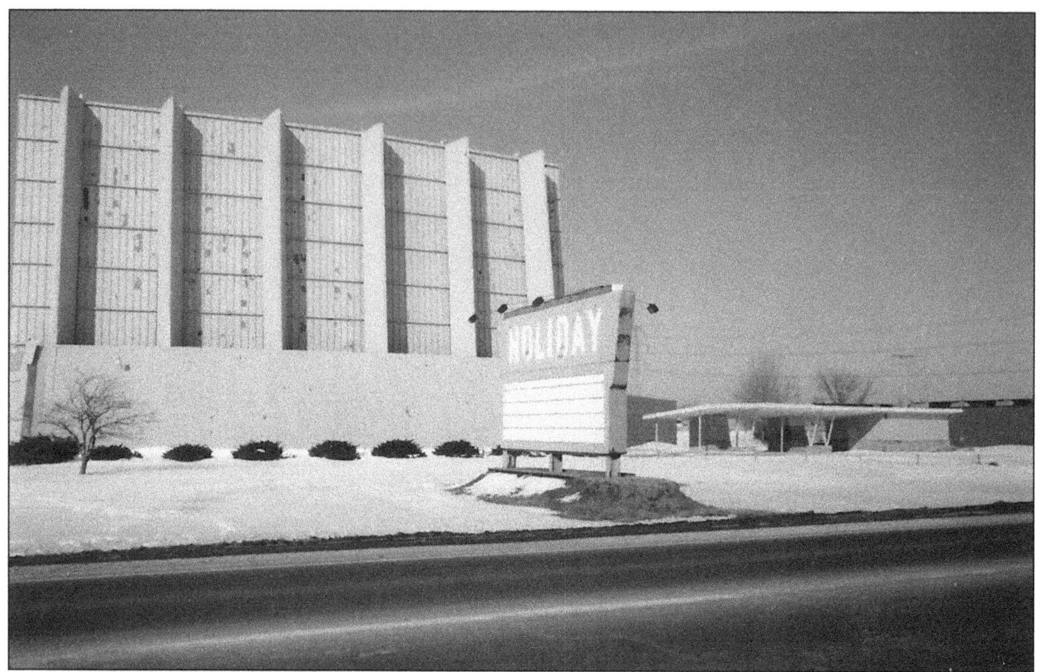

Another Giant. The Holiday, located at 23000 West Road in Woodhaven, was another late and massive theater, with a capacity of 1,140. Constructed in 1956, its screen was distinctive of those intended for Cinemascope pictures. It was also similar to the other city giants in being located fairly close to the road with little screen setback and minimal approach lane length.

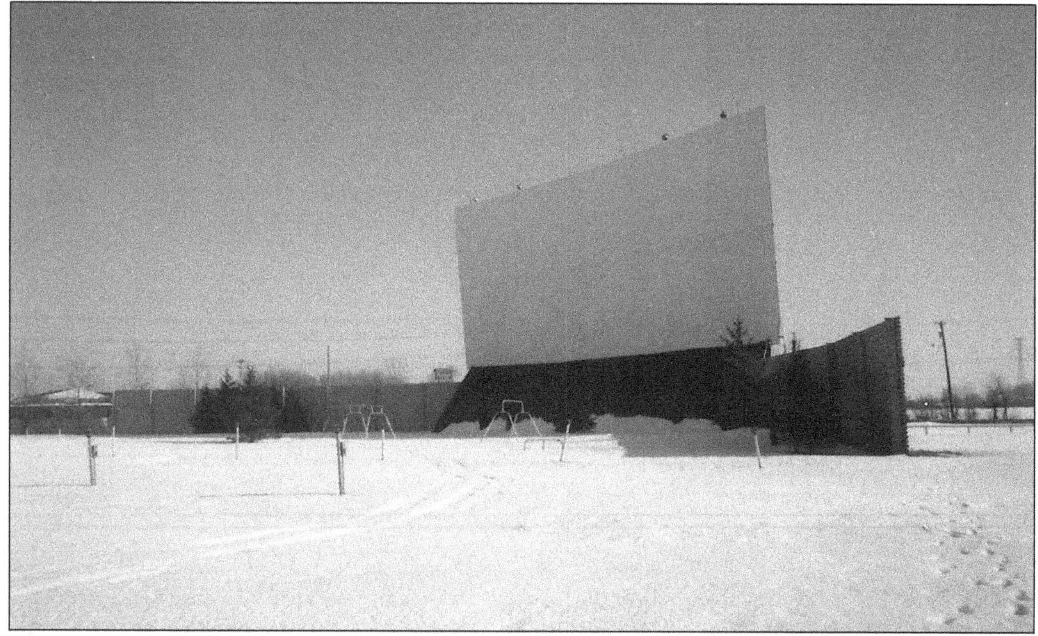

Another Snowy Lot. A 1985 newspaper article suggested that a number of Detroit-area drive-ins would succumb to various pressures and not reopen in the spring; among these was the Holiday. Seen here in March 1985, the theater is snow-covered but intact and could easily have reopened—it never did.

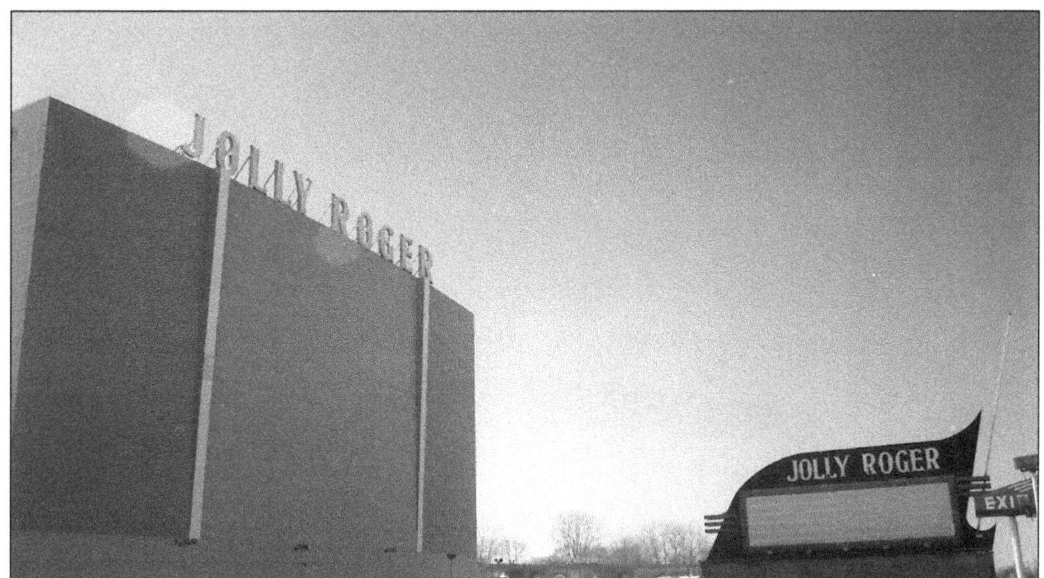

Aarrgh. The Jolly Roger Drive-In also opened in 1956 with a capacity of 1,000 cars, on Van Born Road, west of Telegraph Road in Dearborn. From the beginning, its theme was nautical, and the original marquee and screen tower had a much more blatant pirate motif, which was later minimized. Perhaps patrons should be grateful that as another Nick George theater it was not renamed the Jolly Roger-George.

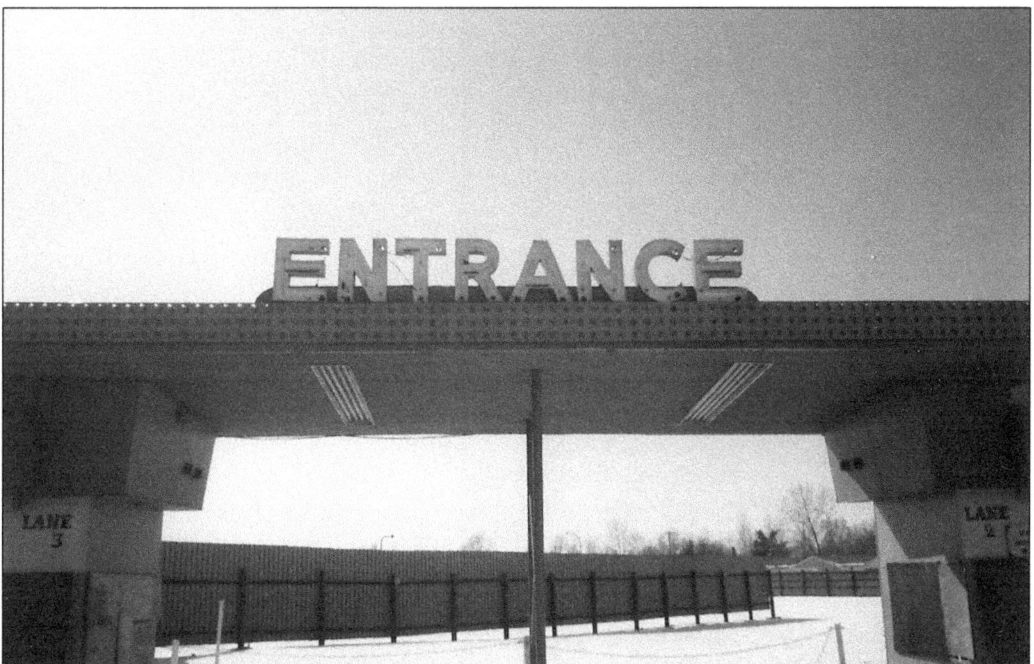

Enter Here, If Ye Dare. The Jolly Roger's box office was well marked, if not particularly nautical. The screen tower originally had a pirate ship painted on it, which must have been difficult to deal with when it came time to repaint. The marquee was also designed to suggest the prow (or stern?) of a sailing ship. The playground contained, among other things, a Ferris wheel and a merry-go-round.

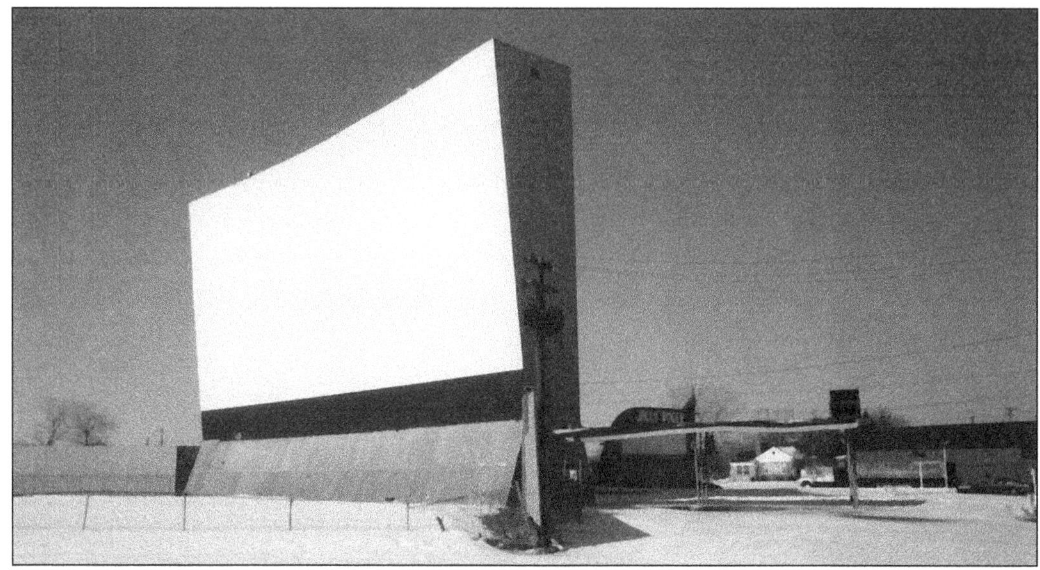

STATE OF THE ART. The Jolly Roger's screen, aside from being quite large, was part of a state-of-the-art exhibition system. Standard for the later theaters—after projection technology had improved with the advent of high-intensity projection lamps—the concession and projection operations were consolidated within one building. The high-tech sound system also included very expensive stereo speakers, which held three speakers, one for each channel, within one aluminum housing.

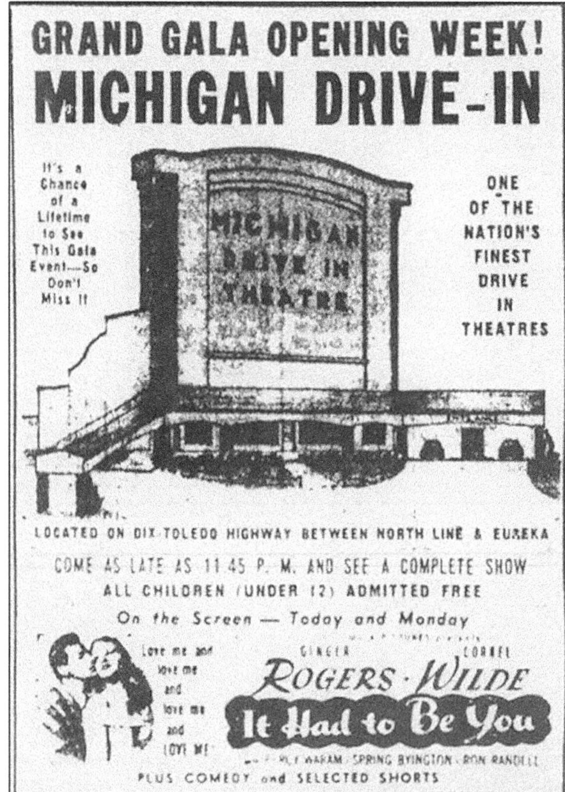

GRAND GALA OPENING WEEK!

MICHIGAN DRIVE-IN

It's a Chance of a Lifetime to See This Gala Event—So Don't Miss It

MICHIGAN DRIVE IN THEATRE

ONE OF THE NATION'S FINEST DRIVE IN THEATRES

LOCATED ON DIX-TOLEDO HIGHWAY BETWEEN NORTH LINE & EUREKA

COME AS LATE AS 11:45 P. M. AND SEE A COMPLETE SHOW

ALL CHILDREN (UNDER 12) ADMITTED FREE

On the Screen — Today and Monday

Love me and love me and love me and LOVE ME

GINGER ROGERS · CORNEL WILDE

It Had to Be You

SPRING BYINGTON · RON RANDELL

PLUS COMEDY and SELECTED SHORTS

GRAND GALA OPENING WEEK! The 1948 opening of the Michigan Drive-In was heralded in a typically showman-like manner with a number of extravagant ads trumpeting its wonders. The Michigan, which was huge for its time with a 1,000-car capacity, was located on Dix-Toledo Road in Wyandotte, and had an oddly shaped tombstone-like screen tower, no doubt implying a very good time indeed.

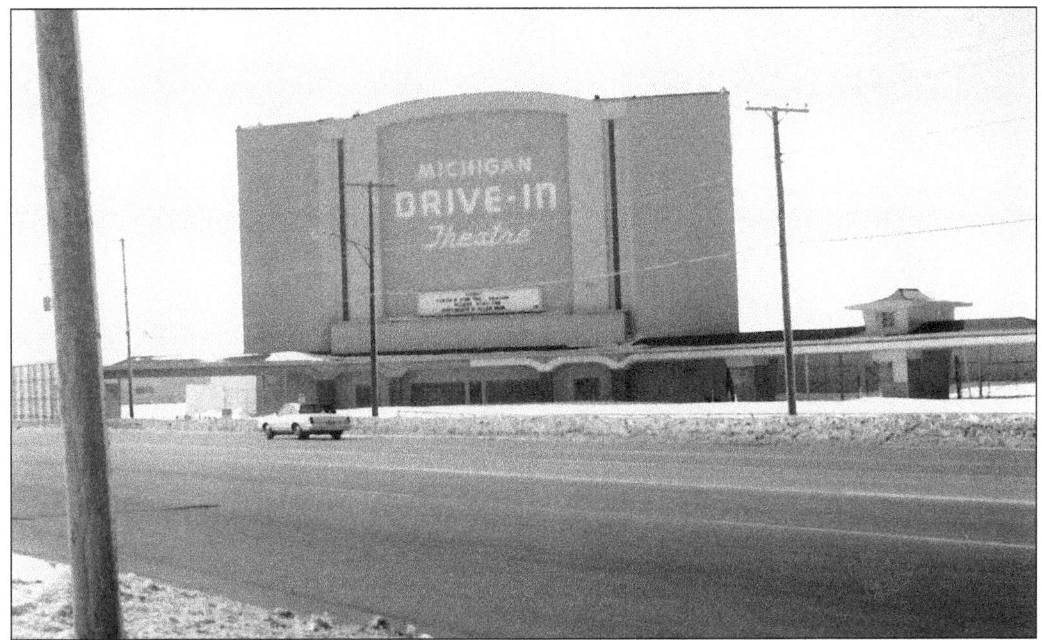

TOMBSTONE WITH WINGS. To allow the showing of wide-screen pictures, the Michigan was required to add on to its screen, just like everyone else. This was more obvious with the Michigan than many others. Also located quite close to the road, the Michigan was another Nicholas George theater.

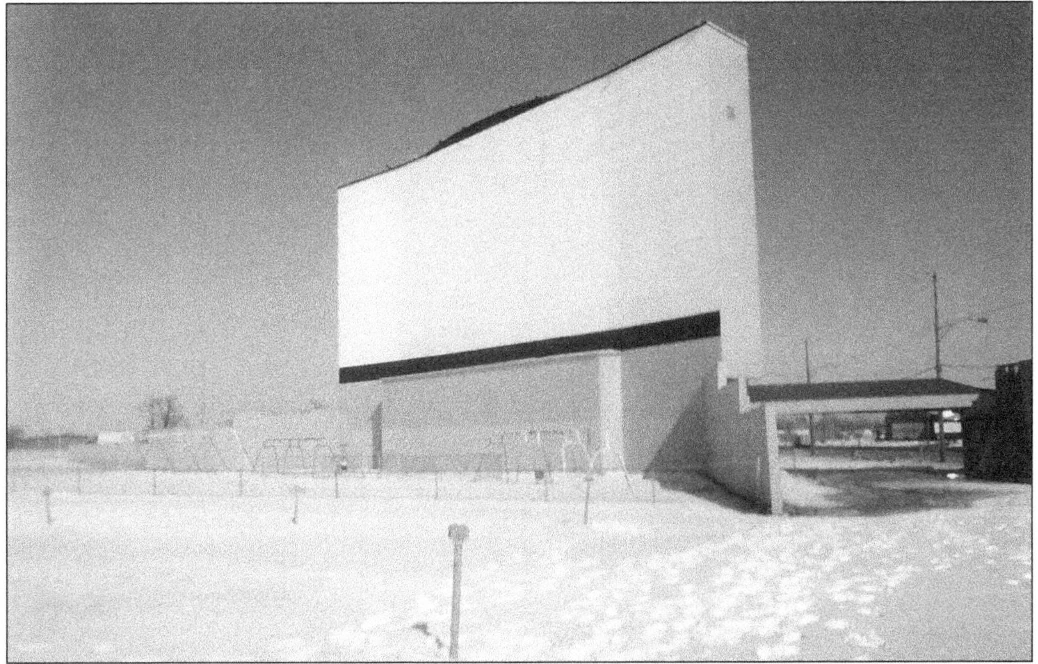

NO GRACEFUL CURVE THIS. The screen addition was not quite so deftly handled at the Michigan as at others. Seen here from the picture side, it is obvious that the addition did not incorporate a uniform curvature, but only two angled wings. This arrangement would have resulted in a less perfect picture than could have otherwise been achieved. Probably, no one ever noticed.

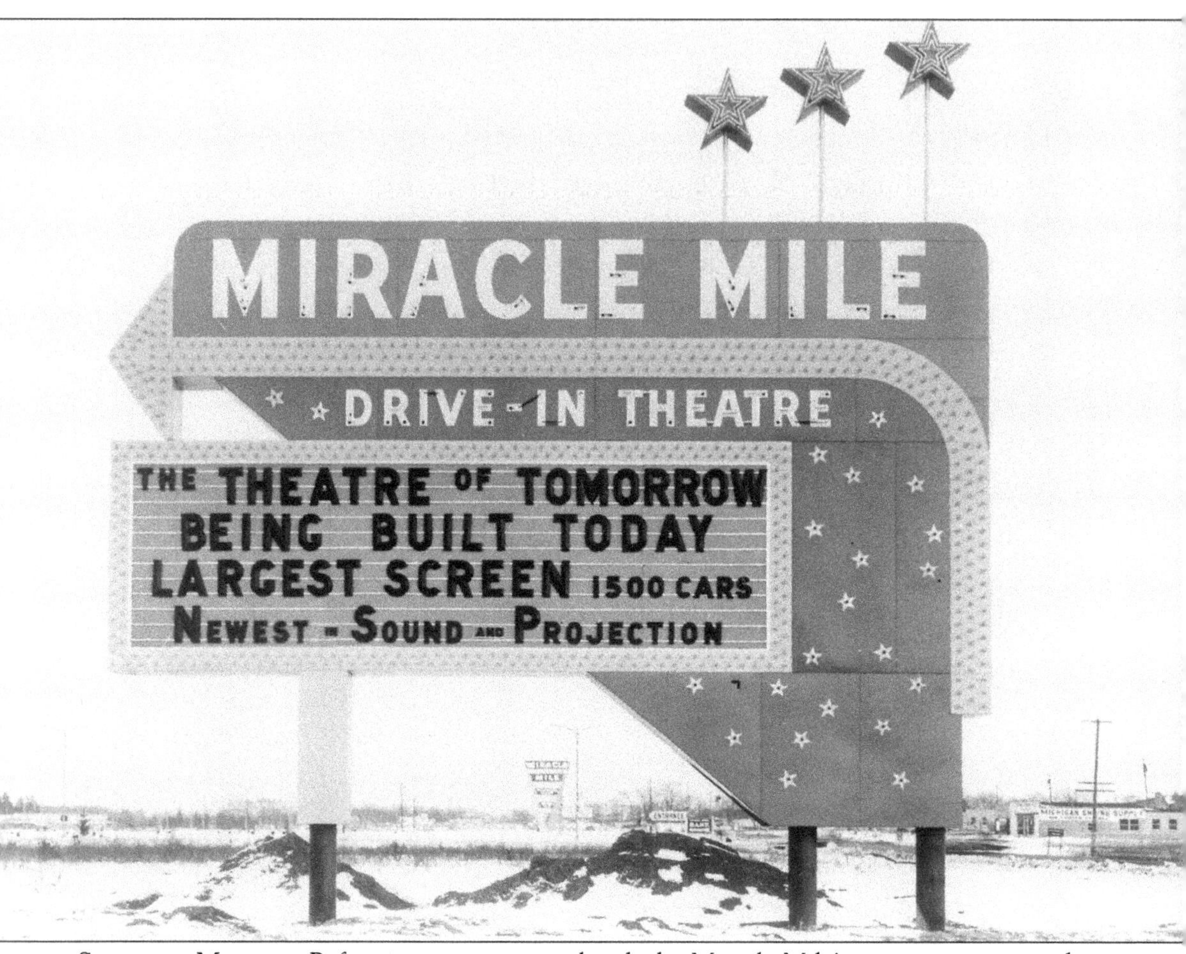

Sign of a Miracle. Before it was even completed, the Miracle Mile's marquee trumpeted its pending arrival. Located on Telegraph Road at Square Lake Road in Pontiac, the Miracle Mile was a late-1960s drive-in and the ultimate drive-in-going experience. It was one of the few drive-ins built with 70-millimeter projectors, guaranteeing a superior picture, and it had a capacity of 1,540 cars. The tower was 85 feet high and 140 feet wide, and the main concession counter was said to be 100 feet long. This masterpiece of drive-in architecture closed in 1986. (Courtesy of Ron Gross.)

More Ballyhoo. The Pontiac Drive-In, located on Dixie Highway near Telegraph Road in Pontiac, was a much more modest theater than the urban giants. With a capacity of 720 cars, it opened during the peak years of drive-in construction, in 1950. It soldiered along until 1990 with only its one original screen; although, in the late 1950s, its capacity was increased to over 1,200. It was one of the few to continue operation in the winter.

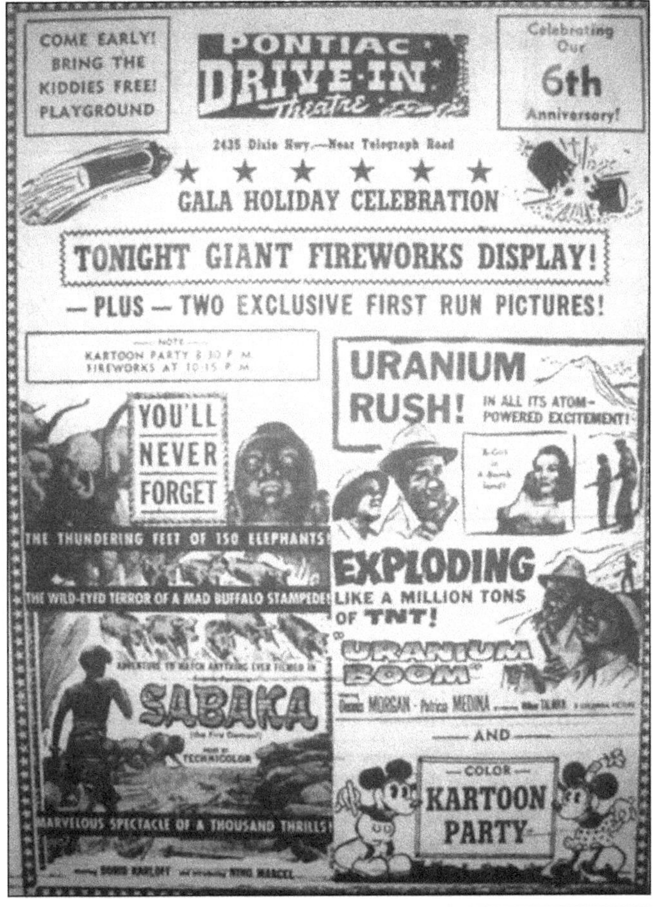

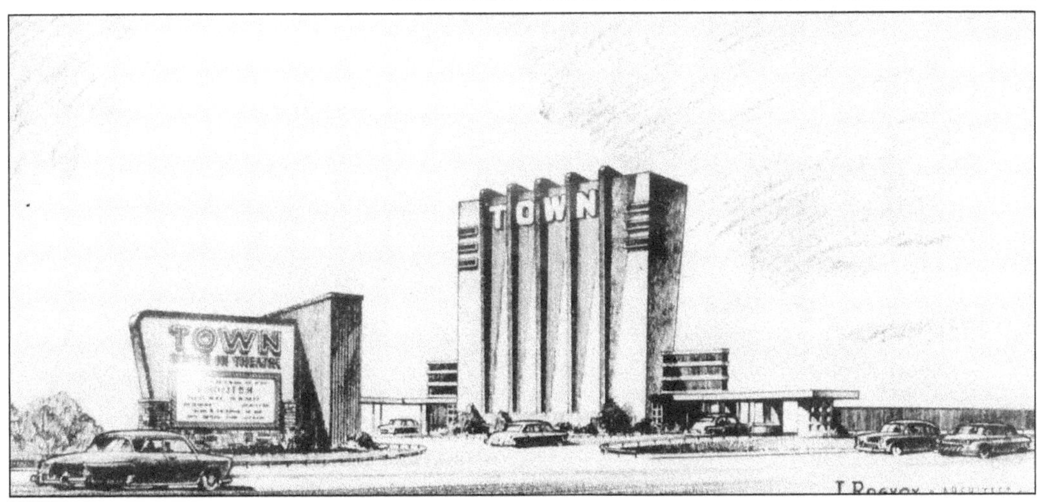

Architect's Rendering. The Town Drive-In, seen here in the original architect's pencil drawing, was built exactly as seen. Another Rogvoy design, like the Gratiot, the Town was constructed in 1949 at Telegraph Road and West Chicago Boulevard in Redford Township and had a capacity of 1,000 cars. It was an early casualty, being torn down in 1963 to make way for a Korvettes store. A scale-model passenger-carrying locomotive circumnavigated its playground.

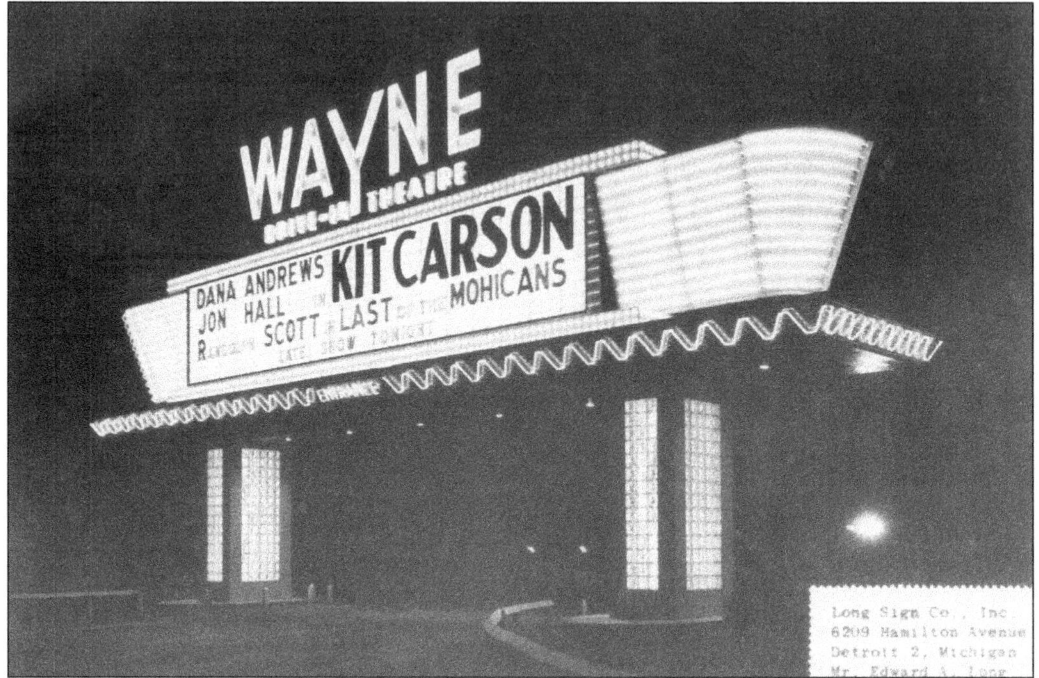

Another Sign of the Times. The magnificent original marquee of the Wayne Drive-In was constructed by the Long Sign Company, of Detroit. Long was responsible for the construction of many drive-in signs, including those of the Ford-Wyoming and Miracle Mile. Unfortunately, these neon-encrusted beauties were difficult and expensive to maintain and often were reduced to mere shadows of their original glory. (Courtesy of Ron Gross.)

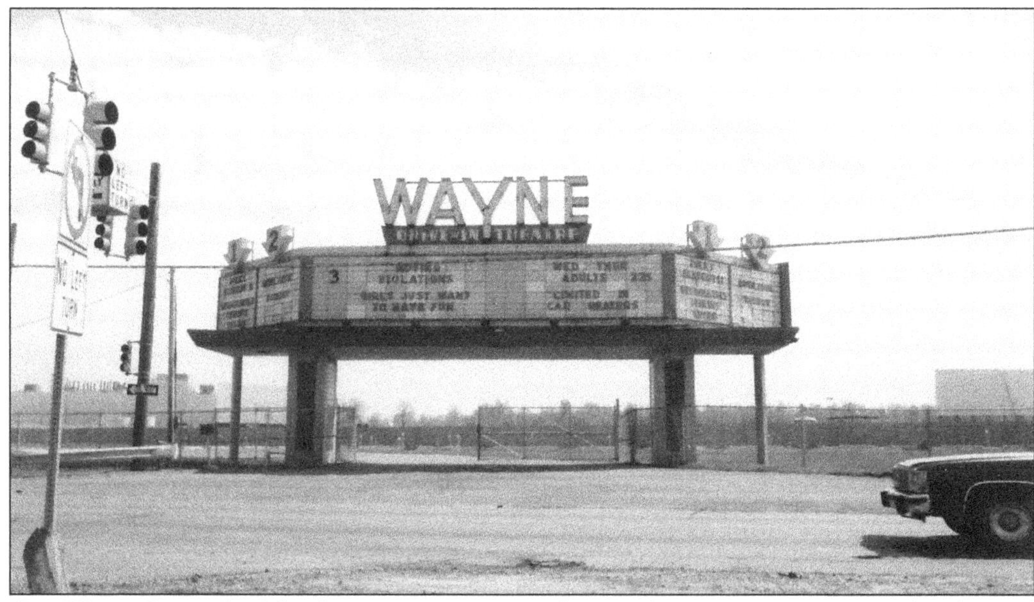

The Wayne Drive-In. The theater was constructed on Michigan Avenue near Newburgh Road in 1949, with a capacity of 842 cars. It was twinned in 1971 and then split again. By the time it closed in 1990, it was said to have a capacity of 2,000 cars. At the time of this 1985 photograph, it appears to have three screens in operation.

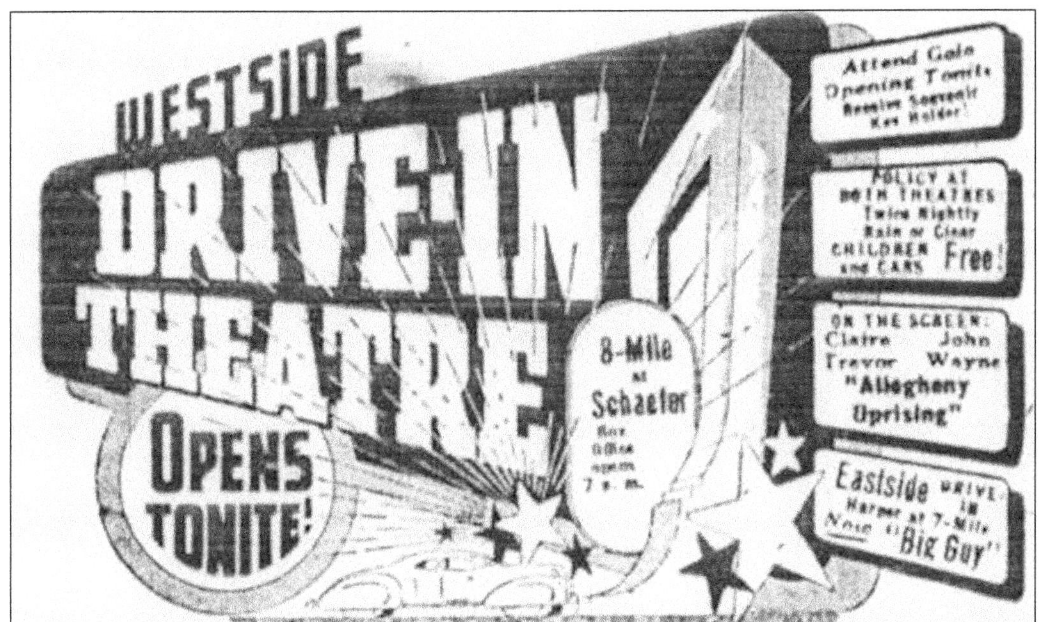

The Westside! It may not have been possible to create a more enthusiastic opening night ad for a theater than this 1941 ad for the Westside. The Westside was only the second drive-in in the Detroit area, after the Eastside—both of which names were adopted at later times. Like all early drive-ins, the Westside was just called "Drive-In Theater," but it eventually became necessary to differentiate between them. Located at 14350 West 8 Mile Road, near Schaefer, the Westside had a capacity of 700 cars.

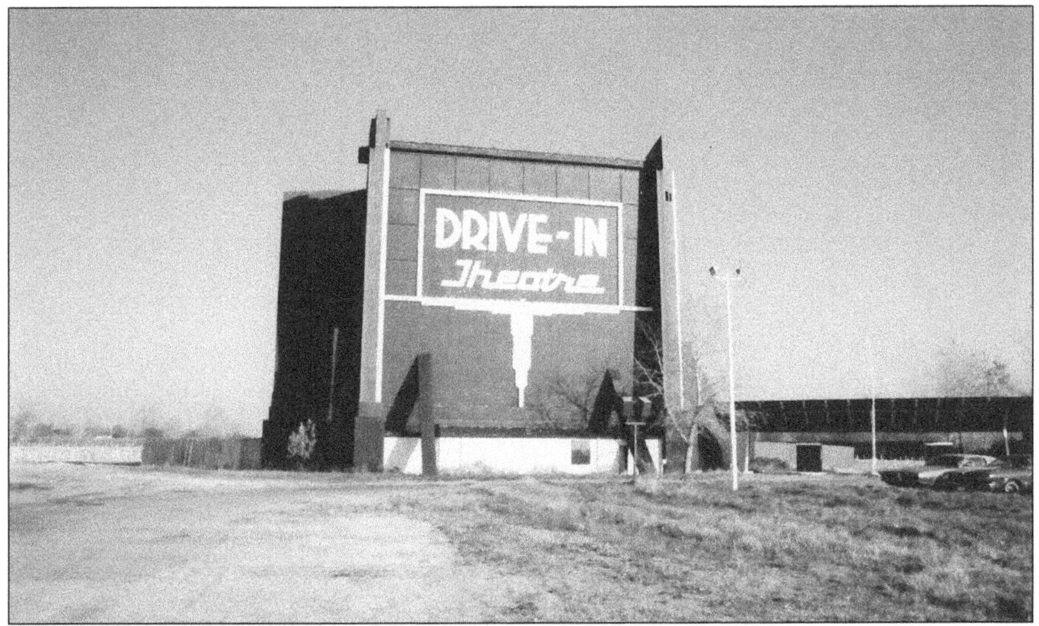

In Later Days. The Westside, seen here after its closing in 1984, was a shadow of its former glory. Its barely evident wide-screen addition hardly obscures its original configuration. After its demolition, it remained a vacant lot for some time. It was, however, ultimately immortalized as it originally appeared, on a popular postcard.

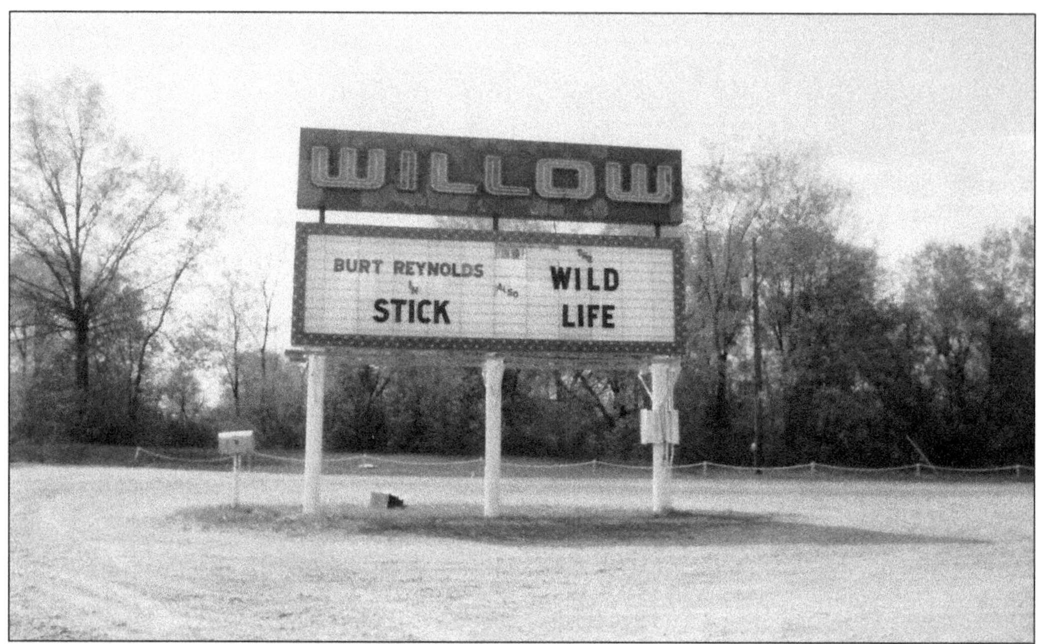

The Willow. The Willow Drive-In, in Belleville, was further out on the fringe than most Detroit-area theaters and built at a later time, in 1966. It had a 1,000-car capacity on an oddly asymmetrical lot with a truncated side to fit within a narrow property line. The large screen was said to be 118 by 50 feet. Despite some claims to the contrary, it was still in operation until 1985.

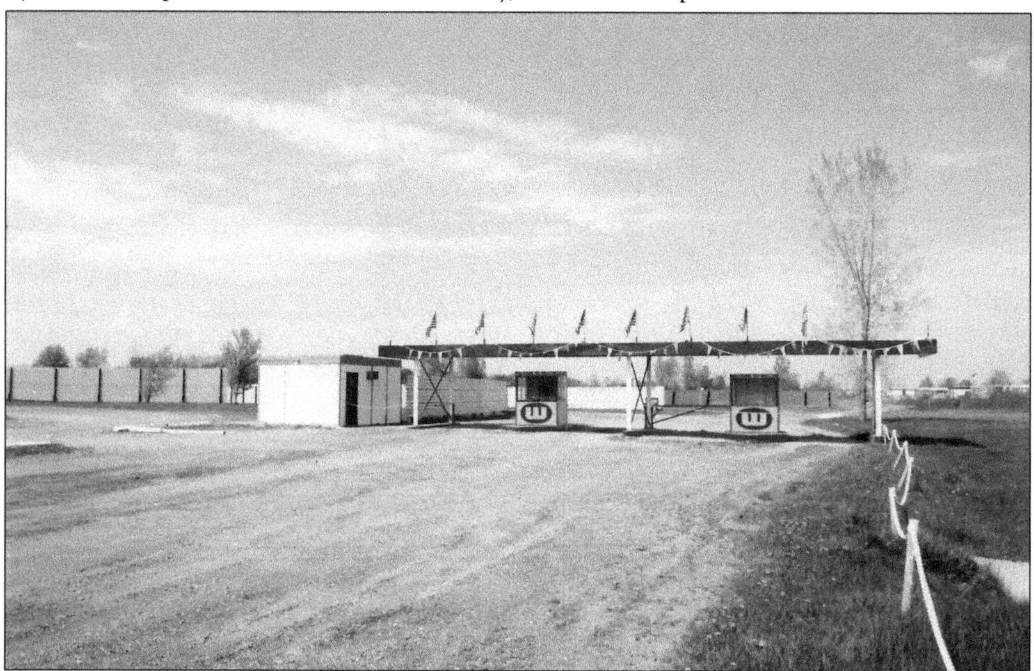

Spacious yet Casual. The Willow's entrance drive was unpaved, but the box offices were well maintained and decorated with festive pennants. The Willow was another example of a theater that was kept up until the day it closed and readied for a next season that never came. Wayne Amusements originally built it.

Three

The Southeast

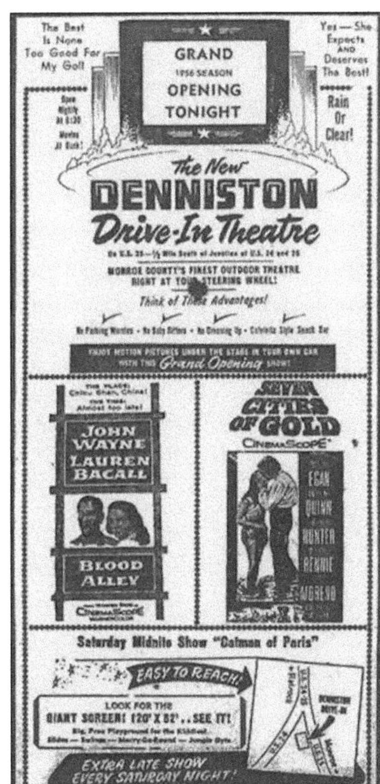

The Denniston. South of Detroit, the Monroe area boasted a phenomenon that was probably unique in the history of drive-ins—a single strip of road containing several drive-ins, all within sight of each other. The Denniston was one of these. The Denniston was fairly large, especially for a small town like Monroe. Opened in 1956, it had a 1,000-car capacity.

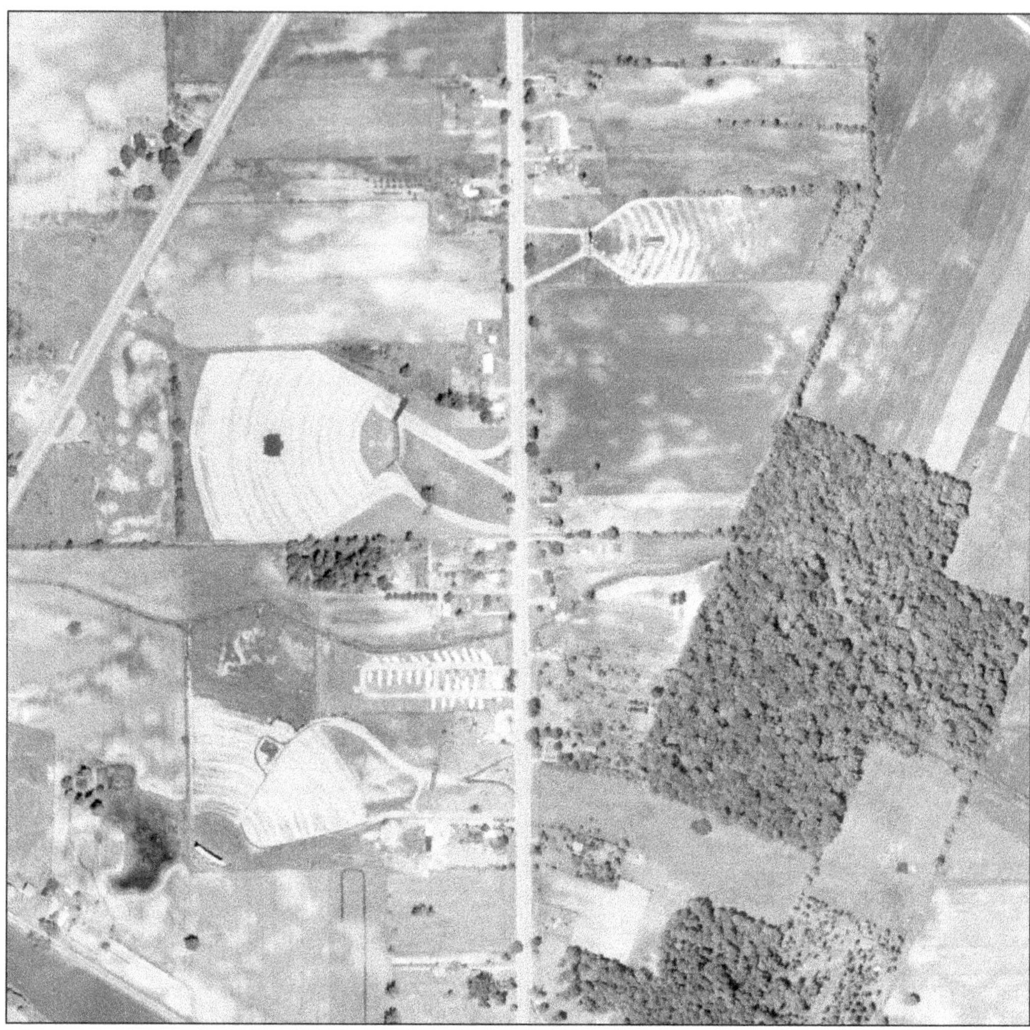

Monroe's Drive-In Mile. The impossible stretch of Michigan Route 151, also known locally as North Monroe Street, seen here, was blessed with three different drive-ins. The drive-ins pictured are, from top to bottom, the Dixie, Denniston, and General Custer. The Dixie opened in 1948, held only 275 cars, and closed in 1966. The Denniston opened in 1956 with a capacity of 1,000 and closed in 1985. The General Custer, also known as Bel Aire Twin, opened in 1955 with a capacity of 800 but was later twinned and closed in 1988. (Courtesy of Historicaerials.com.)

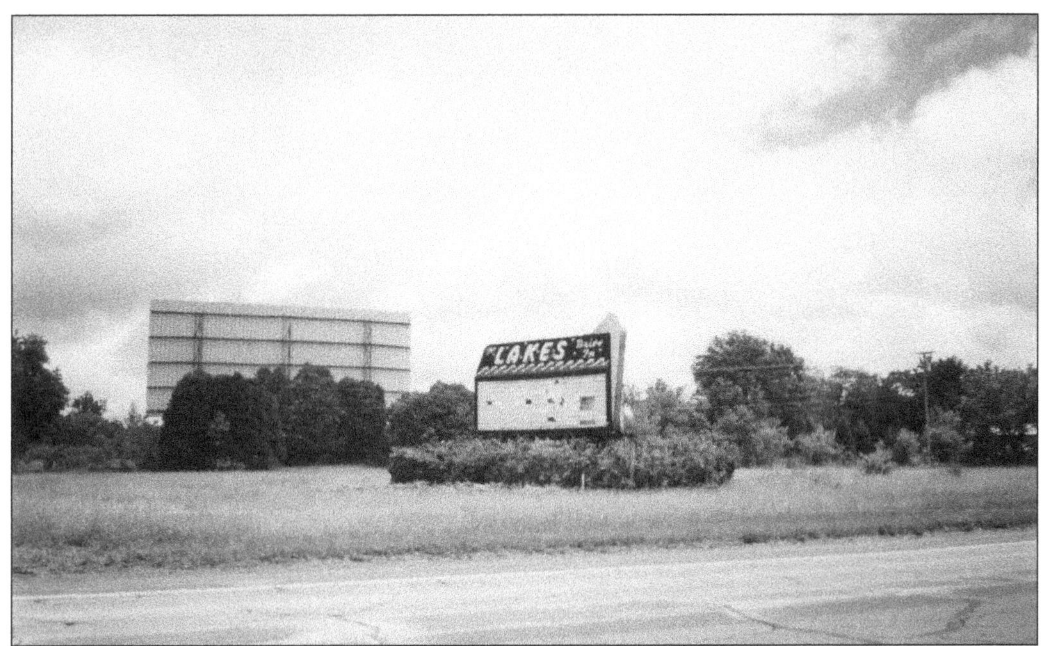

The Lakes, Brighton. The Lakes was located at 10501 East Grand River Road. It opened in 1951 and had a limited but typical capacity of 700 cars. On opening night, orchids were given to the ladies in attendance and it was promised that a playground with free pony rides for the kiddies would soon be available.

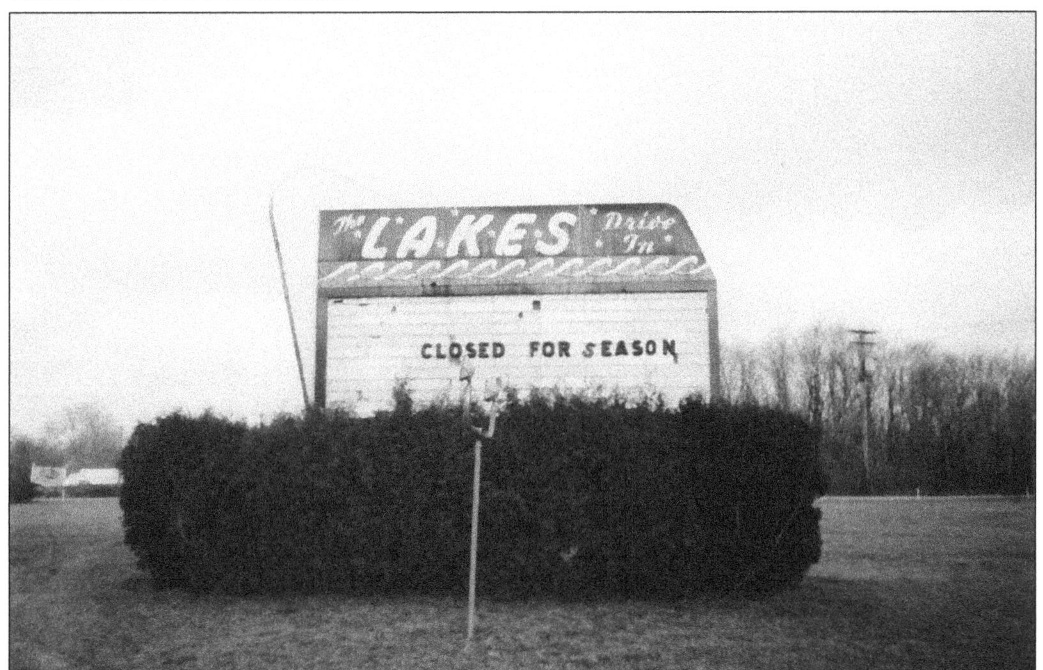

Closed for the Season. The opening night program in 1951 included *Jeepers Creepers* and *Saddle Tramp* projected on its large 66-by-60-foot screen. The Lakes was closed and later demolished to make way for, among other things, an ice rink, in 1989. The marquee shown was originally one of two; the second was facing Interstate 96.

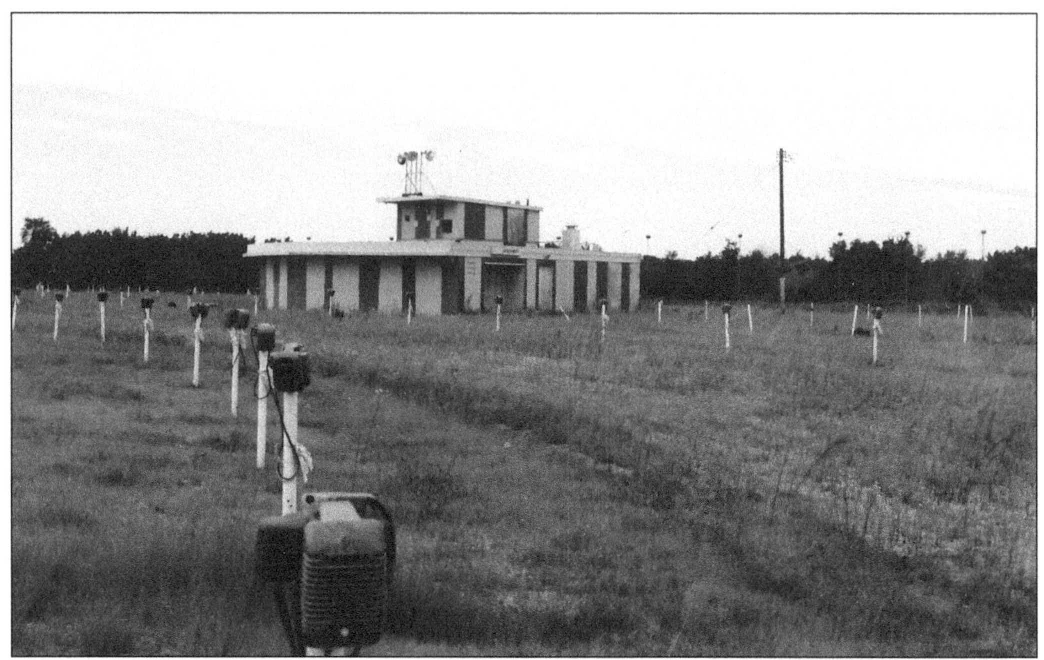

THE SCENIC SCIO. Of the three drive-ins in the Ann Arbor area, the Scio was the furthest west, being located on Jackson Road West of Zeeb Road. Only holding 400 cars, the Scio was nonetheless well maintained, as can be seen in this 1988 photograph. The Scio's design was somewhat atypical for a theater of its size in that it had a projection booth elevated above the concession stand.

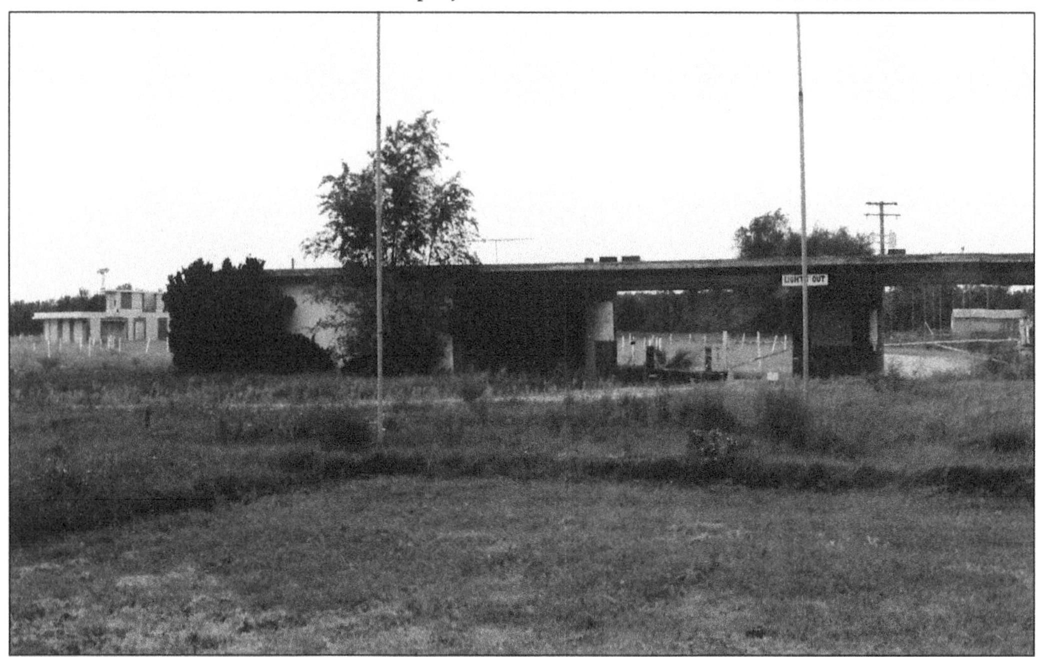

THE SCENIC BOX OFFICE. Actually, the box office was fairly standard for a small theater and equally well maintained. The concession building, visible in the background, avoided the chance of pedestrians walking into the projection beam with its elevated booth. At the time of this photograph, the Scio was showing X-rated films, which were notorious for low concession sales.

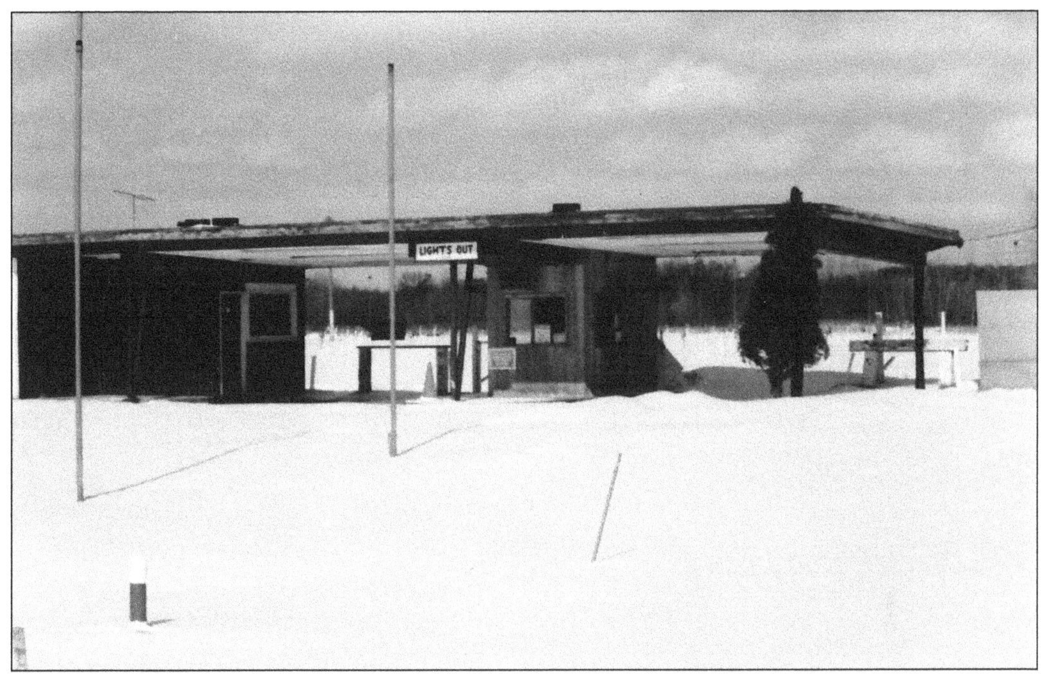

No Ticket Sales Today. The Scio was not one of those theaters that stayed open during winter months—almost no small ones ever did, as the greatly reduced profits did not justify the cost. Although the Scio started life as a family venue, it switched to X-rated films in 1974. In 1977, its capacity was said to be 700.

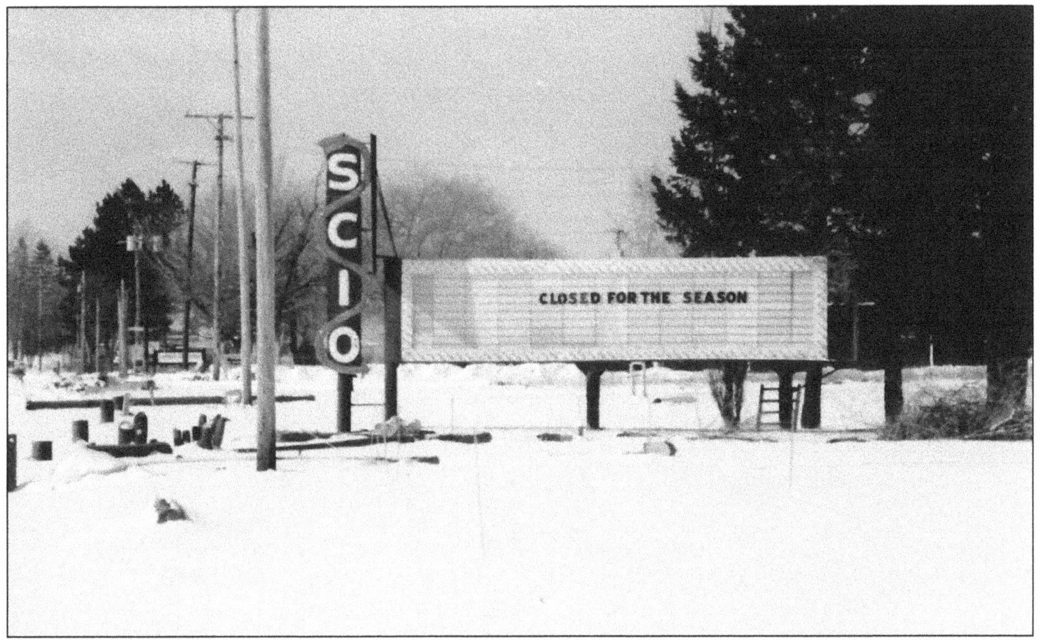

A Simple Marquee. The Scio's marquee, seen here in 1986, was a humble affair, as befit a small rural theater. The sign lingered on in the weeds for years after the theater's closing in 1988 but was later rescued and revived by a rabid drive-in enthusiast. An even more dedicated aficionado rescued the giant Gratiot sign.

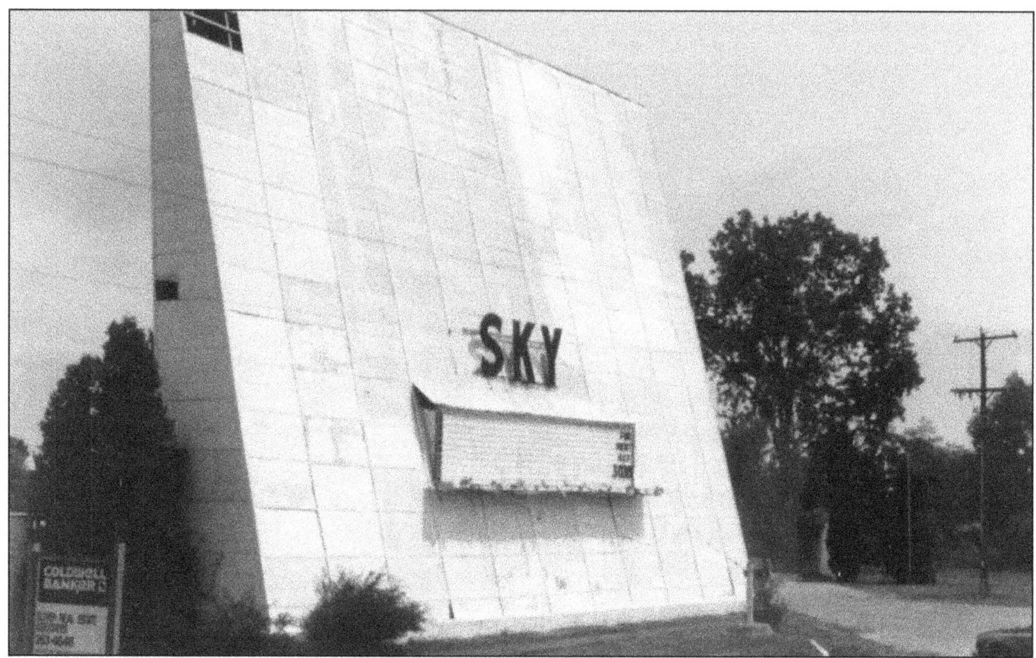

The Sky Drive-In, Adrian. The Sky Drive-In clocked in at a tiny 280-car capacity, which did not prevent it from being cute as the proverbial button. Not only did a playground front the screen, but also in the early years, a winter skating rink was created at the screen base, with music piped in from the sound system. It was built in 1949.

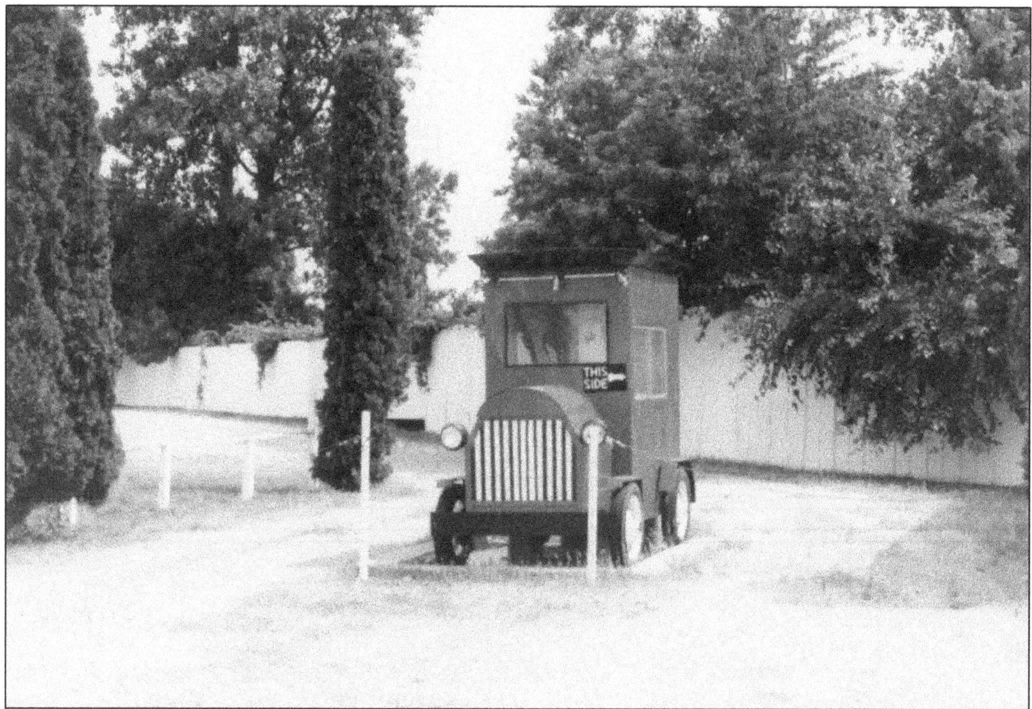

The World's Cutest Box office. It is probably a replacement, but in 1987, the Sky's box office was a tiny red truck. Photographs exist of a much larger, more typical pre-truck box office.

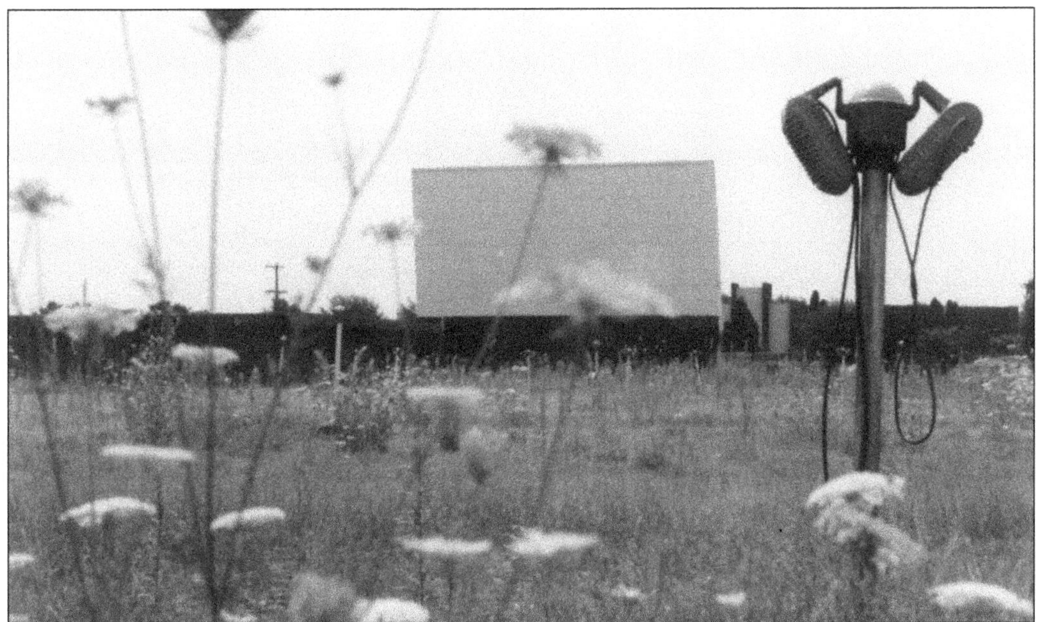

Overgrown for the Season. By 1987, the Sky was closed, and the lot, although intact, was already overgrown and filled with weeds. As with most rural theaters, it was economics, not property values, that did it in, and the Sky, as with many others, stood for some time empty and forlorn as a sad and lonely ghost drive-in.

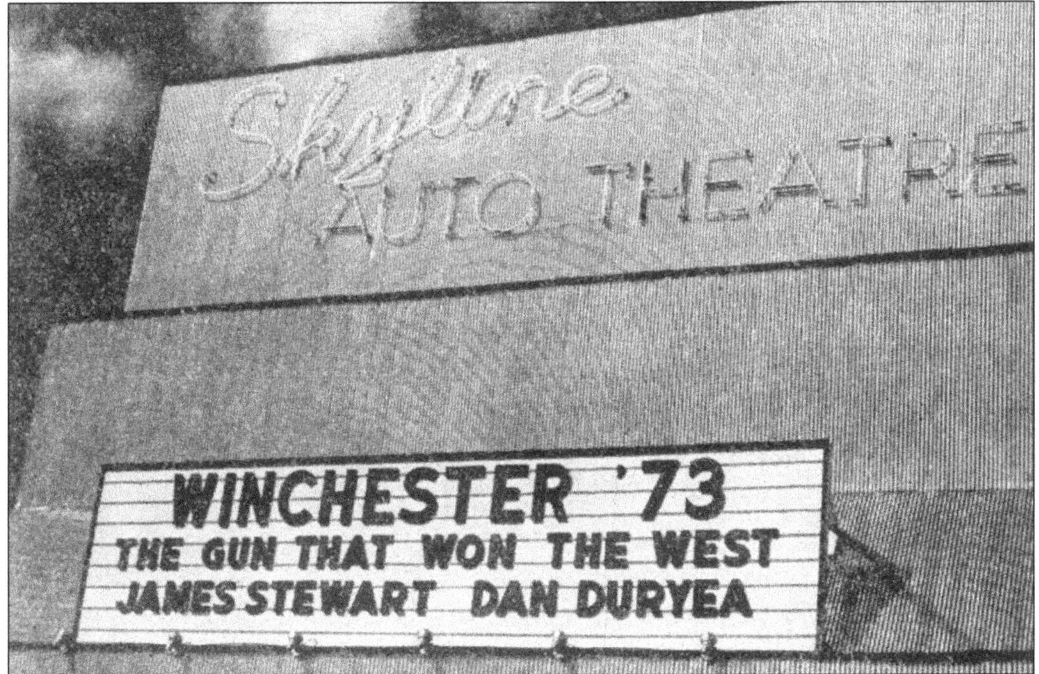

The Skyline Auto Theatre, Morenci. Located literally within feet of the Ohio state line, the tiny Skyline Auto Theatre had to be the closest Michigan drive-in to the state line. Its capacity of 200 cars also made it one of the smallest in the state. It vanished from official drive-in inventories around 1963 and was never seen again. The film on the marquee is from 1950.

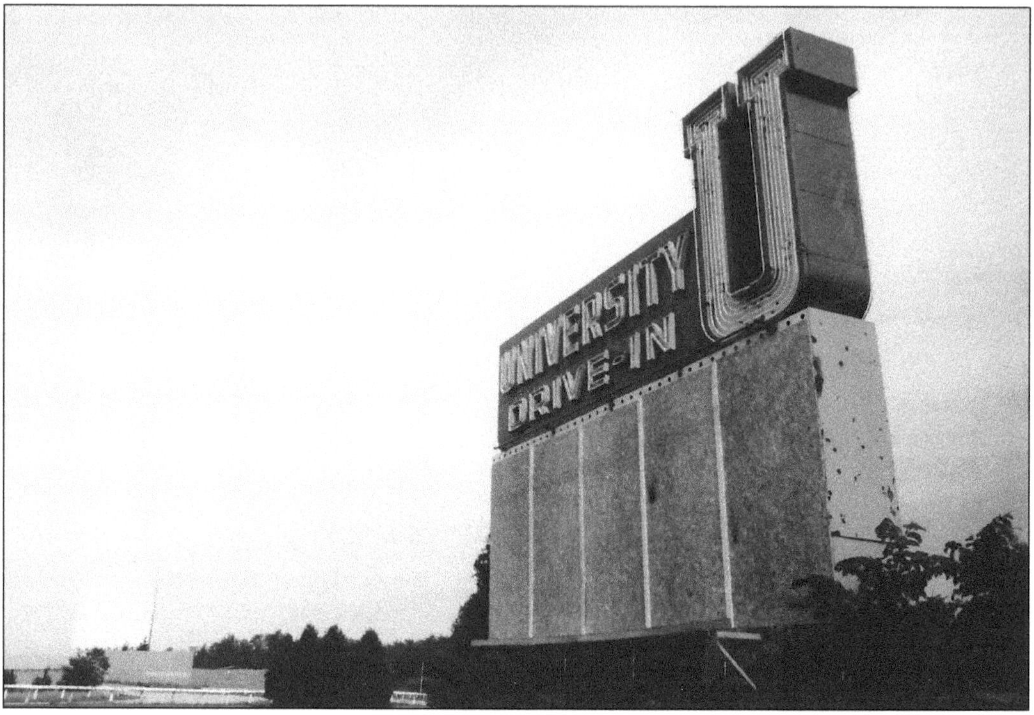

Going to the University. The University was the largest and most modern drive-in in the Ann Arbor area. Located at 4100 Carpenter Road, it opened in 1965 with an estimated construction cost of half a million dollars. With its 1,033-car capacity, it would have been inordinately large for a small-town drive-in if not for its strategic location between the college towns of Ann Arbor and Ypsilanti.

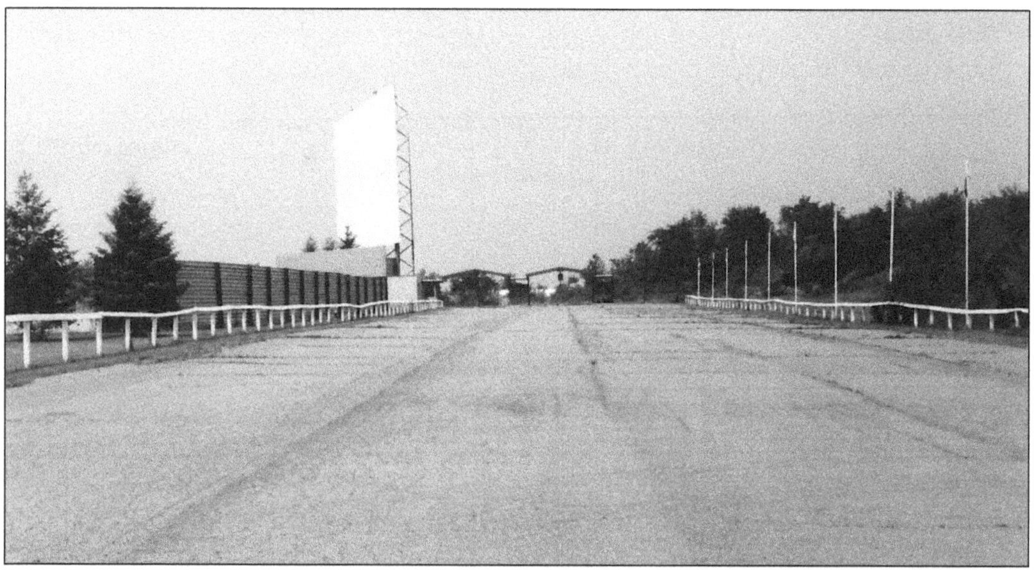

A Long, Long Drive-In. Again typical of a highly evolved later drive-in, the approach by way of a broad, lengthy driveway was virtually guaranteed to prevent traffic jams on the road leading to the drive-in. This thoroughfare was attractively landscaped and well lighted, as was the rest of the property.

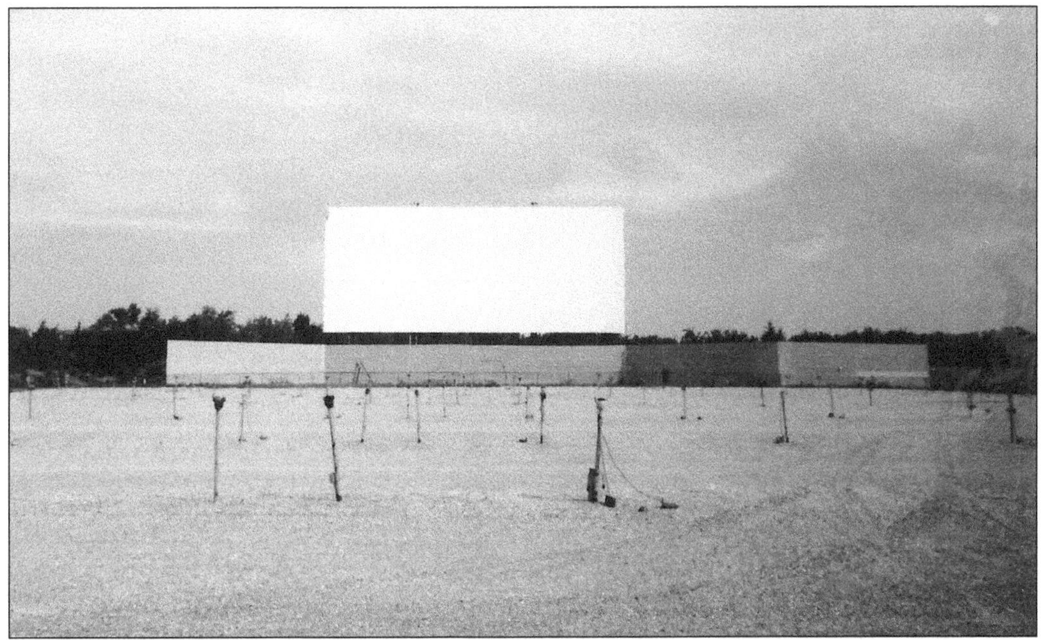

A Lot of Lot. The vast expanse of the University's lot made for a healthy walk to the combination concession-and-projection building. By this time, high-intensity projection lamps made the long throw to the screen possible without undue loss of brightness. The University was probably still using in-car speakers when this photograph was taken in 1985.

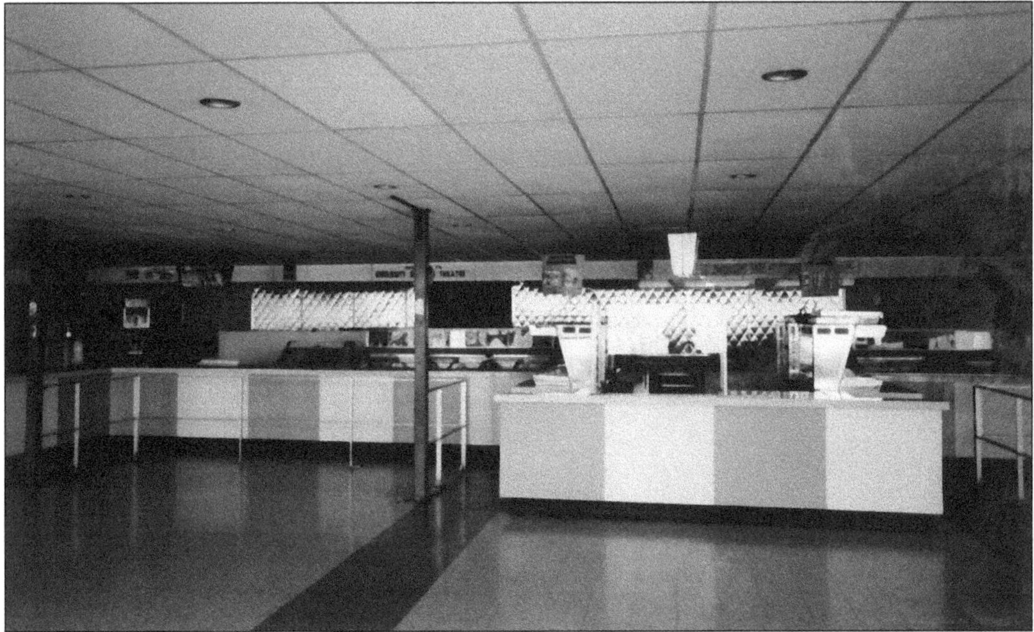

No Concessions to Be Made. The concession stand at the University is seen after its closing in 1985. As with so many others, the University's concession stand was in pristine condition when it closed down at the end of the 1985 season, never to reopen again. The University was torn down to make room for a multiscreen Showcase Cinema, the entrance drive of which was in the same location as the drive-in's.

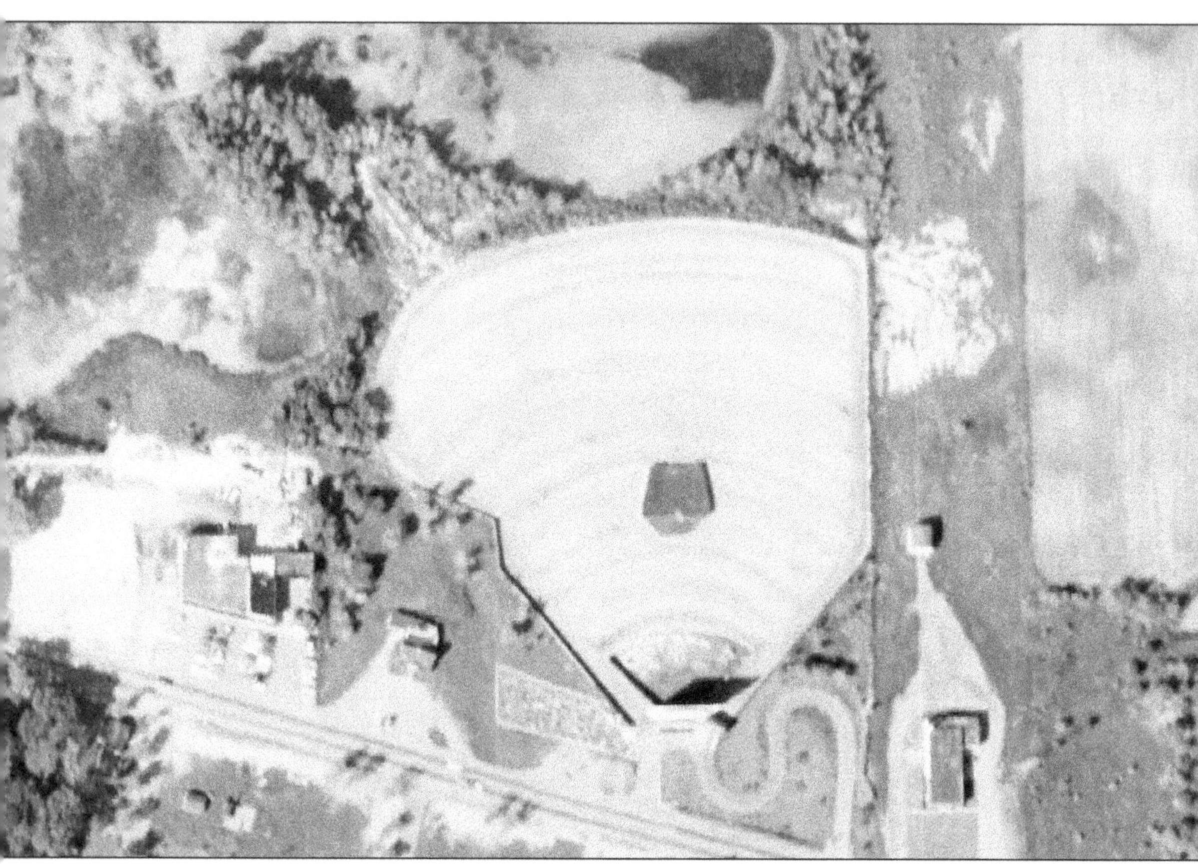

The Ypsi-Ann Drive-In. The Ypsi-Ann was a modest-sized 500-car theater at 4675 Washtenaw Avenue, between Ypsilanti and Ann Arbor. It was constructed in 1948, making it the first drive-in in the vicinity. Eventually, it would be overshadowed by the construction of the University Drive-In, only a few miles away. The Ypsi-Ann was ultimately closed and demolished, probably in 1978, to make room for a shopping center. This aerial photograph is from 1963. (Courtesy of Historicaerials.com.)

Four

The Thumb

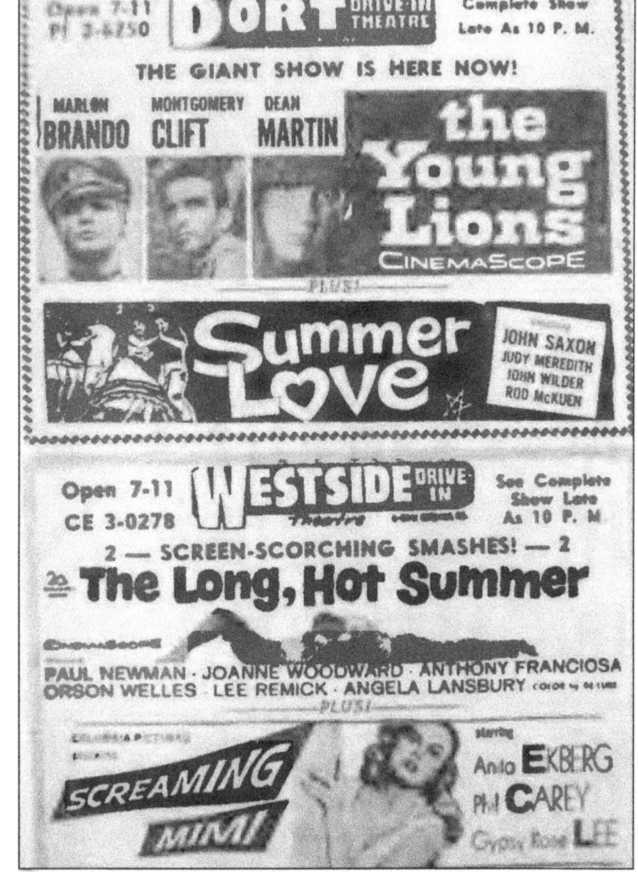

The Dort and Westside Drive-Ins. This ad from 1958 is for two of the Flint area's drive-ins, the Dort, also known as Dort-Eastside, and the Westside. The Dort was opened 1946 and was an attractive theater, with a 700-car capacity, but closed in 1963. The Westside opened in 1947 and closed in 1984. It had a 500-car capacity.

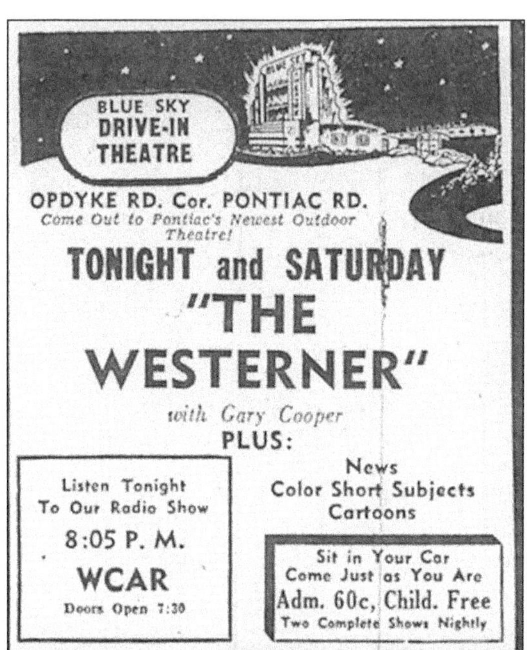

Blue Sky Ad. This Blue Sky Drive-In was located at 2150 North Opdyke Road in Pontiac. It opened in 1948 with a 700-car capacity. It was similar to the Dort in construction and closed in 1987 to make way for another Showcase Cinema. Although in proximity to the thumb area, this drive-in could also be considered a Detroit-area theater but is presented here so as to not confuse it with the Blue Sky in Caseville.

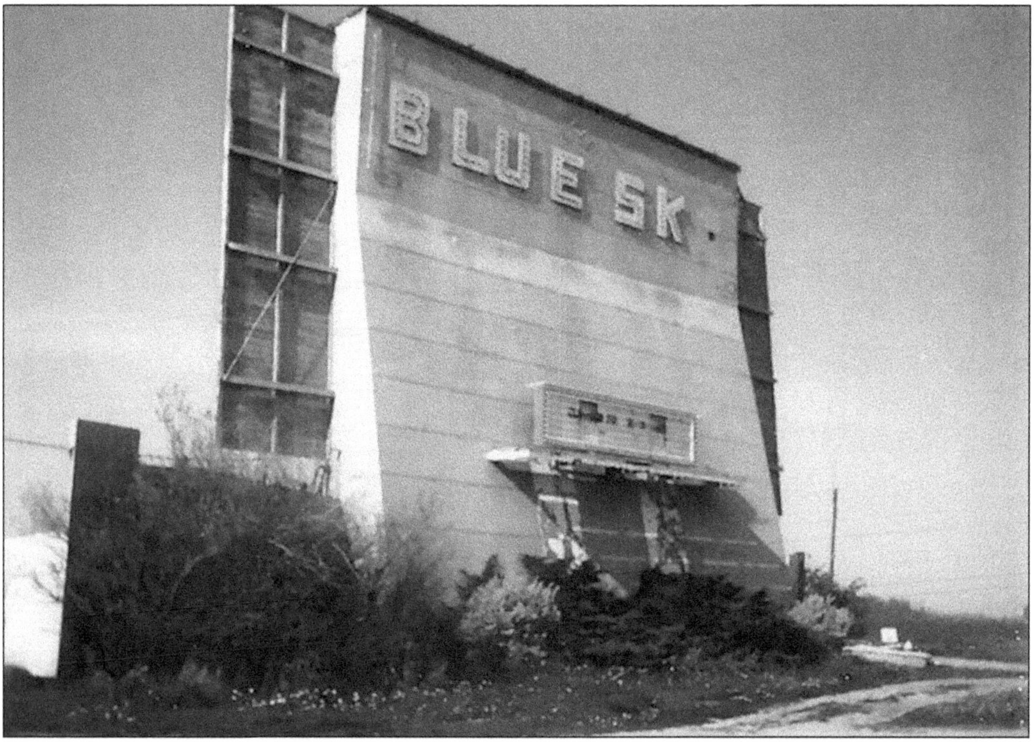

The Blue Sky Drive-In, Caseville. This Blue Sky was on Kinde Road in Caseville and had a 250-car capacity. It was constructed probably around 1950 and operated most of its life as a legitimate drive-in but turned to X-rated in the 1970s. It most likely closed sometime between 1980 and 1985. During the X-rated era, neighbors picketed in front, while others snuck in the back. (Courtesy of Curt Peterson.)

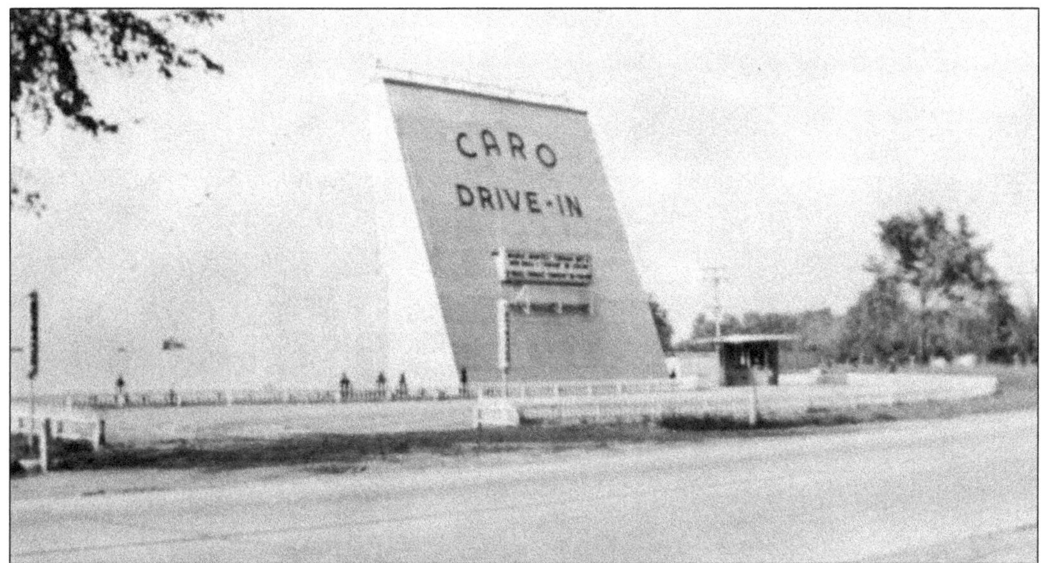

The Caro Drive-In. The Caro Drive-In was located at 1123 East Caro Road in Caro. It opened in May 1950 with a 500-car capacity, and R.J. Ashmun, who also operated the Strand Theatre in Caro, owned it. Built for a reported $65,000, the Caro was a modest yet efficient affair, suitable for such a small town. Note the screen tower's similarity to that of the Blue Sky.

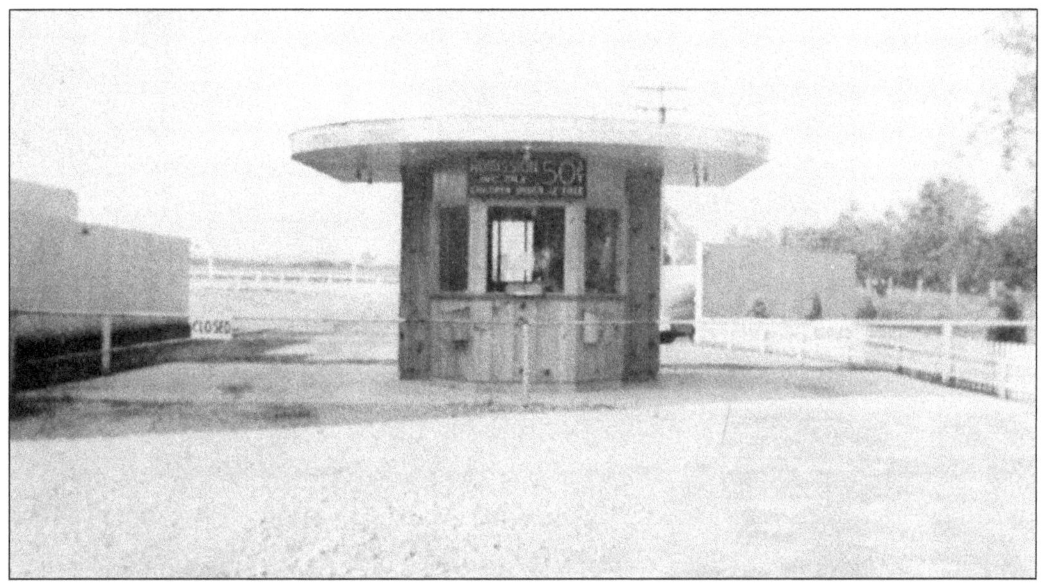

Box Office Beauty. Seen here when new in 1950, the Caro's box office was pretty typical but was also a fine example of what could be accomplished on a limited budget. Unlike the giant Gratiot of only two years earlier, box offices by this time were built with a window for each lane of cars and not merely as a home location for roving ticket takers.

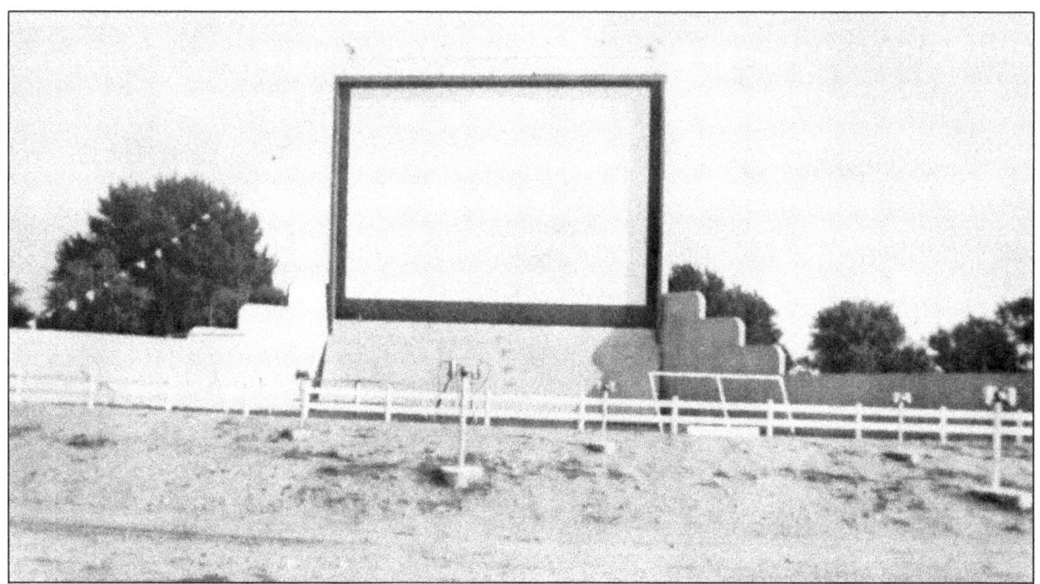

The Caro's Screen. Strings of pennants descend from the screen of the new Caro, seen here at its opening. Despite the venue's small size, the architect took the time to include the waterfall decorative elements, also seen here on either side. The Caro's small playground is also visible within the fenced-in area. It included the usual slides, swings, and teeter-totters—no railroad here.

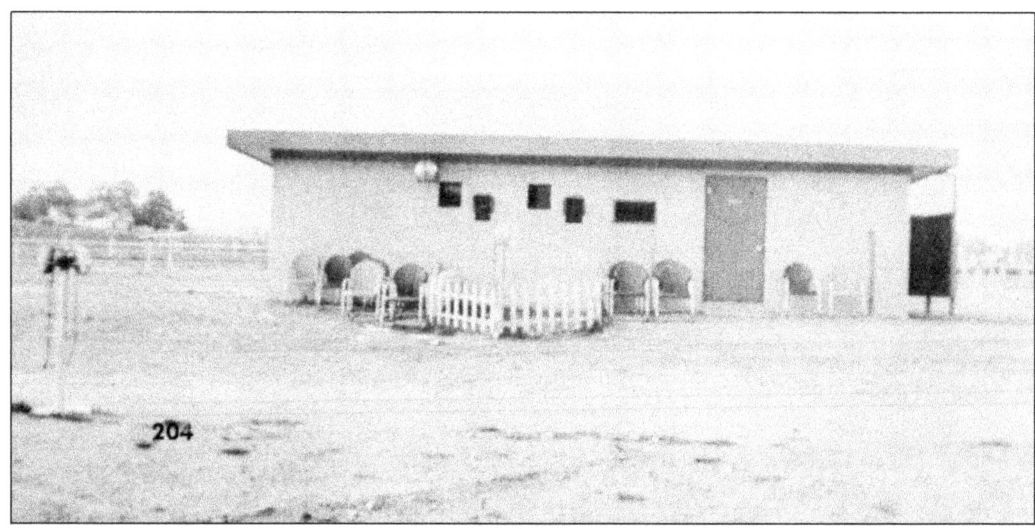

Concession Stand. The Caro's concession building was an equally humble affair. The door in front is apparently to the projection booth, and restrooms are accessed on the right. The tiny white picket fence is of course to keep people from walking into the projector beams, and the metal chairs are available for those waiting near the building.

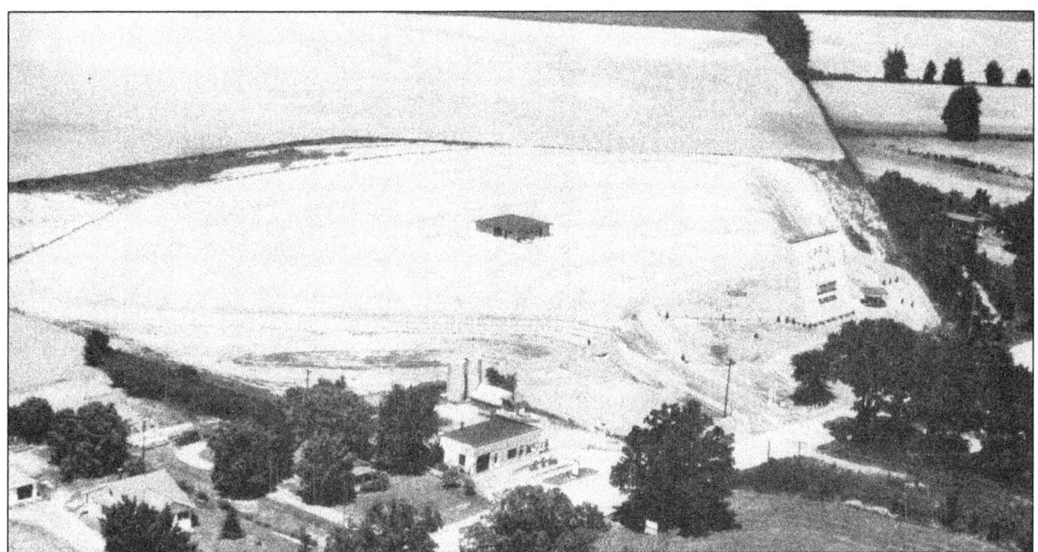

Aerial View. The essentially rural situation of the Caro is visible in this aerial photograph. Although the landscaping is still undeveloped, the tiny pine trees planted to decorate the theater are visible in front. The screen was ultimately another victim of the elements and was blown to the ground by high winds in 1988.

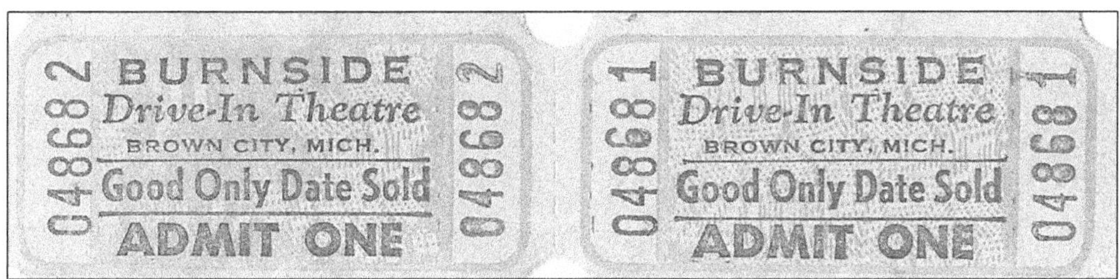

Two Tickets to Paradise. The Burnside Drive-In was located in the tiny village of Burnside, about eight miles from Imlay City. It was opened in 1951 and had a capacity of 300–400 cars. The screen tower was decorated with a mural depicting a pheasant rising from a cornfield. After its closing, it sat abandoned for years. Eventually, the property was used as an archery range.

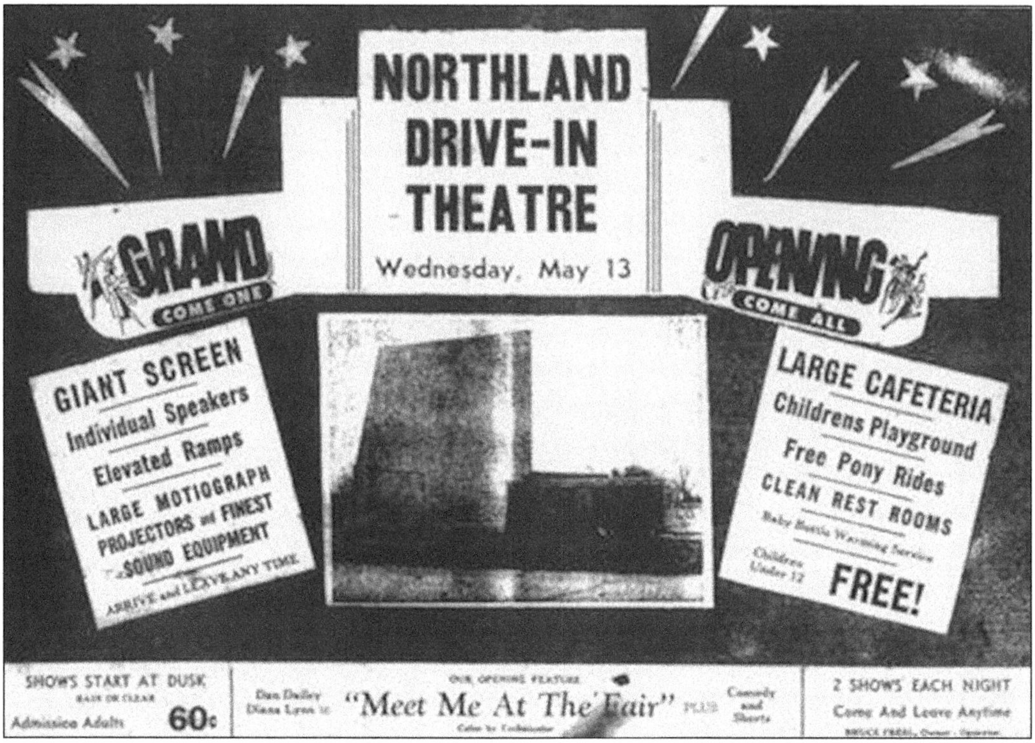

NORTHLAND
DRIVE-IN
THEATRE
Wednesday, May 13

GRAND
COME ONE

OPENING
COME ALL

GIANT SCREEN
Individual Speakers
Elevated Ramps
LARGE MOTIOGRAPH
PROJECTORS and FINEST
SOUND EQUIPMENT

LARGE CAFETERIA
Childrens Playground
Free Pony Rides
CLEAN REST ROOMS
Children
Under 12
FREE!

SHOWS START AT DUSK
Admission Adults 60¢

Dan Dailey
Diana Lynn in
"Meet Me At The Fair" PLUS Comedy and Shorts

2 SHOWS EACH NIGHT
Come And Leave Anytime

NORTHLAND DRIVE-IN, PETOSKY. The tiny Northland Drive-In nonetheless had a spectacular ad to herald its opening in 1953. With an original capacity given as 282 cars, the Northland still had pony rides for the kids (at least during the grand opening). Some time after 1974, it was enlarged, if one is to believe the accounts, to 400 cars. It closed in 1986.

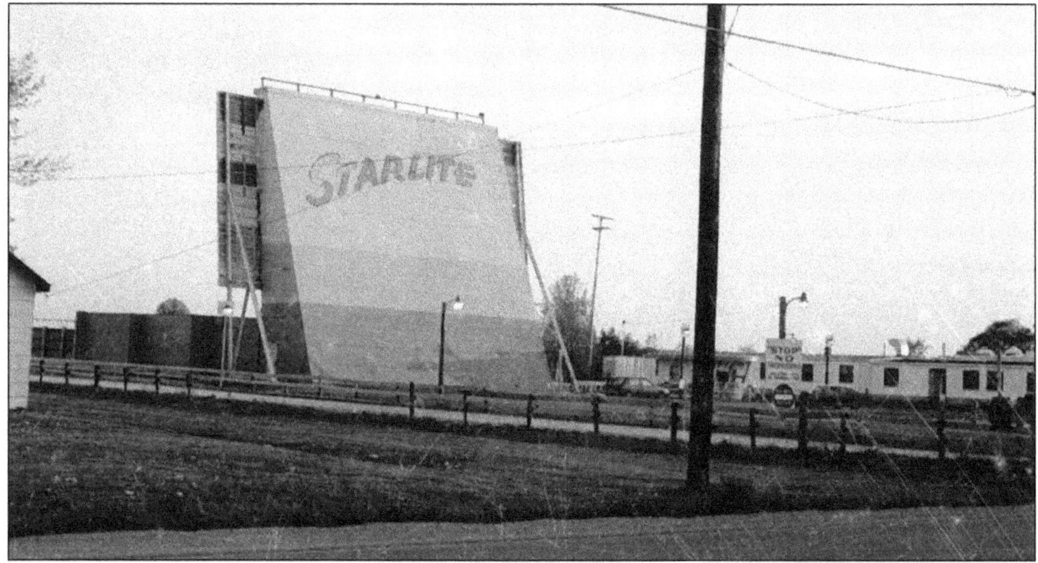

THE STARLITE, BAY CITY. The Starlite, also known as Starlight, was situated at 2400 Midland Road in Bay City. It opened in 1950 with a capacity of 700 cars, and R.J. Ashmun, also of the Caro, operated it. In 1982, it was twinned and renamed the Starlite Twin. It closed in July 1987. (Courtesy of Curt Peterson.)

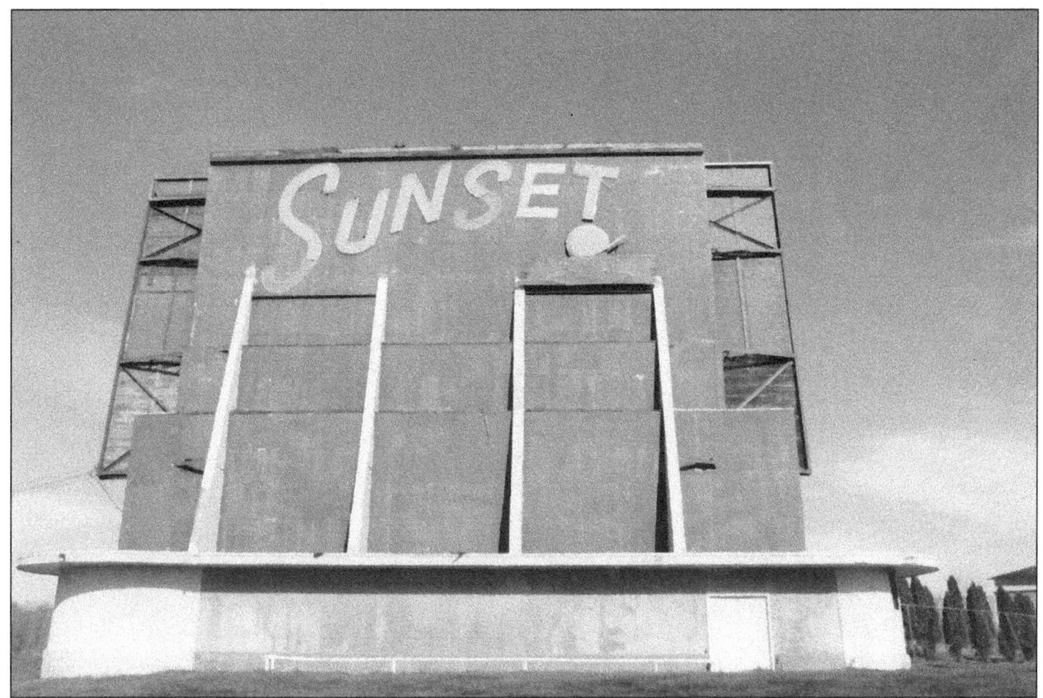

THE SUNSET DRIVE-IN, LAPEER. The Sunset, seen here in 1984, was located at 1455 Imlay City Road, between Lapeer and Imlay City. It opened with a 400-car capacity. The screen structure not only proclaimed its name in tall neon-outlined letters but also depicted a neon sunset, with the setting sun reflecting in neon waters.

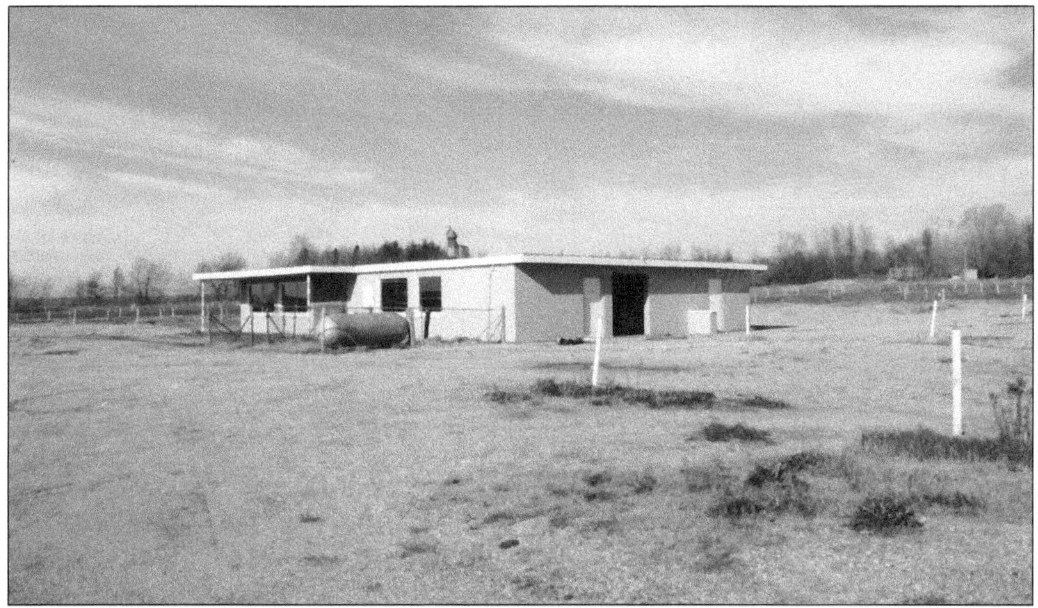

CONCESSION STAND, 1984. Despite its small size, the concession building was well designed and maintained, but its remote location required the use of a propane tank to supply heat and for kitchen equipment. Large windows and a small outside canopy allowed patrons to view the film from the concession stand.

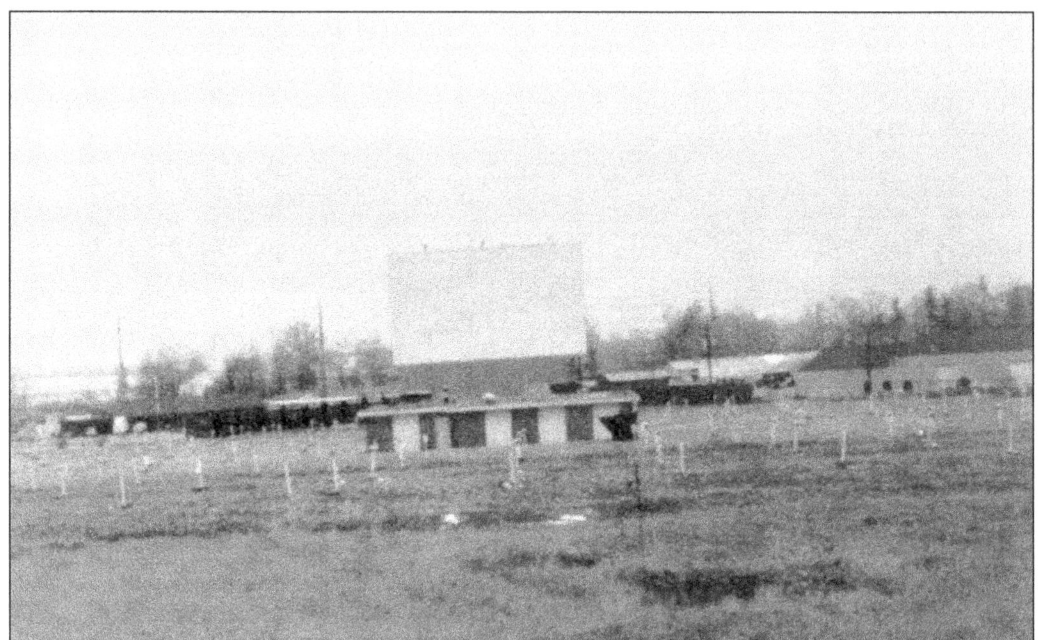

Sunset Lot, c. 1970s. This earlier image of the Sunset includes the lot, screen, and striped concession building. Several of the theaters operated by Harry Mohney and Curt Peterson indulged in this candy-striped paint job, another among them being the Scio. In later years, the Sunset ran adult films, much to the consternation of the locals. Its last year of operation was 1984.

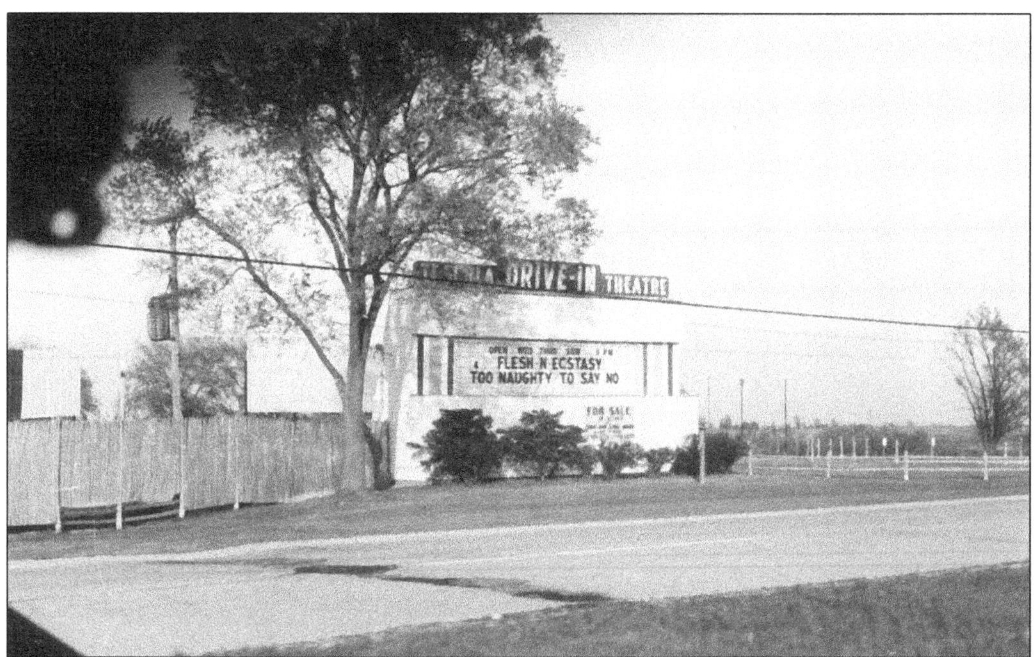

The Tuscola, Bay City. The Tuscola was located at 537 Tuscola Road in Bay City. It was a pretty large theater at the time of its opening in 1948, having a capacity of 800 cars, and Ashmun also operated it. It also went to X-rated fare later in life and also irritated the neighbors sufficiently that their complaints to the city had it closed by the mid-1980s. (Courtesy of Curt Peterson.)

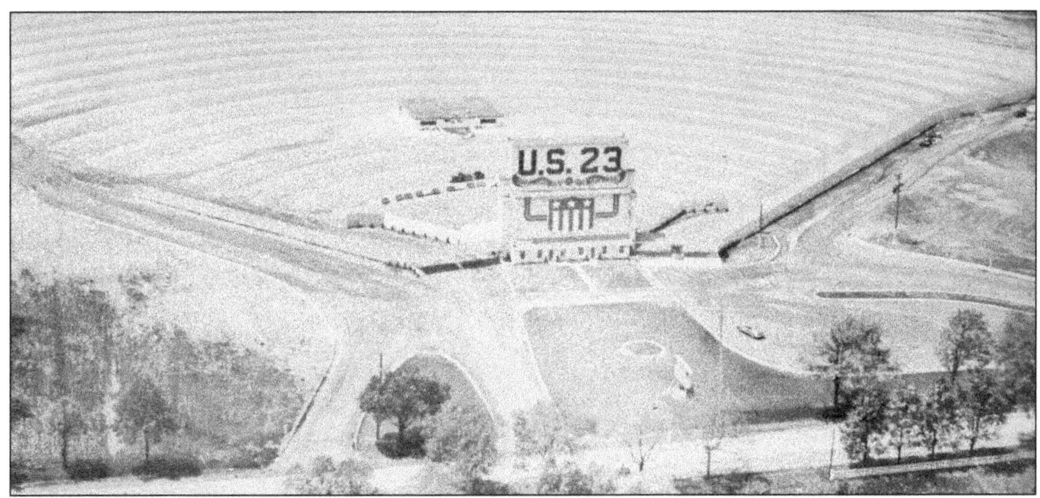

The US-23, Flint. Though located on Fenton Road, the US-23 was, not surprisingly, named for its proximity to US Route 23. It was built in 1952 as a very large 1,250-car theater, and its 25-acre expanse can be appreciated in this aerial photograph. The combination concession-and-projection building is closer to the screen than the lot's center, requiring those customers in the back rows to take quite a walk.

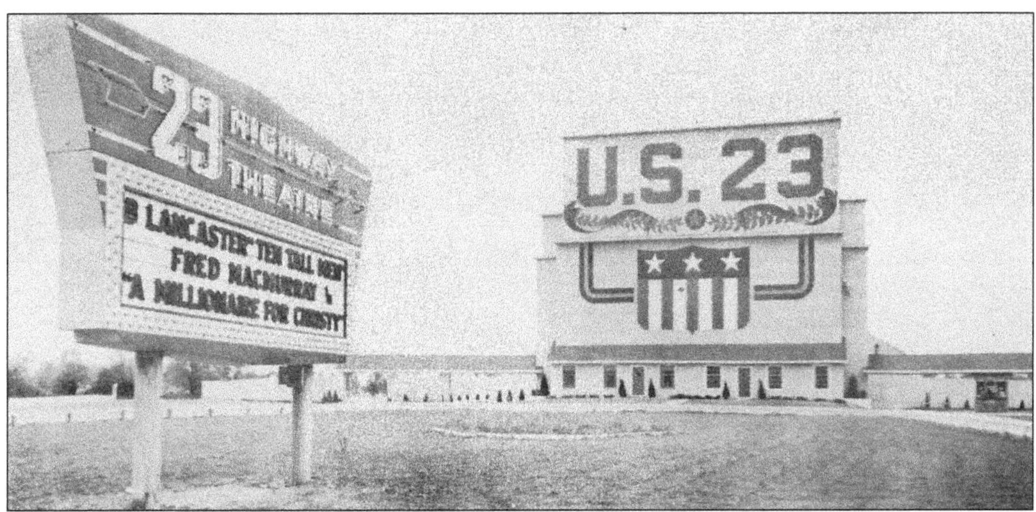

A Patriotic Screen. The screen tower is of a late-1940s design and incorporates both the manager's office and a five-room apartment. Designs similar to this could also be seen at the Toledo and Jackson Drive-Ins. Even the Gratiot's screen tower contained an apartment.

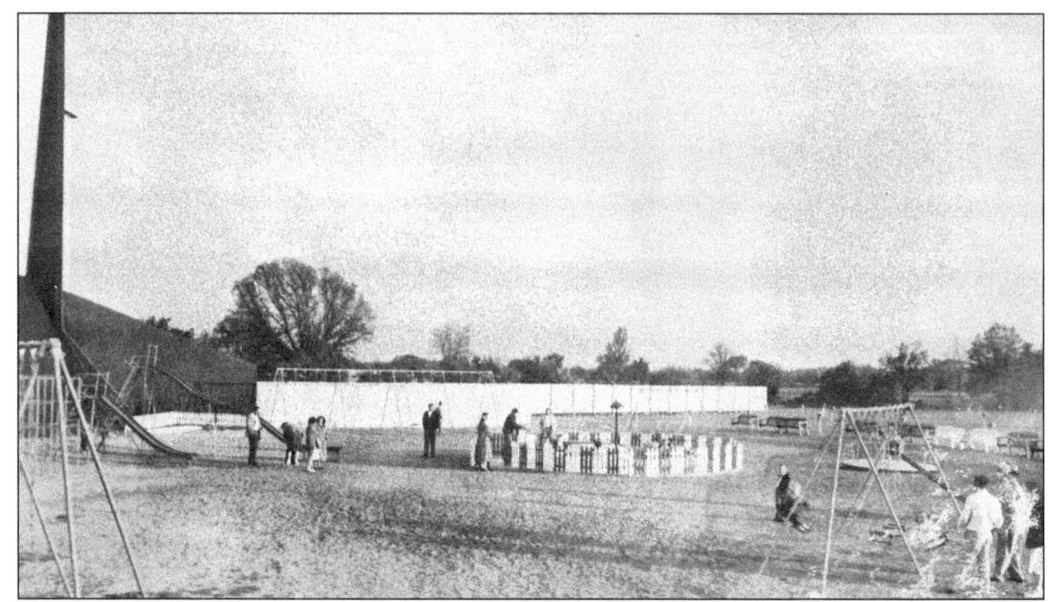

Rub-A-Dub-Dub. The playground equipment included swings, slides, a merry-go-round, and a small motorboat ride within a water-filled tank (visible in the center). Chairs and benches located around the playground's fence provided convenient seating for attentive or weary parents. Architect Frank Boomer designed the theater and its playground.

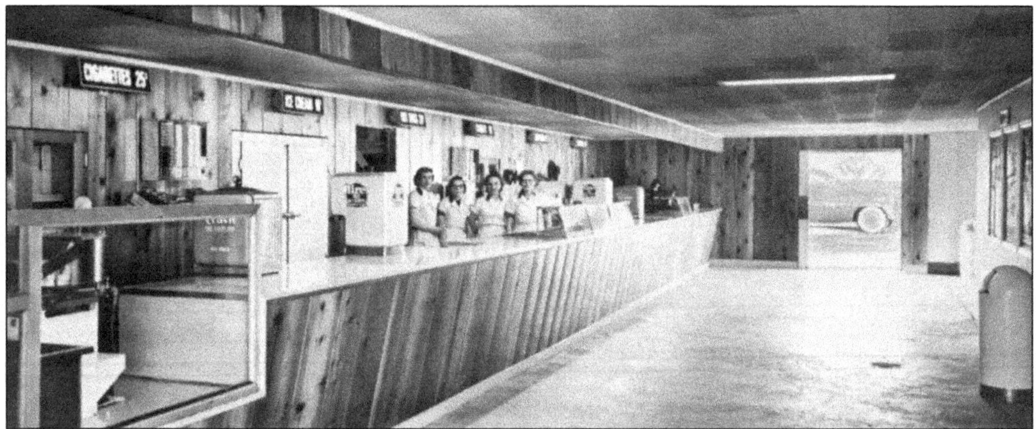

Concessions and Cars. The 23's concession stand is described in the *Motion Picture Herald* as "remarkably inviting, with its varnished pine paneling, acoustical board ceiling, and recessed fluorescent illumination." It is large, but of the typical non-cafeteria-style construction popular at the time. Close examination suggests that the car visible outside the far door is, in fact, a drawing added later.

Five

South-Central

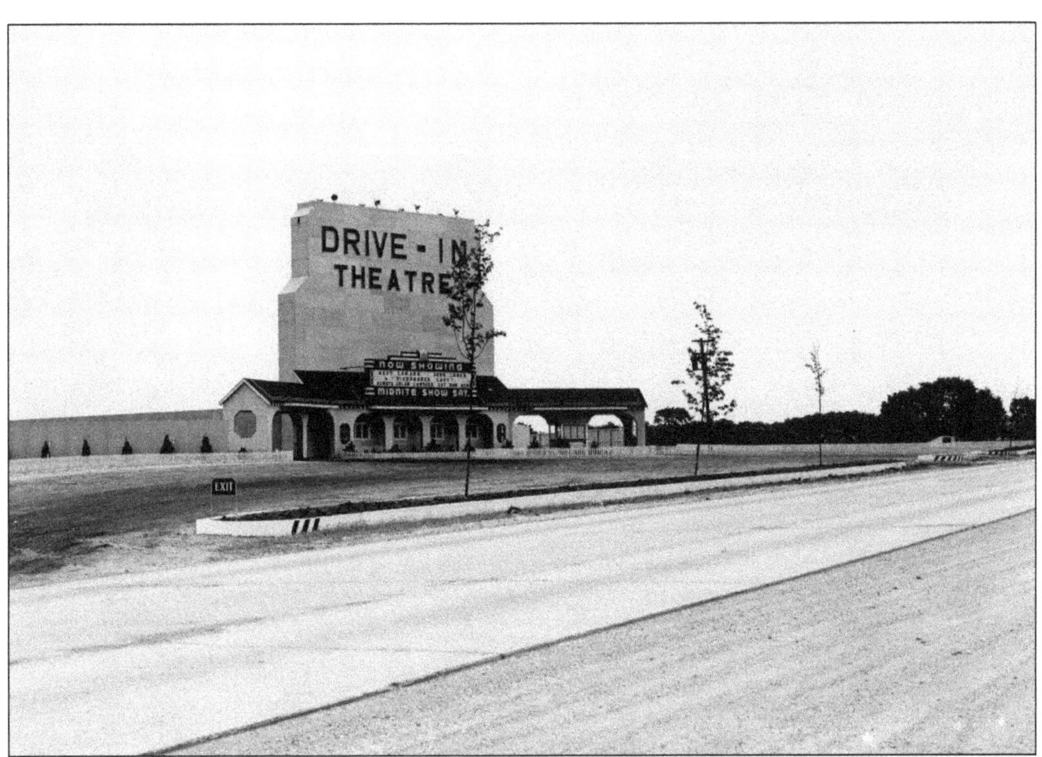

The Jackson Drive-In. Located at 4400 Ann Arbor Road in Jackson, it opened in 1948, and Lawrence J. Aubry originally owned it. Its original capacity was 520 cars. The Jackson, Lansing, and Toldeo Drive-Ins are similar in construction and suggest the same architect, if not the same blueprints. It closed at the end of the 1987 season and was later demolished. (Courtesy of the Bentley Library.)

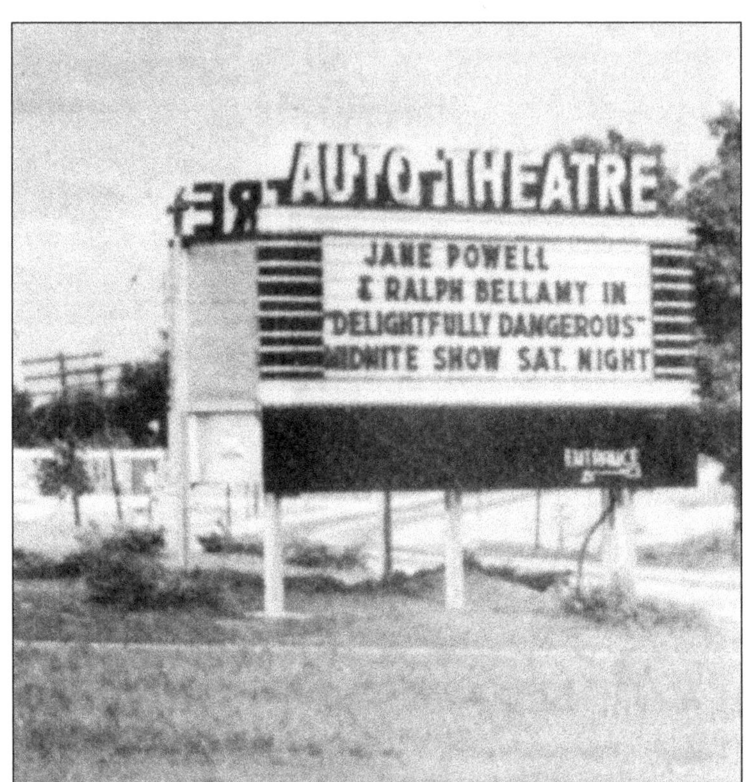

The Battle Creek Auto Theatre. The Battle Creek Auto Theatre, also known as Battle Creek Auto Drive-In, was on East Highway 12, at Cady Road. Its original capacity is given as 500, and while the theater remained a single screen, the car capacity grew to 900. It was strategically located about midway between Battle Creek and Marshal, with this attractive marquee poised to entice customers.

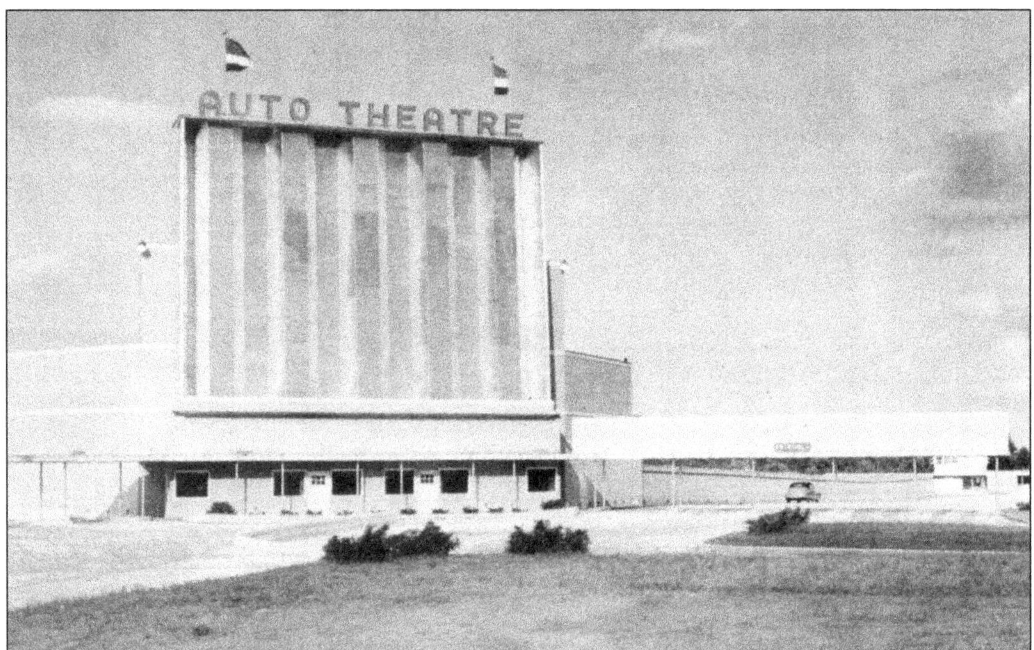

Screen Tower. For a relatively small theater, the Auto Theatre presented a very attractive screen tower of Moderne and relatively unique design. Although this appears to be another drive-in with an apartment in its tower, it bears little resemblance to the Jackson and its brethren, looking much more streamlined and less funereal.

The Inviting Entrance. Pennants adorn the shiny new Auto Theatre box office at its opening. The two-story manager's office allowed the manager to oversee the functioning of the theater from an elevated perch. The theater opened June 22, 1948. The theater landscaping was incomplete at the time.

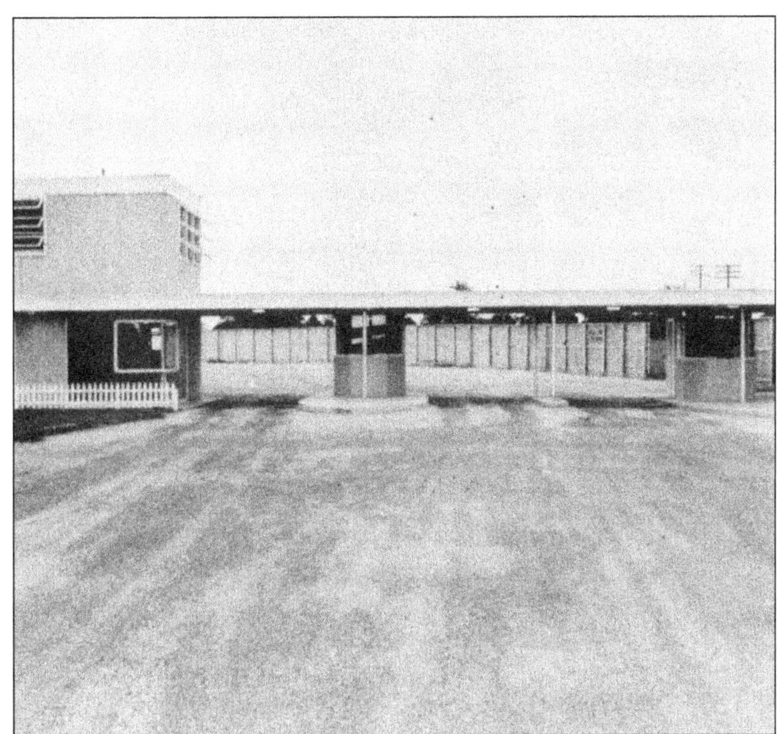

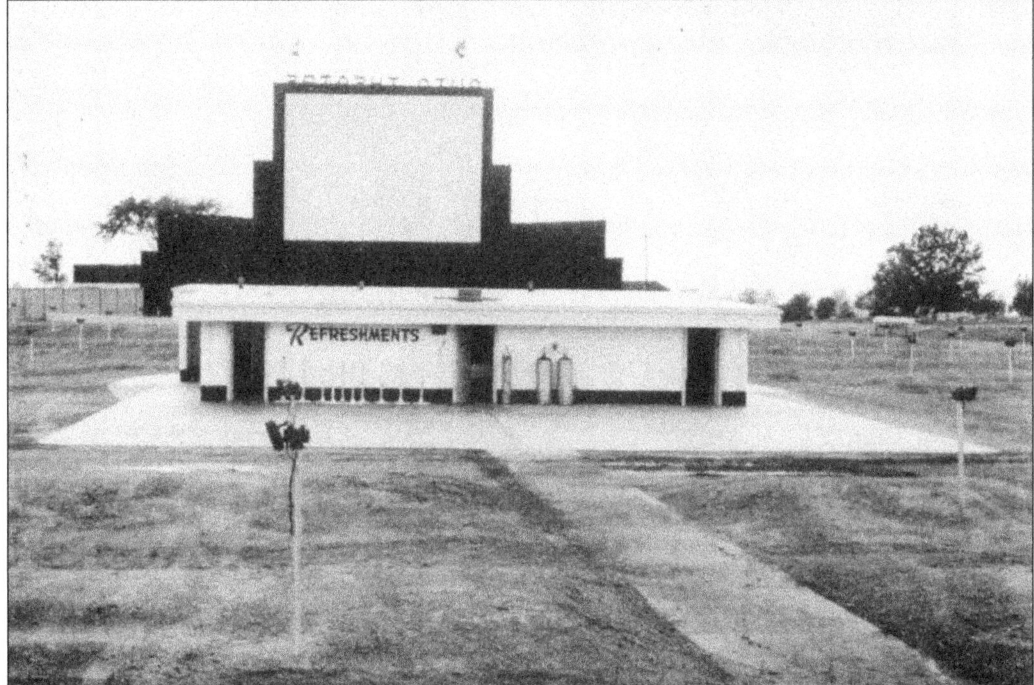

The Concession Stand. The Auto Theatre's concession building was an attractive, tidy little affair with a sign helpfully proclaiming "Refreshments!" Like other rural facilities, the Auto Theatre required propane tanks to operate the warmers, grills, and building heat. A surfaced area surrounds the building to minimize wear and the tracking in of dirt.

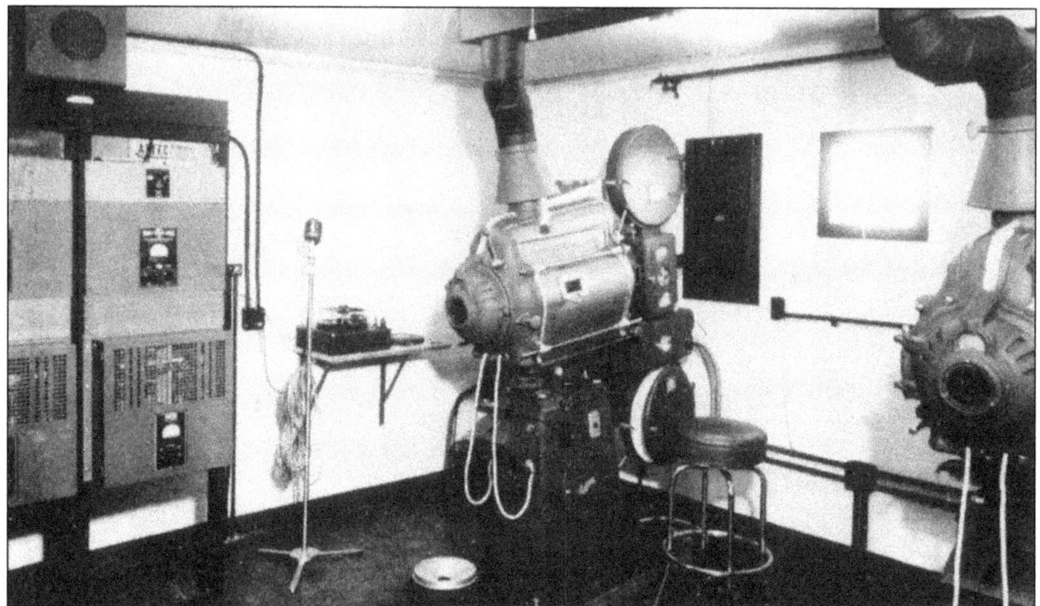

The Auto Theatre's Projection Booth. The state-of-the-art 1948 projection booth of the theater is seen here. In the center is one of the theater's two 35-millimeter projectors. To its left can be seen the record player for pre-movie music and the microphone for announcements. On the far left are the racked Altec amplifiers.

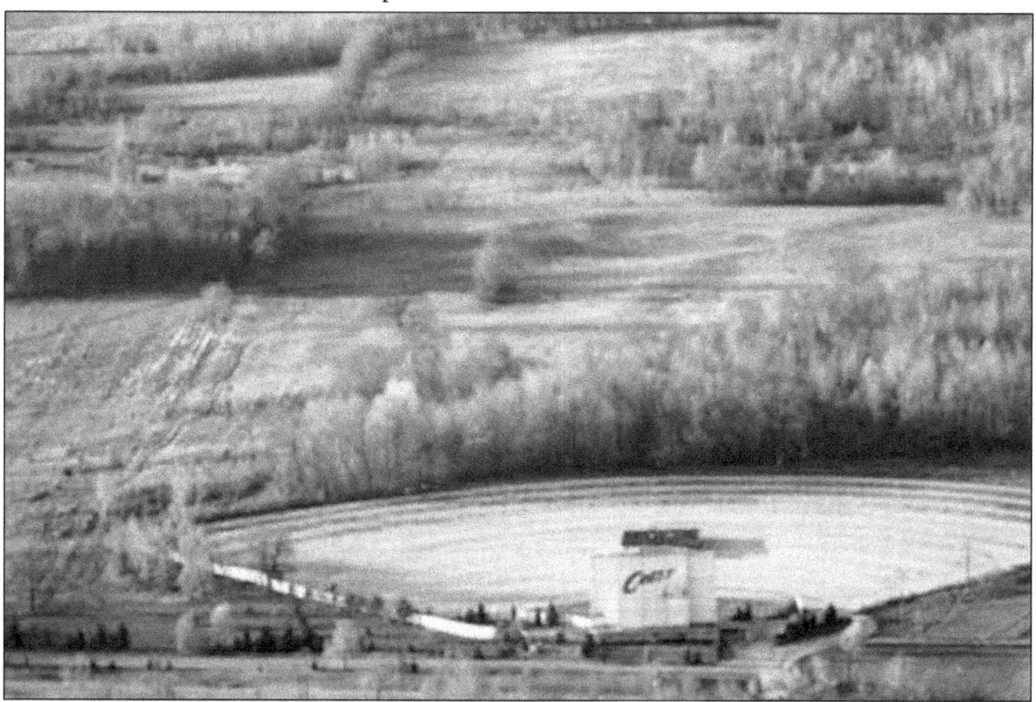

The Crest, Lansing. The Crest was at 1096 West Grand River, technically in Okemos. It was constructed in 1950 and had a capacity of 800 cars. As seen in this aerial view, it was a textbook fan-shaped drive-in, which, like so many others, had an apartment in the screen tower. It also converted to X-rated films later in life. It closed in 1990. (Courtesy of Curt Peterson.)

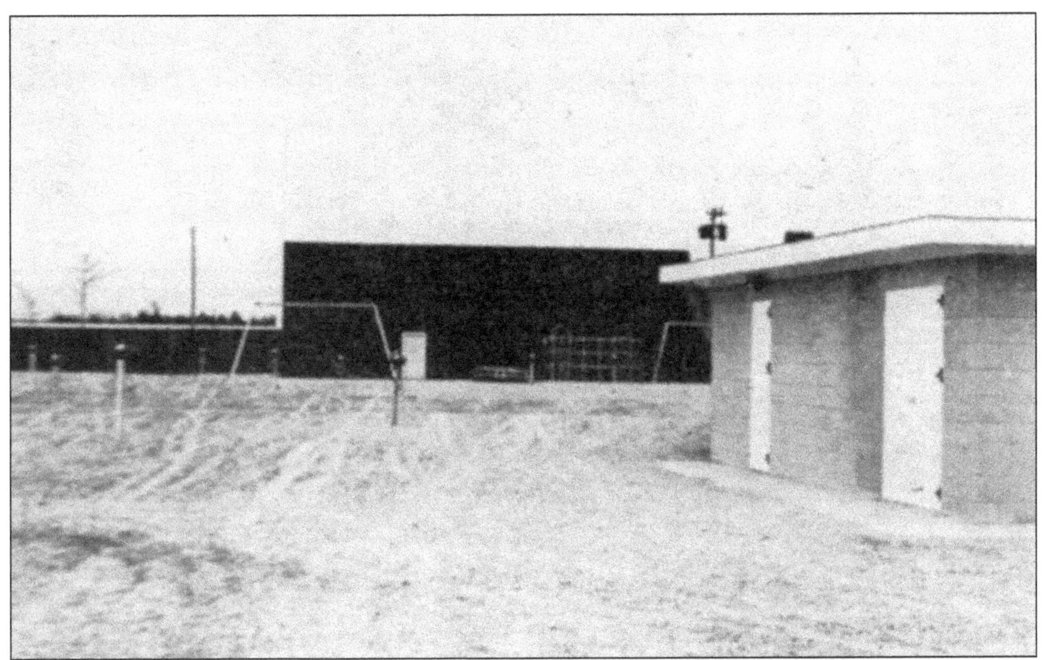

The Hilltop Drive-In, Escanaba. The Hilltop was a standard smaller drive-in with 500-car capacity. It was located at 4965 Danforth Road and opened in 1953. This rare photograph shows an unremarkable screen, concession building, and playground, which were perfect for a small town. It closed in 1989. There is now a subdivision called Hilltop Estates on the site.

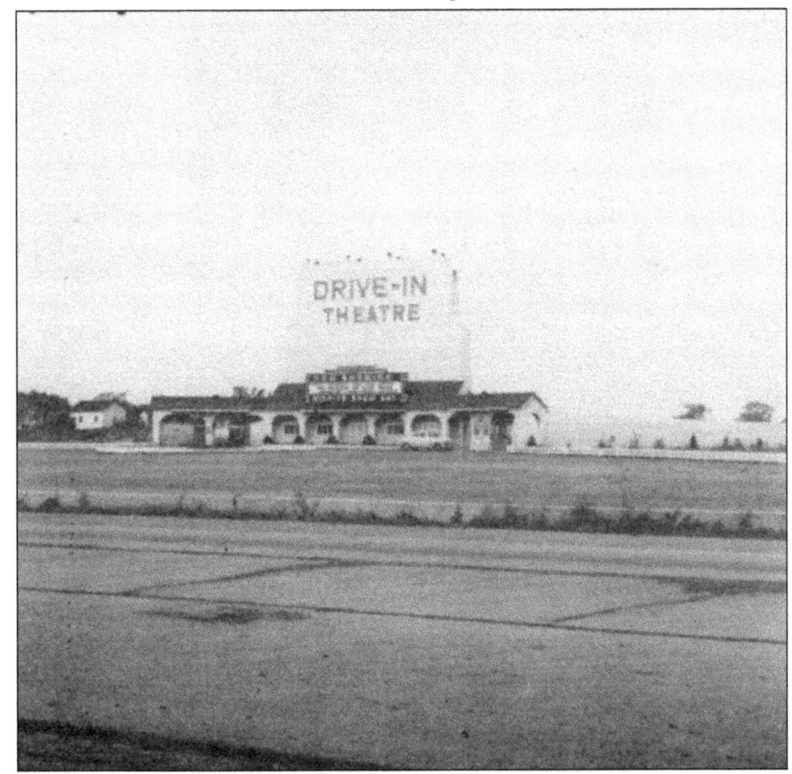

The Lansing Drive-In. The Lansing Drive-In looks so much like the Jackson Drive-In in this photograph that it is tempting to believe that one of them was mislabeled. There are, however, differences in landscaping and so on. The Lansing was on US Route 127, south of the city, and was Lansing's first drive-in. It held 700 cars initially but was later enlarged to accommodate over 1,000.

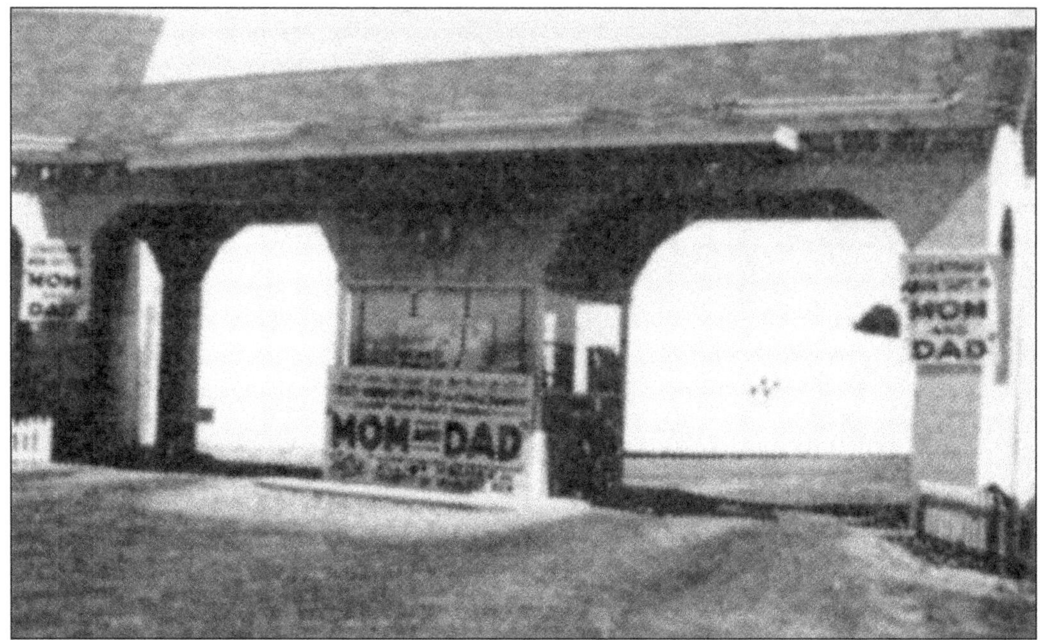

Ticket Booths. These photographs of the Lansing probably date from 1948 to 1949. The banners and other signage indicate that it was in the midst of a ballyhoo binge in connection with the notorious 1945 "hygiene" (that is, sex exploitation) film *Mom and Dad*. The so-called hygiene films were constructed to attract customers with promises of lurid content, but avoided censorship by cloaking the prurience of the film in a mantle of "public service."

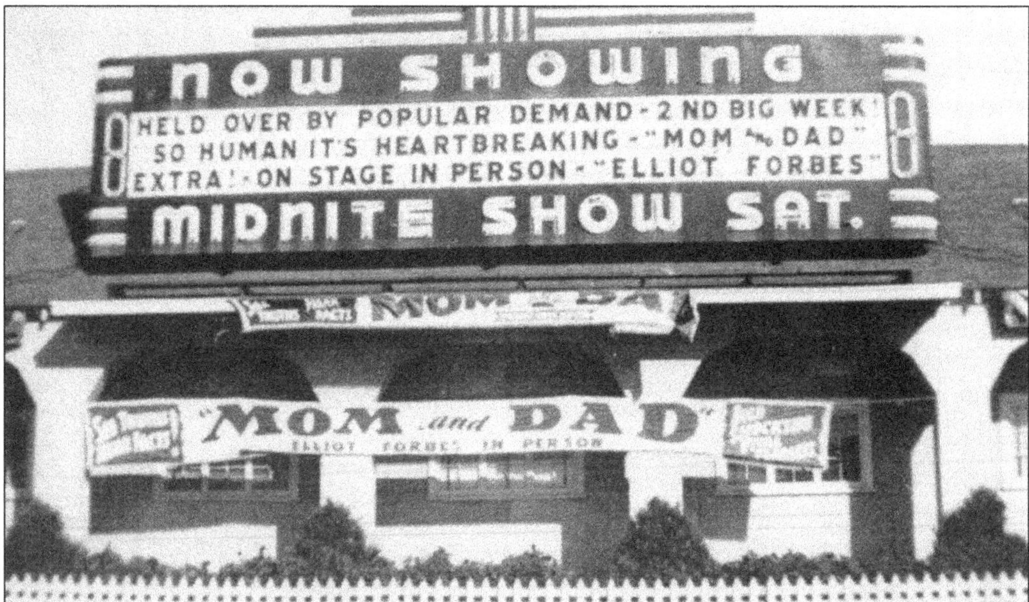

More Ballyhoo. The plot of *Mom and Dad* concerned a teenage girl who becomes pregnant because her mother refuses to allow her access to books explaining sex. The film's run was always heavily advertised, and its social value was expounded by so-called experts, such as "Elliot Forbes," who was in fact any one of a team of Elliot Forbeses (actors) hired to promote the film. The Lansing closed in 1981.

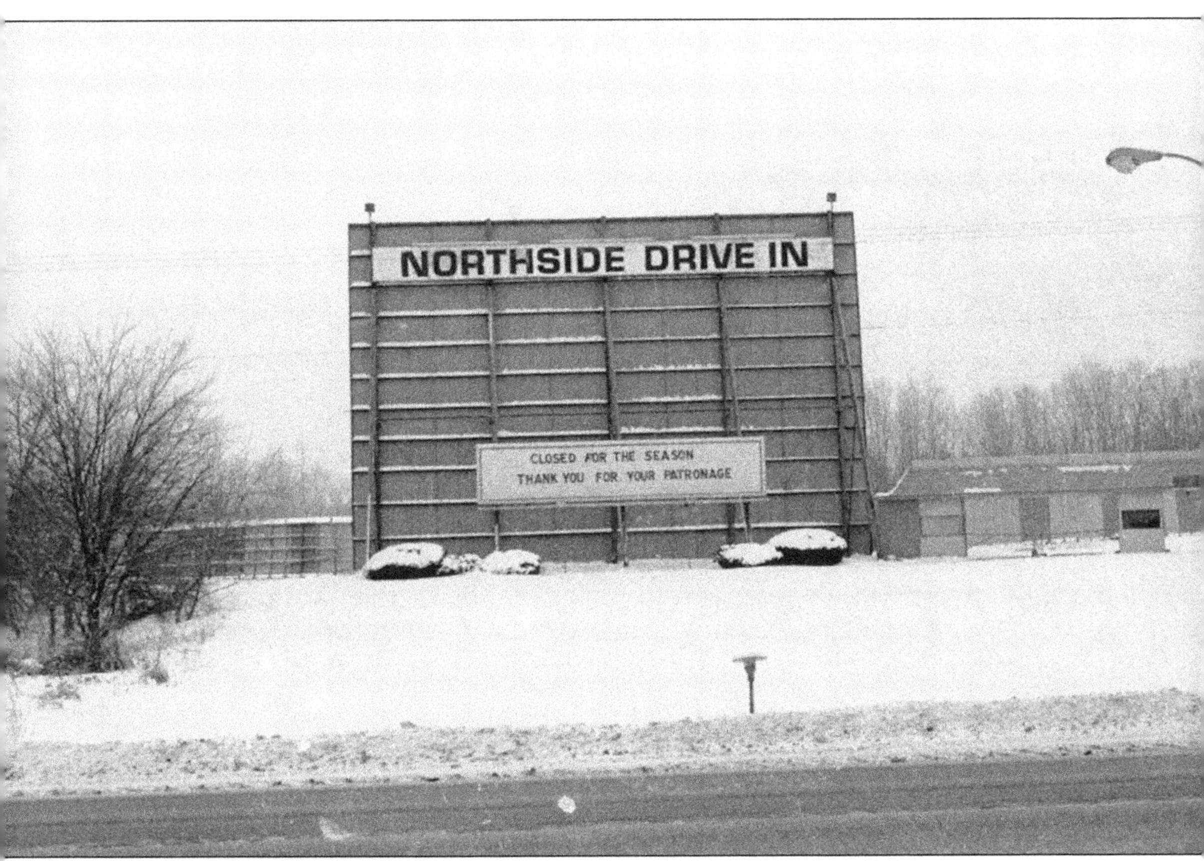

The Northside, Lansing. The Northside was located at North US Route 27 at Stoll Road. It opened in 1952 with a capacity of 400 but was expanded to a three-screen theater in 1984 with an estimated capacity of 750. Immediately before the addition of the second and third screens, it claimed a capacity of 1,000. In the early 1980s, it claimed 800. (Courtesy of Curt Peterson.)

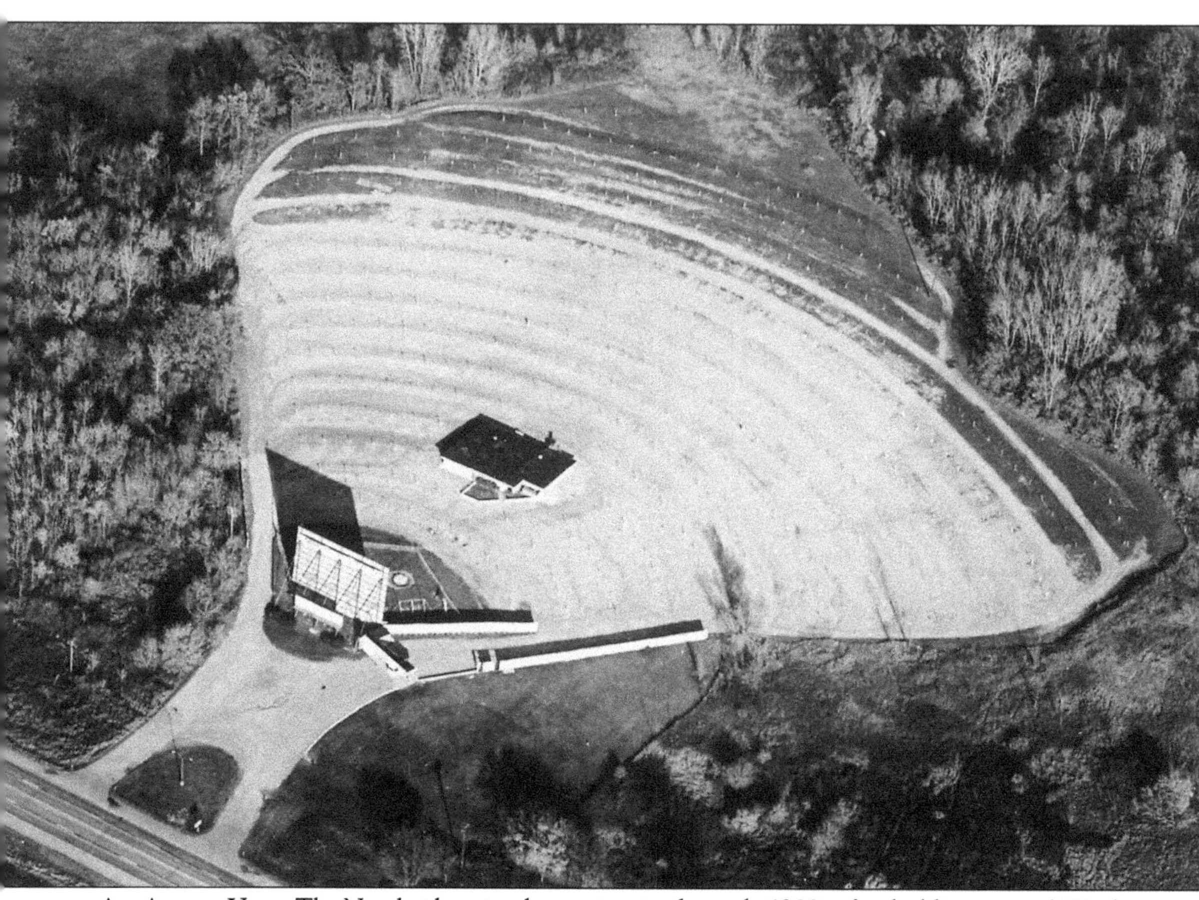

An Aerial View. The Northside gained notoriety in the early 1980s after holding annual "Buck Nights." These were low-admission-cost shows at which live rock-and roll music combined with cheap beer and pervasive drug use to draw in teenagers for a night of merriment much to the consternation of neighbors and local law enforcement officials. It closed in 1988. (Courtesy of Curt Peterson.)

The Starlite Drive-In, Lansing. This attractive marquee announces the current attractions at the Starlite soon after its opening in 1953. Located at 3020 Snow Road, it initially claimed a capacity of 500 or 600 cars (depending on the source), but by 1955, it could hold 700. It occupied a 17-acre lot and was reputed to have cost $85,000 to build.

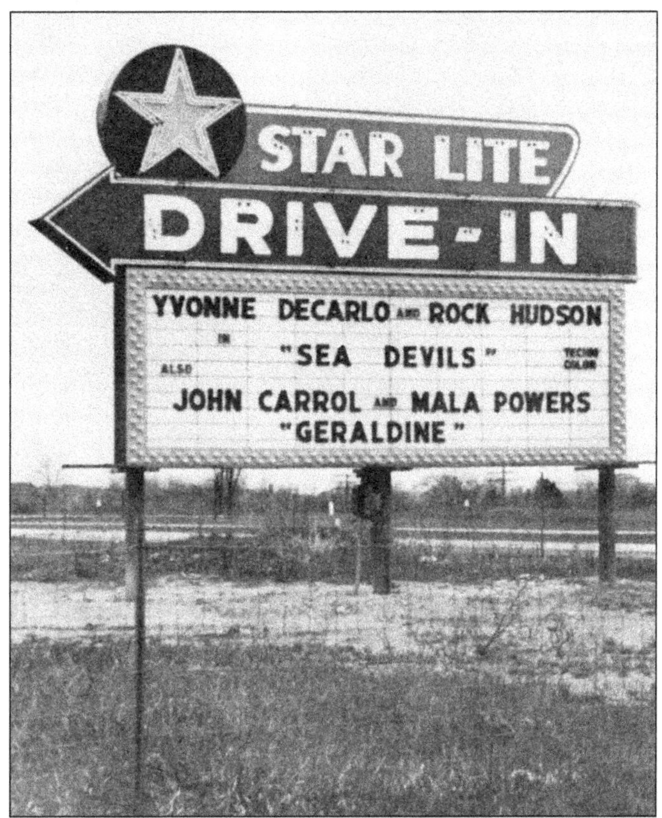

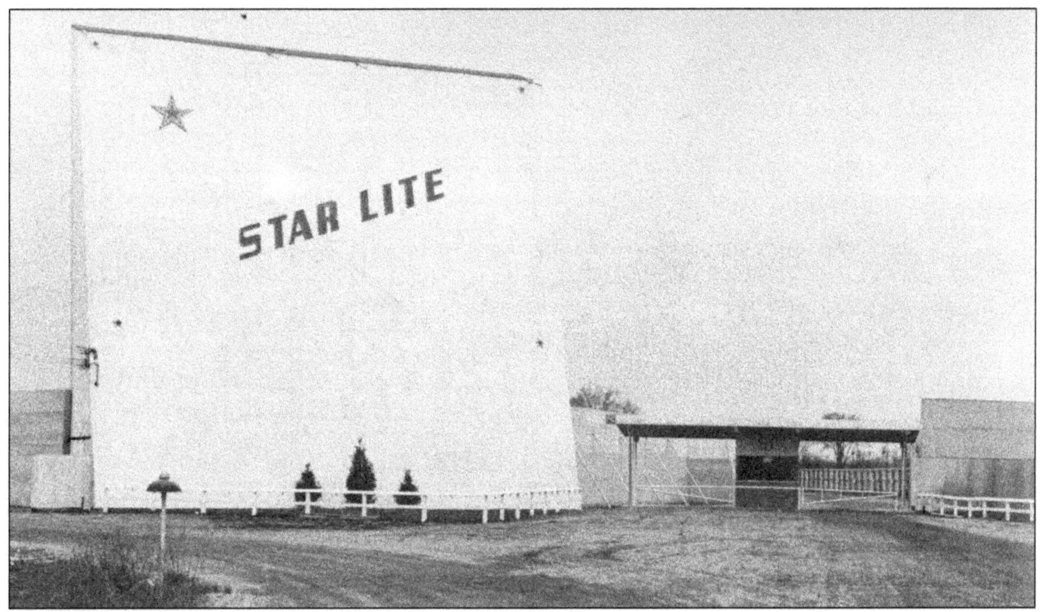

An Attractive Approach. The star-adorned face of the shiny new Starlite welcomes theatergoers to their nightly repast. The landscaping is still fresh, and two lanes of driveway pretty minimal, but the tidy white picket fences and adjacent lights are nice touches that raise the site above the average.

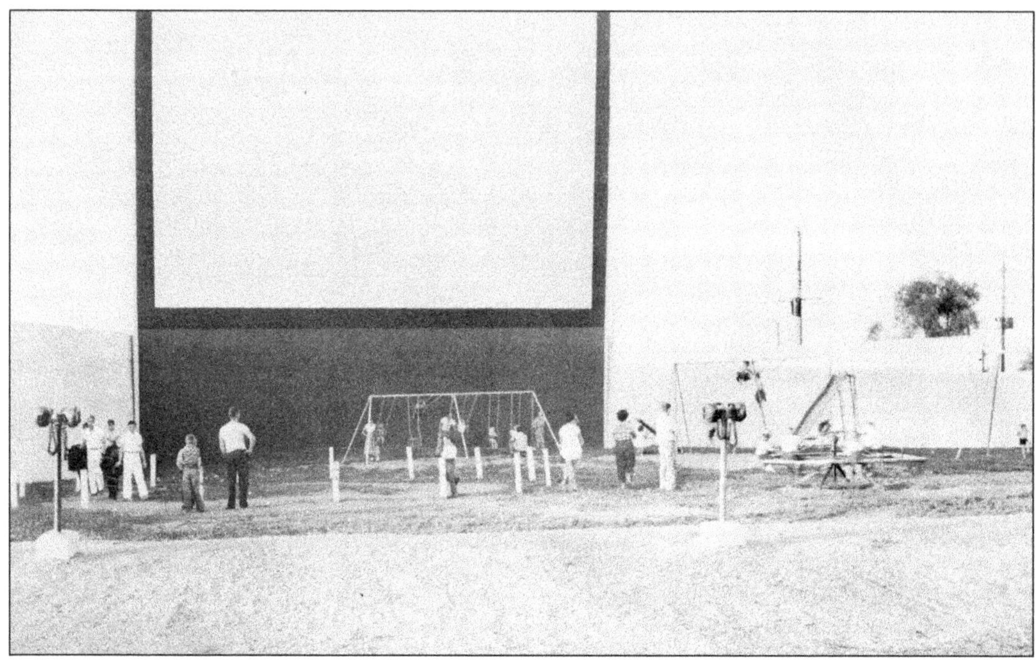

Playing at the Drive-In. At the base of the Starlite's 60-by-60-foot screen, children and their families take advantage of the theater's small playground. The front of the Starlite's screen and its flashing neon marquee were visible from the busy, adjacent Lansing Road, thus maximizing its potential for free advertising.

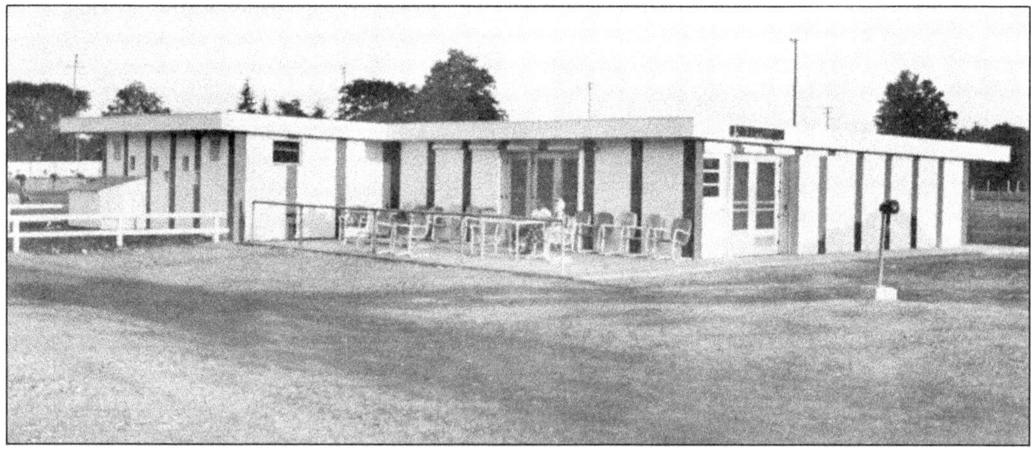

The Concession Building. The Starlite's snack bar was equipped with all the most current conveniences. Double doors at both ends opened in and out of the concession area and also into the outside seating area in front. The region in front of the projection ports is protected by the usual fence, while restrooms hide discreetly in the rear.

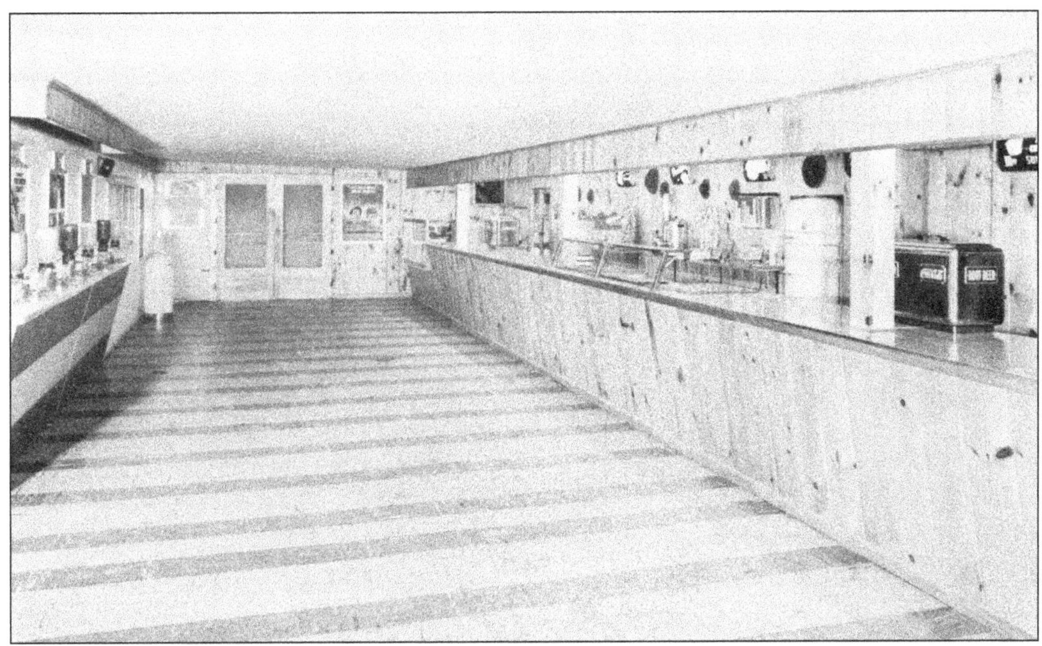

THE FAMILIAR SNACK BAR. The service area of the Starlite is nearly identical to that of the US-23 (see page 64) and hundreds of other early drive-ins, from its walk-up counter to its knotty-pine paneling. In later years, this concession would be converted to the more efficient cafeteria-style layout. The Starlite closed in 1984.

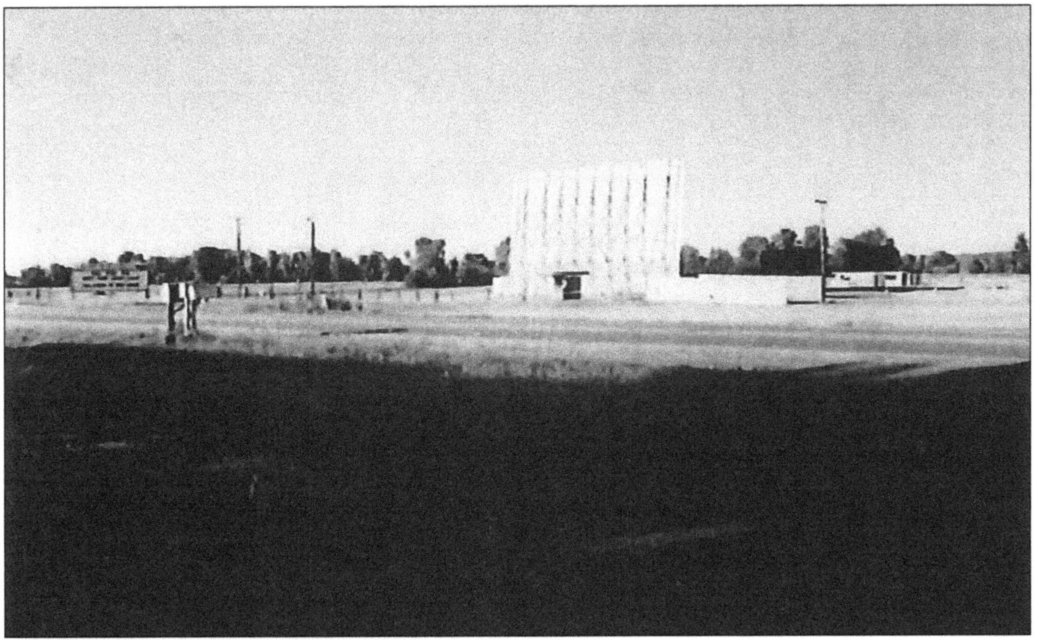

THE UNIVERSITY DRIVE-IN, BIG RAPIDS. It should be noted that the regional divisions in this book are arbitrary, and so it is hard to say if this theater should be "Up North," or "Central," or "West." So for better or worse, here is the University, also known as the Big Rapids, in Big Rapids. It opened some time before 1955 with a tiny capacity of 328. It was at 18580 Northland Drive. (Courtesy of Goodrich Theaters.)

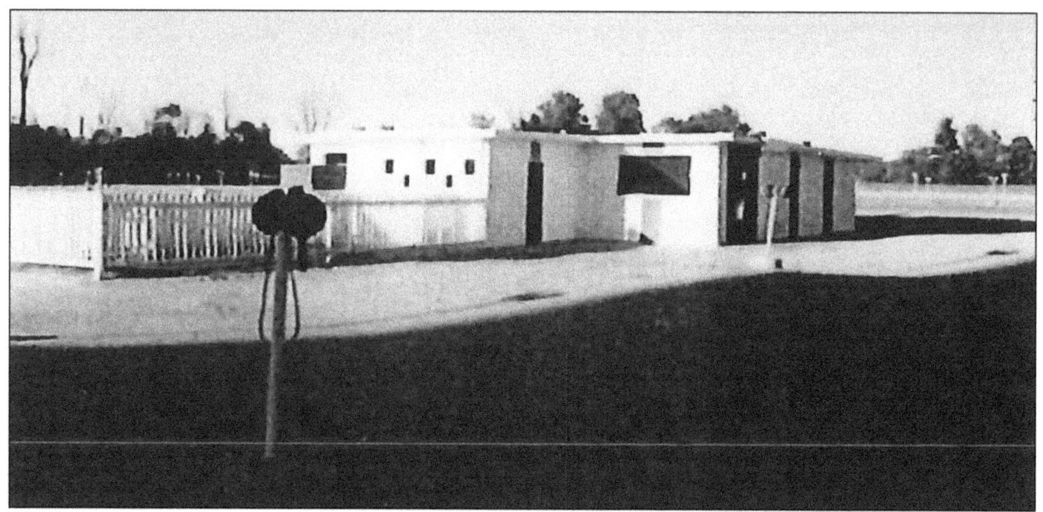

CONCESSION BUILDING. Despite its tiny size, the University had a complete and up-to-date layout and projection-and-concession building. There was even a tiny picture window to allow film viewing from within. The angle from the projectors to the screen must have been shallow, or management's concern high, to call for the very long fenced area in front. (Courtesy of Goodrich Theaters.)

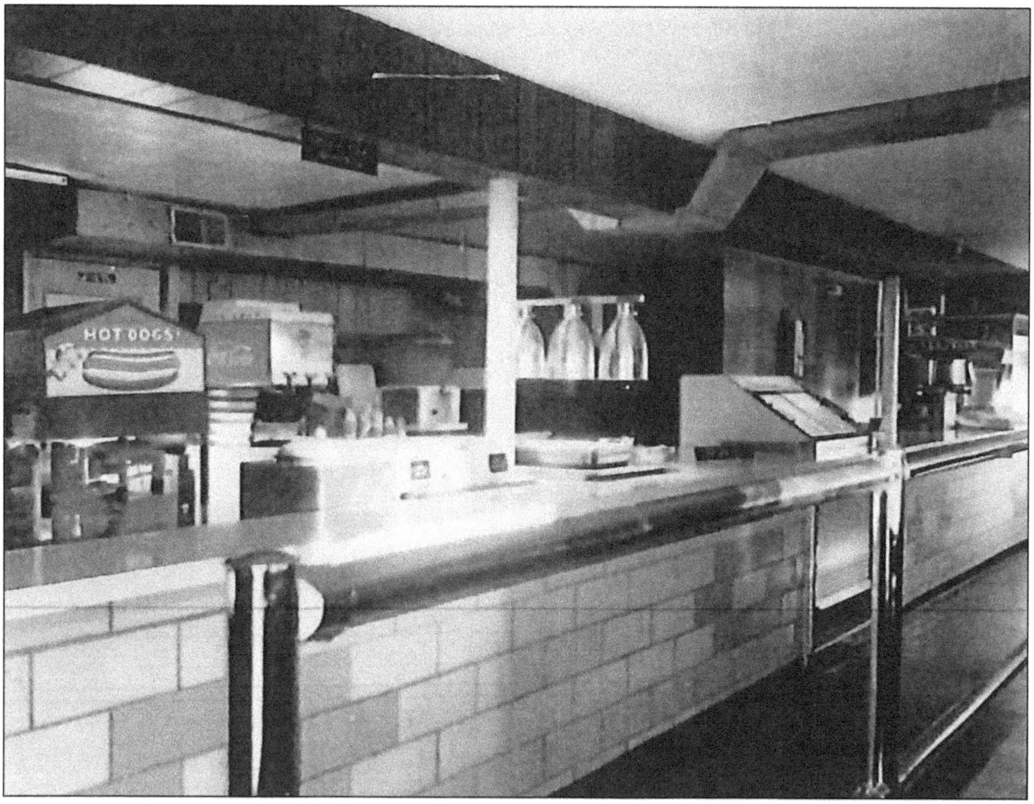

CAFETERIA LINE. Again, tiny but terrific, the cafeteria-style concession was efficiently arranged and carefully executed. Expensive glazed block covers the wearing and washable surfaces of the snack bar, while chrome-plated railings keep the patrons in line. Note the built-in warmer for burgers and hot dogs. (Courtesy of Goodrich Theaters.)

Six

The Southwest

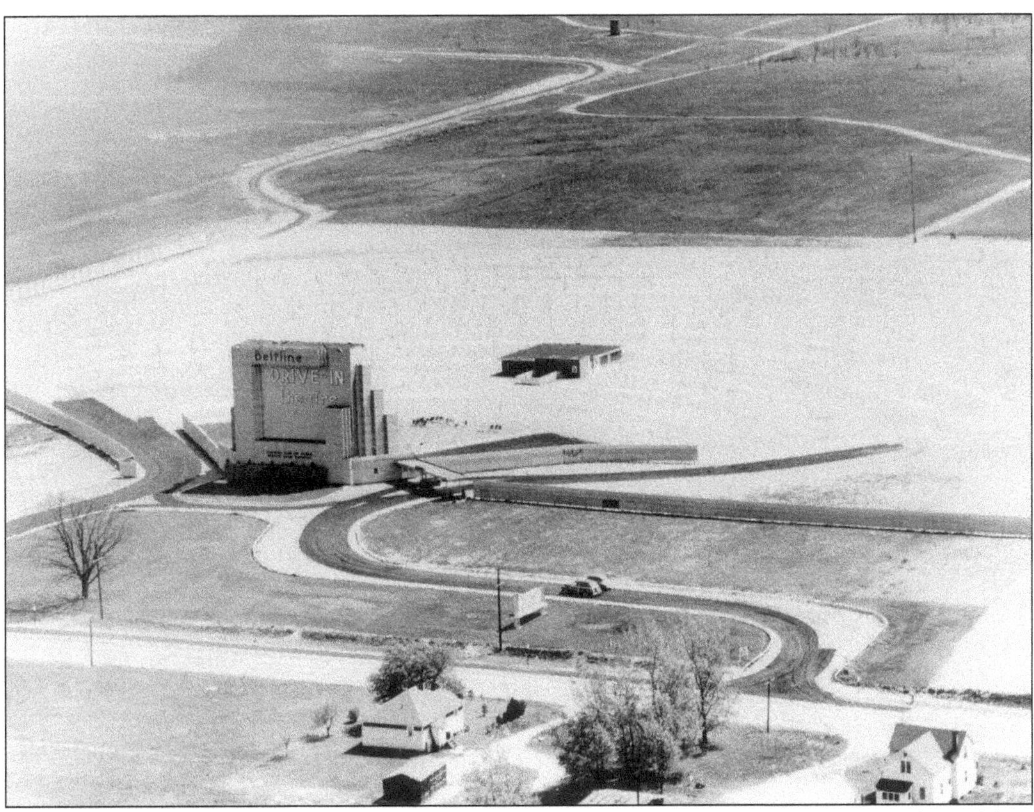

The Beltline Drive-In. Located at 1400 West Twenty-eighth Street in Wyoming, the Beltline exemplified the state of the art for a small theater at the time of its opening in 1948. With an original capacity listed as 250 cars, it grew and shrank and mutated in almost every way possible over its life. This photograph is reputedly from 1954. (Courtesy of Grand Rapids Public Library.)

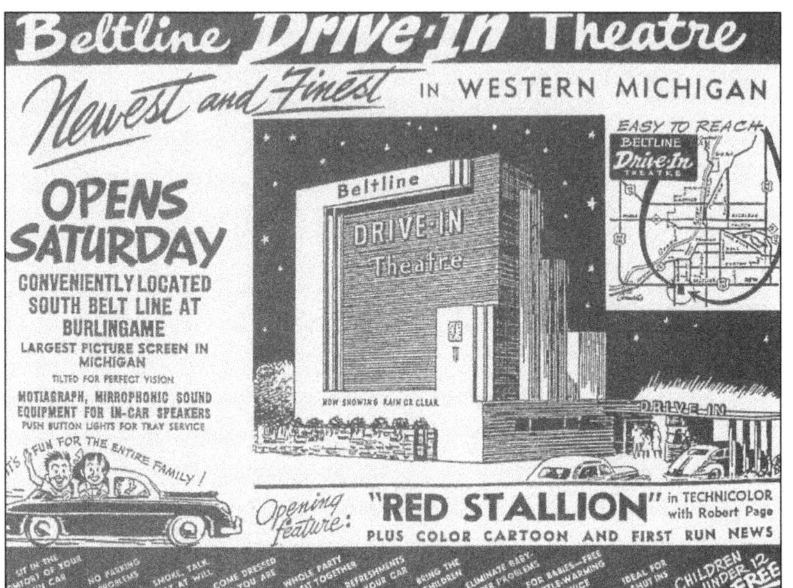

Opening Night Ad. This ad for the opening of the new Beltline expounds its virtues in every way possible, right down to its (misspelled) Motiograph in-car speakers. In-car speakers were fairly new in 1948, with many theaters still dealing with speakers mounted on the screen. Note the Beltline's resemblance to the Dearborn (page 24).

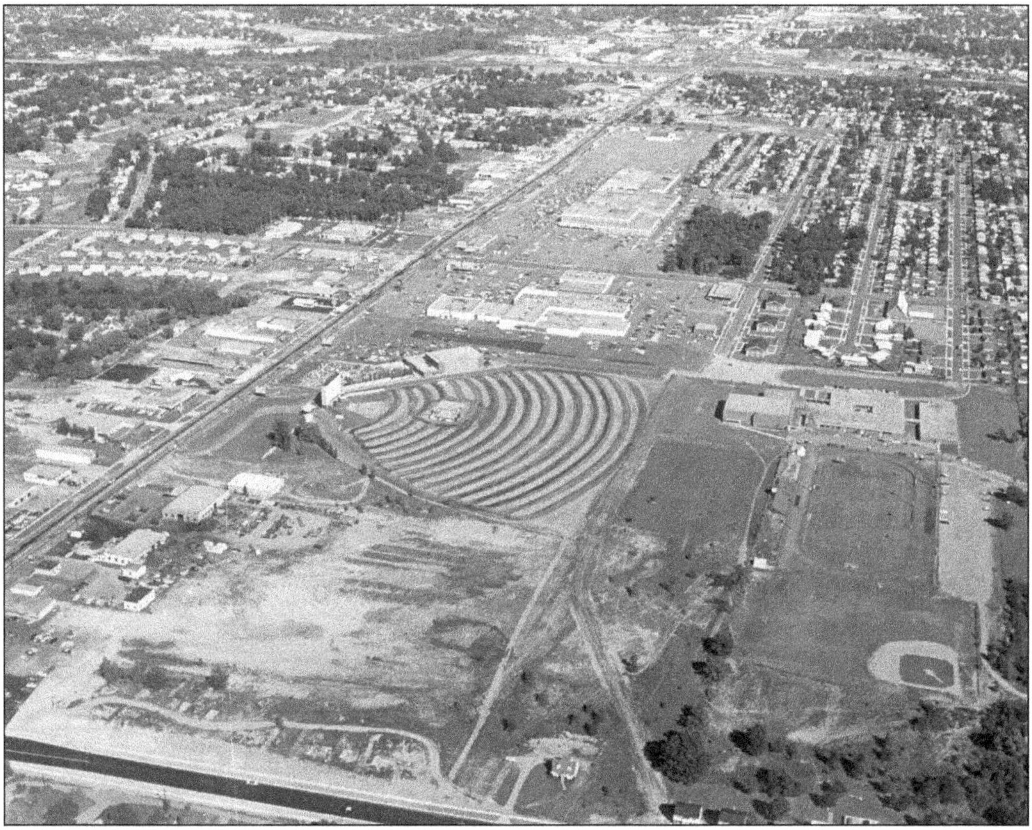

Another Aerial View. This photograph probably dates from the 1960s or 1970s and shows the phenomenal growth that had occurred since the theater's construction. Also visible is the adjacent cinema, the parking lot of which would eventually engulf the ramps of the Beltline (see page 107). (Courtesy of Jack Loeks Collection/Celebration Cinemas.)

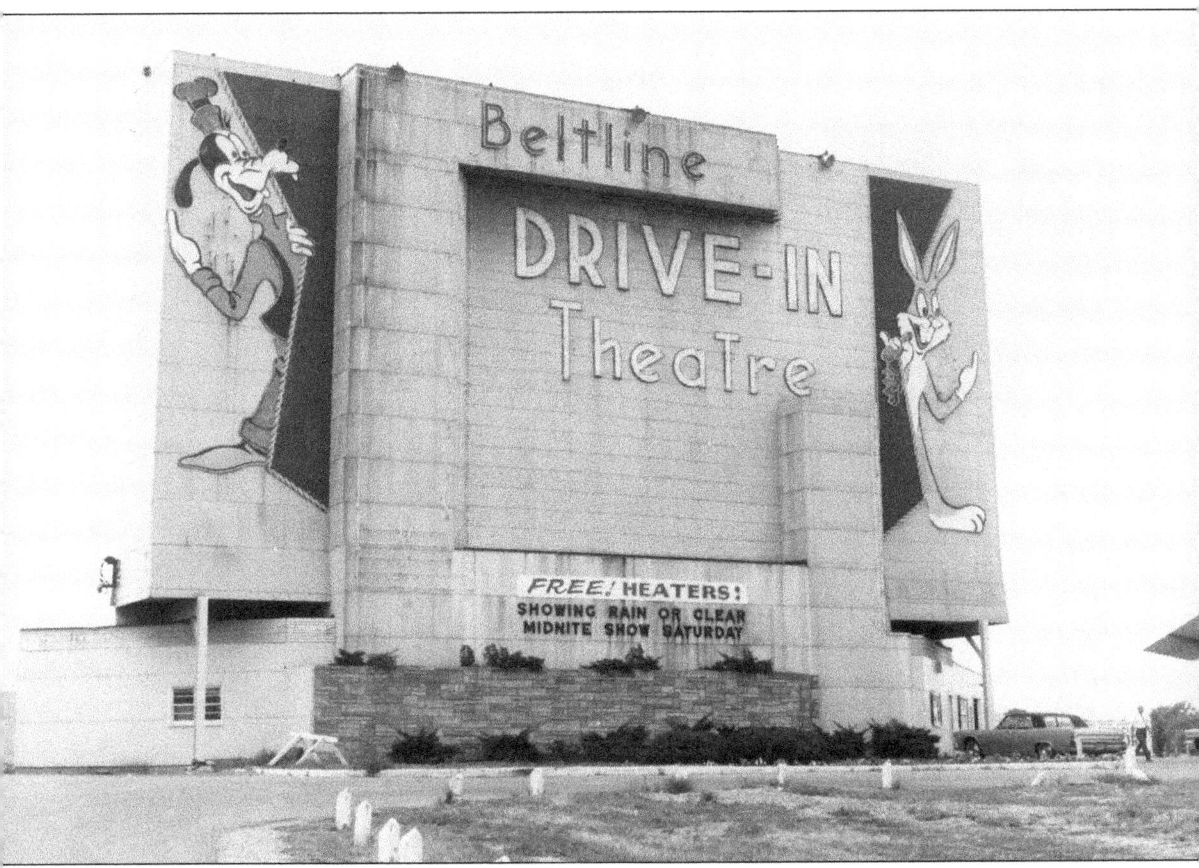

AFTER MODIFICATIONS. The Beltline's screen is seen here (probably in the 1960s), as it is probably best remembered, flanked by Bugs and Goofy. Aside from the gross infringement on Warner Bros. and Disney copyrights, the screen has been widened to allow for the showing of widescreen movies. Bugs and Goofy just took advantage of it. (Courtesy of Jack Loeks Collection/Celebration Cinemas.)

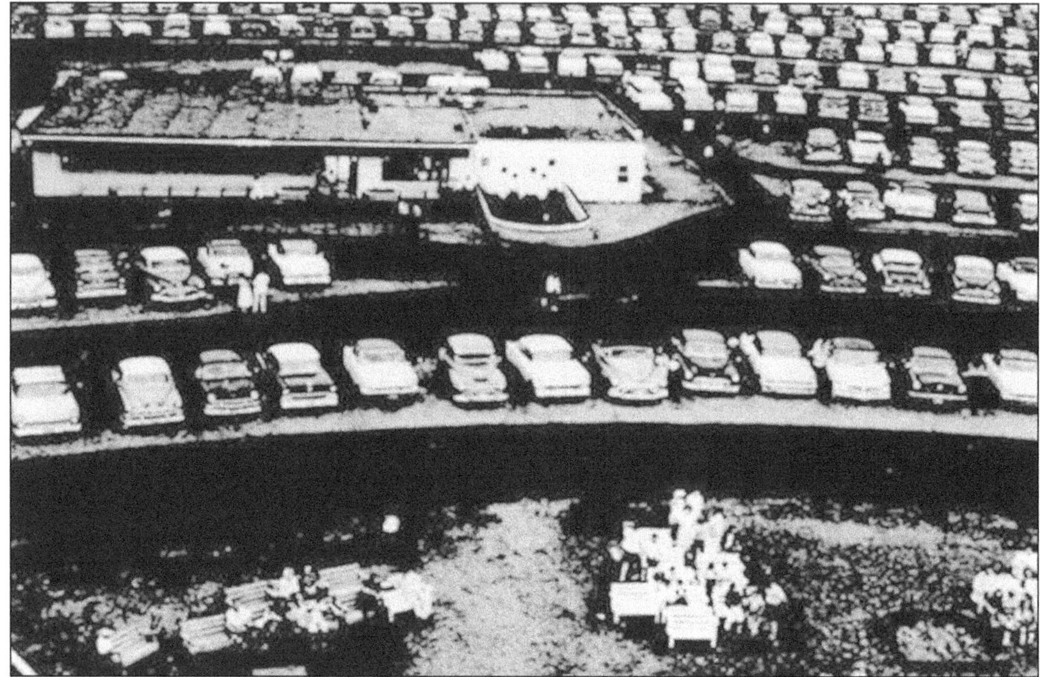

A Lot from Atop the Screen. The Beltline, seen from the screen tower sometime in the 1950s, is a popular place indeed, with hundreds of cars in place for the show. Note the unusually asymmetric concession building, with the booth to the right and snack bar to the left. The longer portion on the left appears to be a later addition. (Courtesy of Jack Loeks Collection/ Celebration Cinemas.)

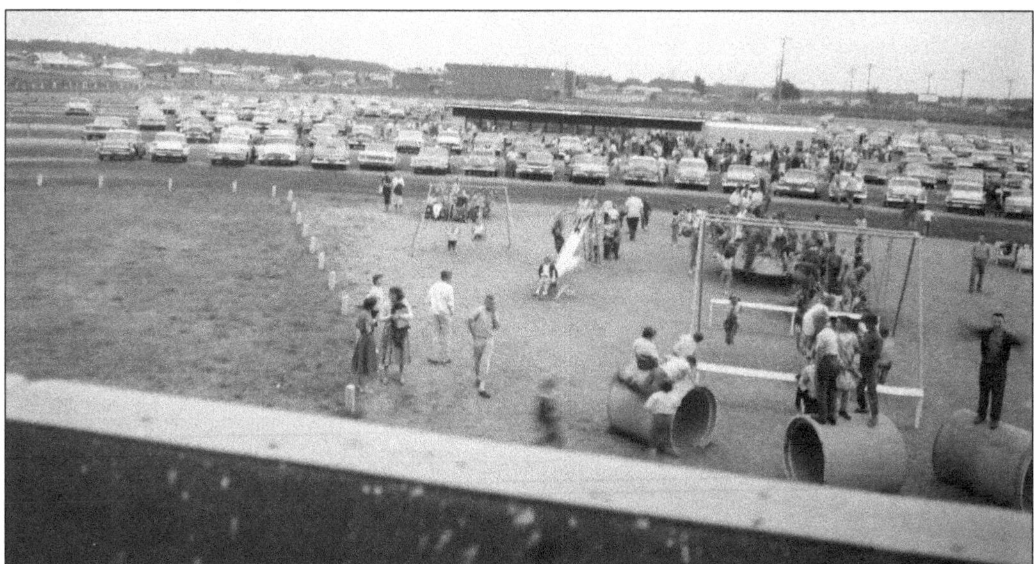

A Lower Vantage Point. Seen from closer to the ground, the playground is more easily visible. In later years, the theater would be tripled into the Beltline-3, with capacity increasing to around 850. Then later still, the portion of the lot to the left in this picture was stolen by the adjacent indoor cinema, which used it as a parking lot. The Loeks chain also owned the land thief. (Courtesy of Jack Loeks Collection/Celebration Cinemas.)

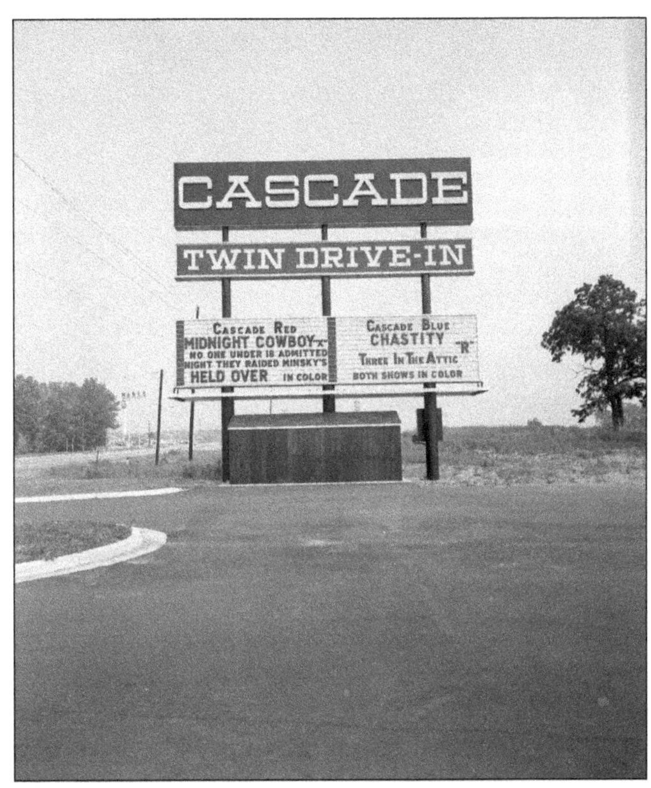

The Cascade Twin, Cascade. Doubtlessly one of the most magnificent drive-ins to ever grace the state or the planet, the Cascade Twin was built by National Amusements and opened with much fanfare in 1969. Located at 5050 Twenty-eighth Street Northeast, the Cascade was also one of the few to start out as a two-screen theater, with the screens located at roughly opposite ends of the lot. (Courtesy of Grand Rapids Public Library.)

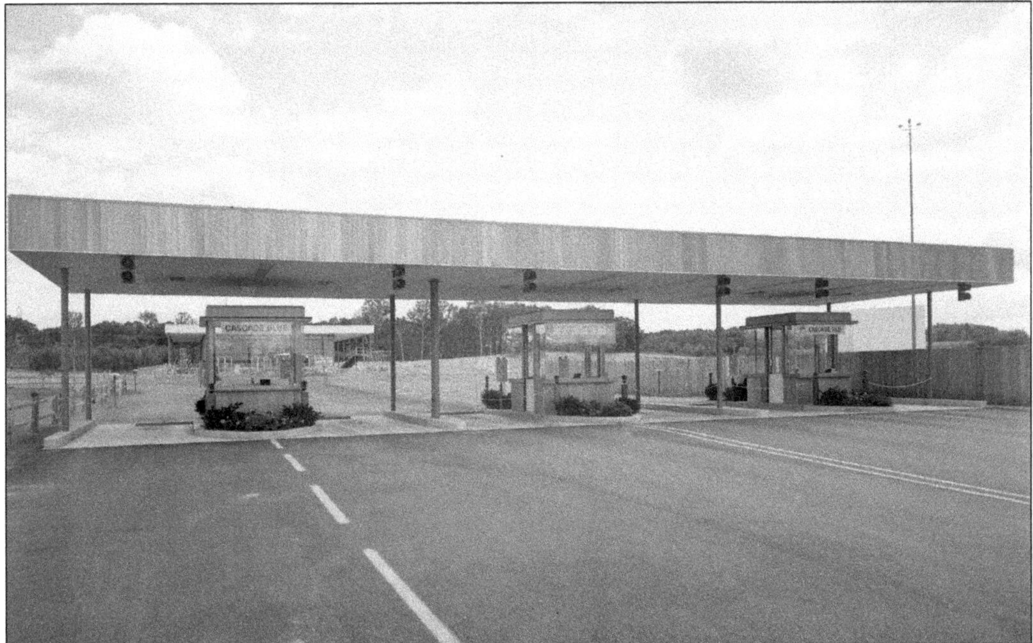

Lanes and Lanes. Three of the six lanes routed patrons to the red screen and the other three to the blue. The vast property had a capacity of 2,500 cars and every imaginable amenity, including a large central playground and a concession stand with huge plate-glass picture windows. It is seen here just before opening. (Courtesy of Grand Rapids Public Library.)

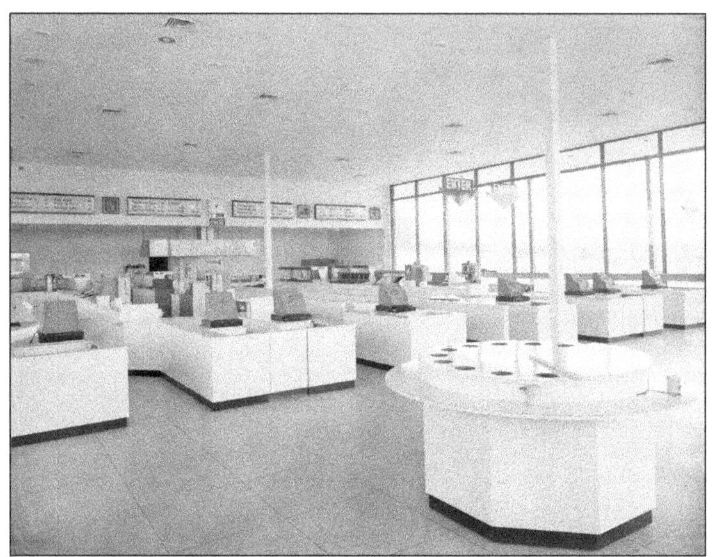

Eight Lanes, No Waiting. The concession facility was nothing short of dazzling, with its spotless counters and floor-to-ceiling windows. No fewer than eight lanes of cafeteria-style counters allowed the staff to efficiently serve the potential thousands of customers expected during a film's intermission. Note that a hamburger is 40¢ and a meatball sub is 55¢. (Courtesy of Grand Rapids Public Library.)

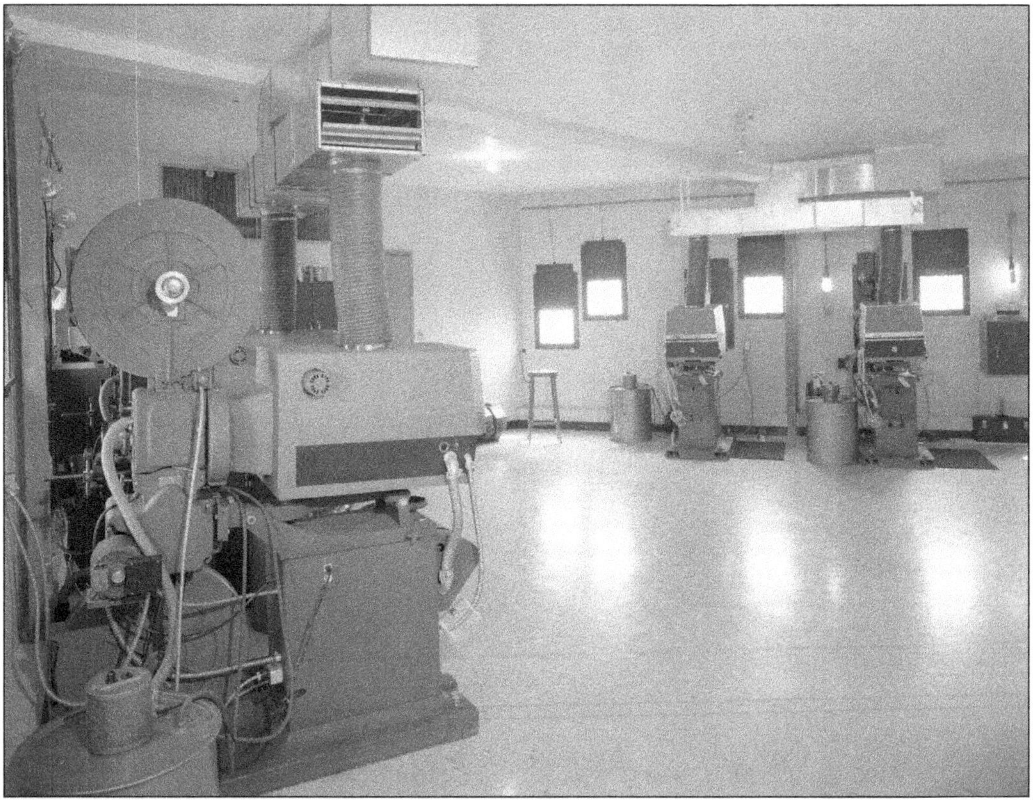

Projection Booth. The mammoth projection booth of the Cascade was located on a second floor, above the concession level. There was no picket fence needed here. In this photograph, the spaciousness of the booth can be appreciated. The two sets of projectors for the two screens are pictured. These projectors have xenon lamps. A third screen was eventually added. The Cascade closed in 1992.

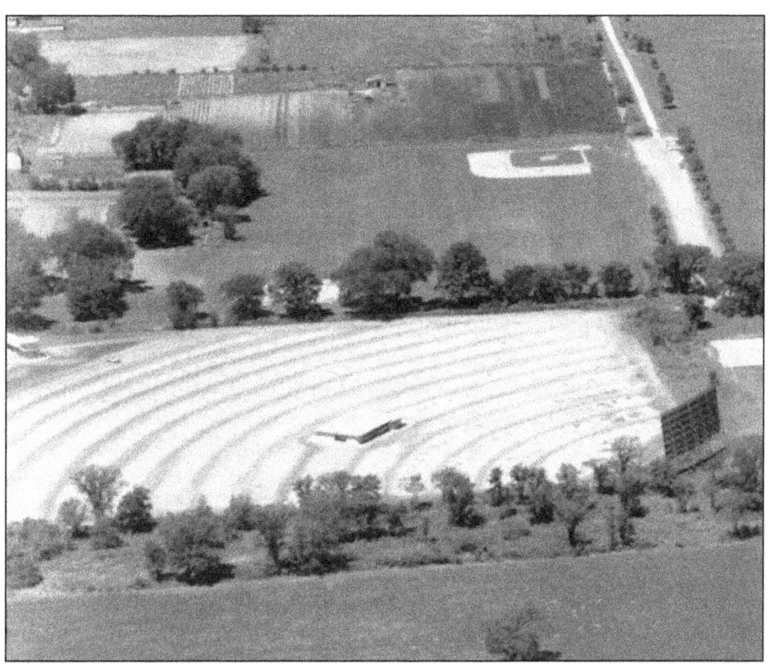

The Douglas Auto Theatre, Kalamazoo. The Douglas stood at 1900 Douglas Avenue in Kalamazoo. It opened in 1955 and had a capacity of 800 cars. The Butterfield Theatres chain operated the Douglas until its closing in 1985, with *Mad Max Beyond Thunderdome* as the last feature. Its restored marquee resides at the Henry Ford Museum.

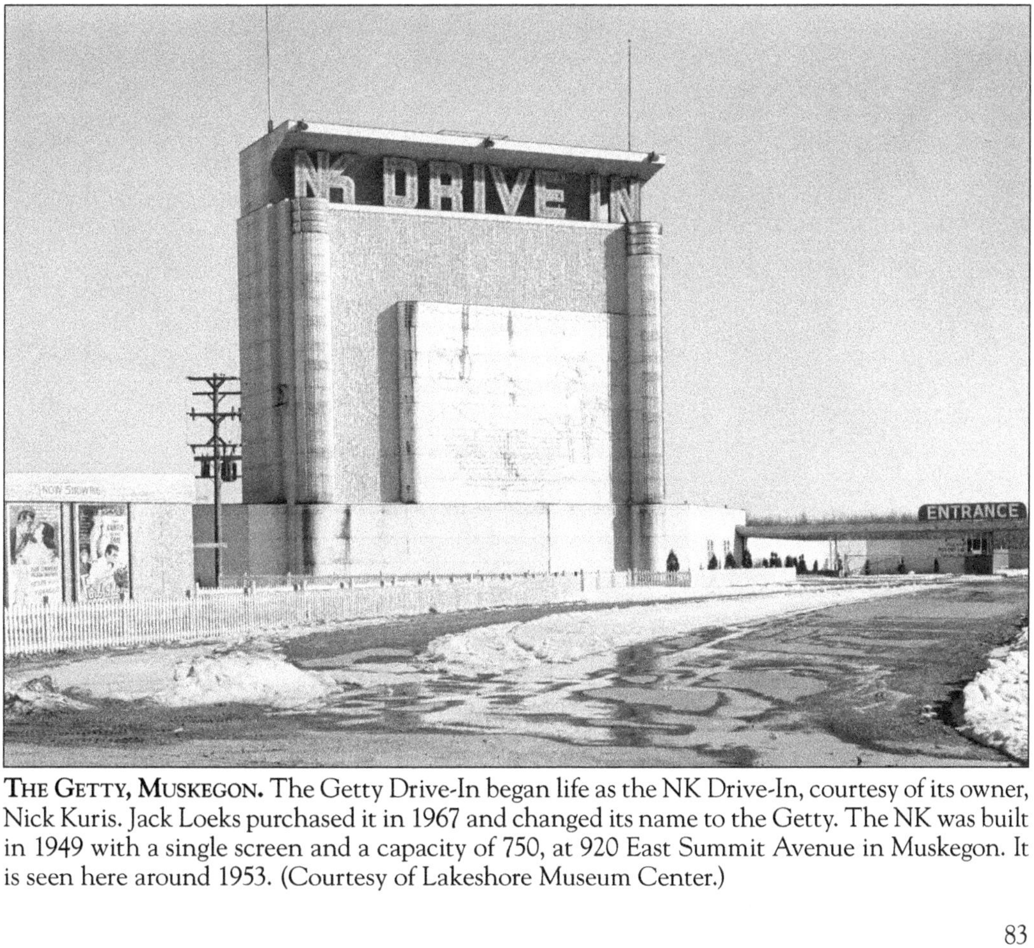

The Getty, Muskegon. The Getty Drive-In began life as the NK Drive-In, courtesy of its owner, Nick Kuris. Jack Loeks purchased it in 1967 and changed its name to the Getty. The NK was built in 1949 with a single screen and a capacity of 750, at 920 East Summit Avenue in Muskegon. It is seen here around 1953. (Courtesy of Lakeshore Museum Center.)

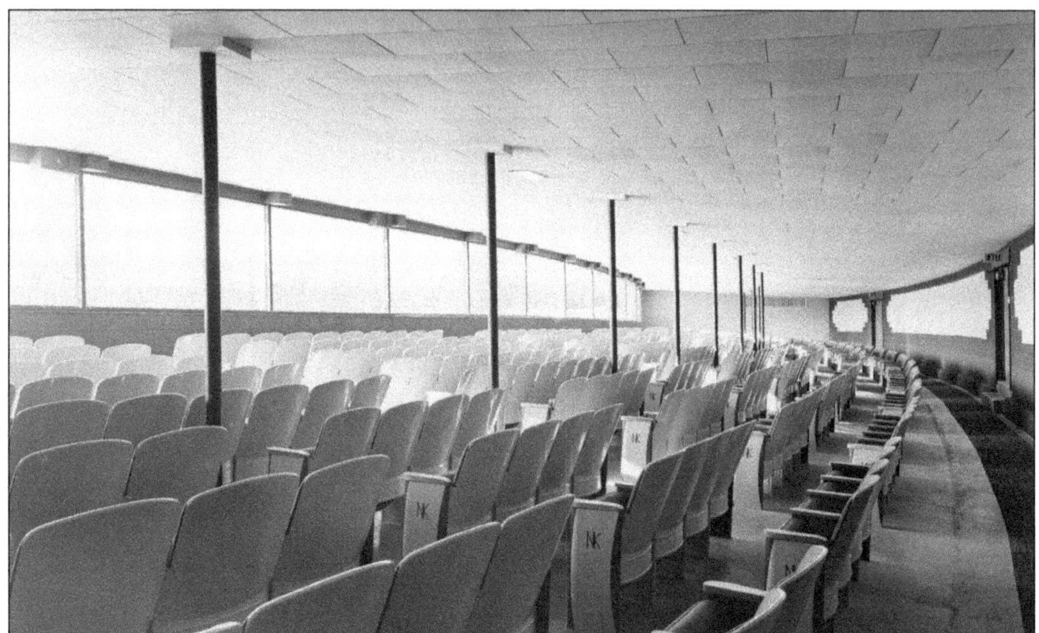

Indoor Viewing Area. The Getty was unusual in having an enclosed area for patrons without cars to watch the film. This unusually vast area was treated as elegantly as possible, even to the extent of having the theaters initials featured on the seats' end standards. One can only wonder if this was really better than going to an indoor theater. The Getty is still operating.

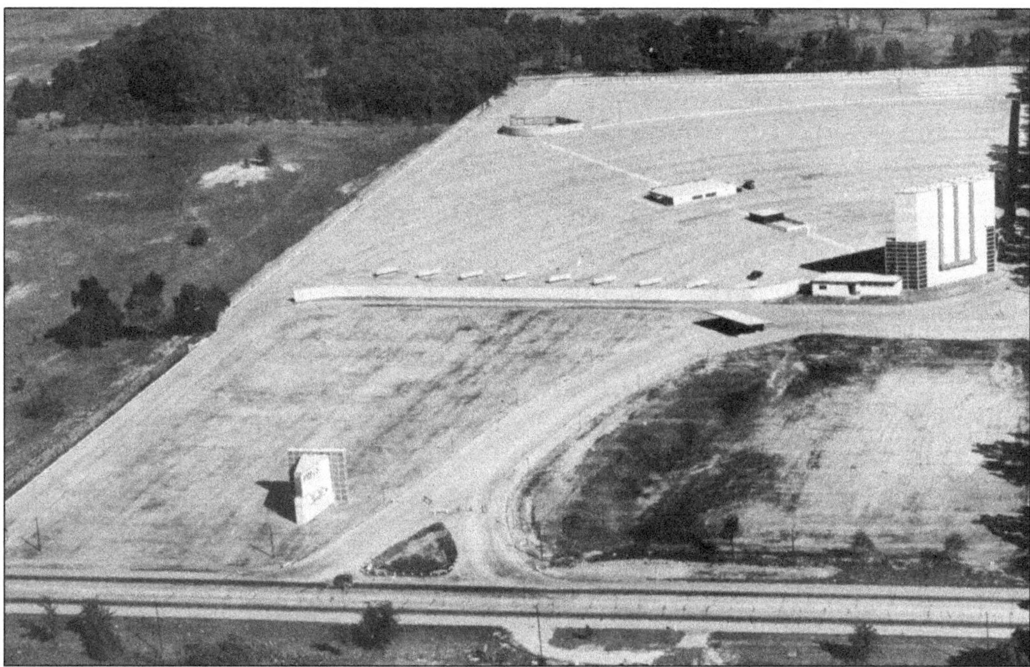

The Niles. The Niles opened in the summer of 1948 at 2141 South Eleventh Street in Niles, with a capacity of 870; different accounts also say that it could hold 970 or 1,000 cars. The general layout can be seen here, along with its uniquely modernistic screen and marquee. Note the separate concession and projection buildings. The lot is paved, an unusual luxury.

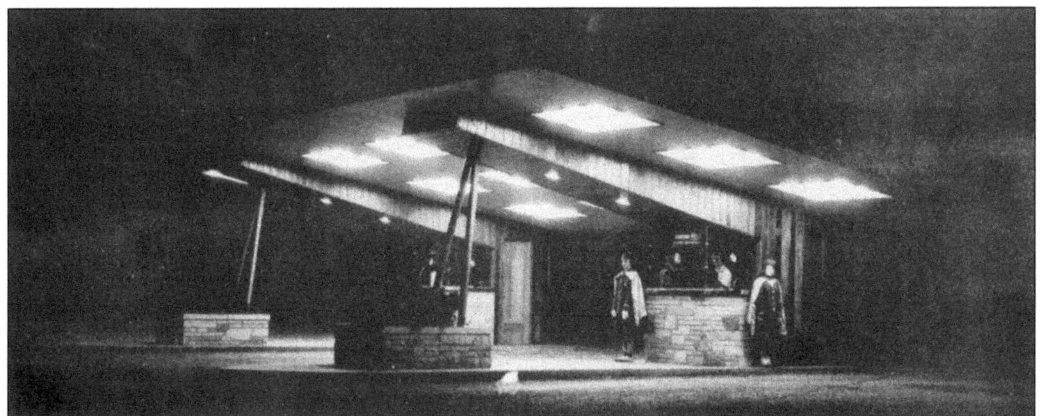

CRACK BOX OFFICE STAFF. Proclaiming itself "America's finest outdoor theatre," the Niles sure looked it, with its uniformed-and-caped box office attendants. This dramatic shot highlights both the elegance of the staff and their appointments and the decidedly modern architecture of the facility, which are all within a pool of cool fluorescent light. The Niles closed in 1985.

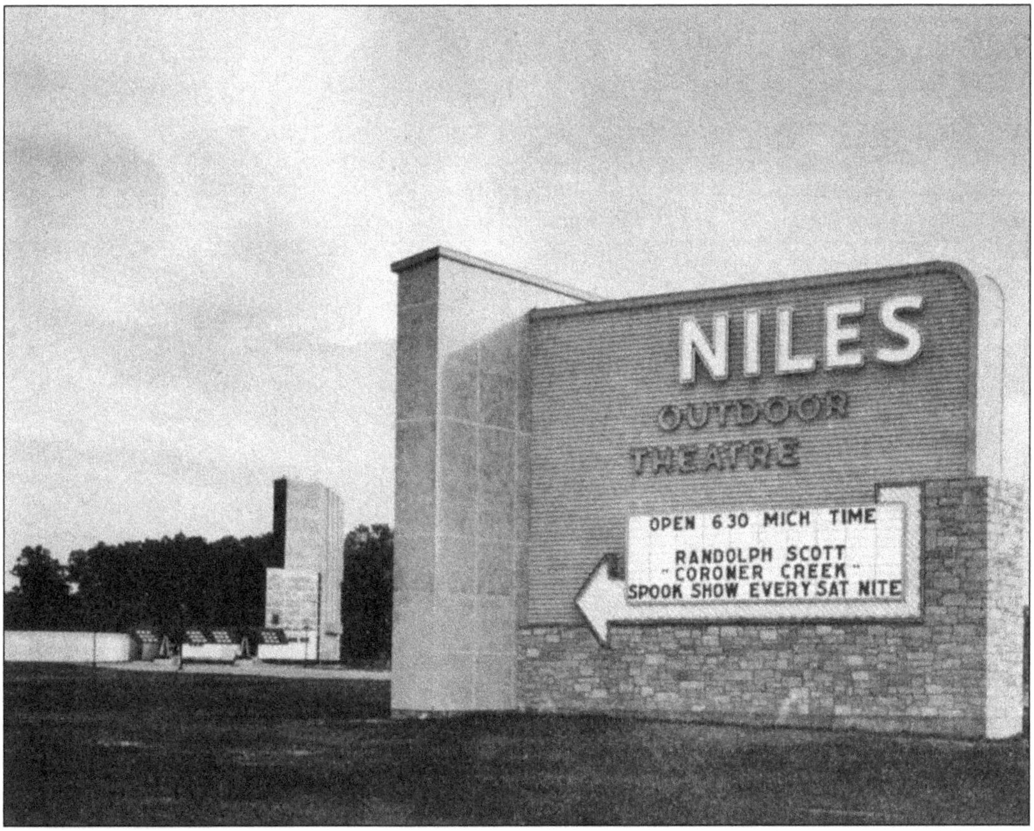

MARQUEE MODERNITY. The unique attraction sign at the Niles features the 1948 Randolph Scott Western *Coroner Creek*. The sign could have been designed a decade later and would have still looked contemporary, with its understated elegance and blend of materials. "Spookshows" combined live magic, scary movies, and spooky fun and were popular kids' attractions after the war.

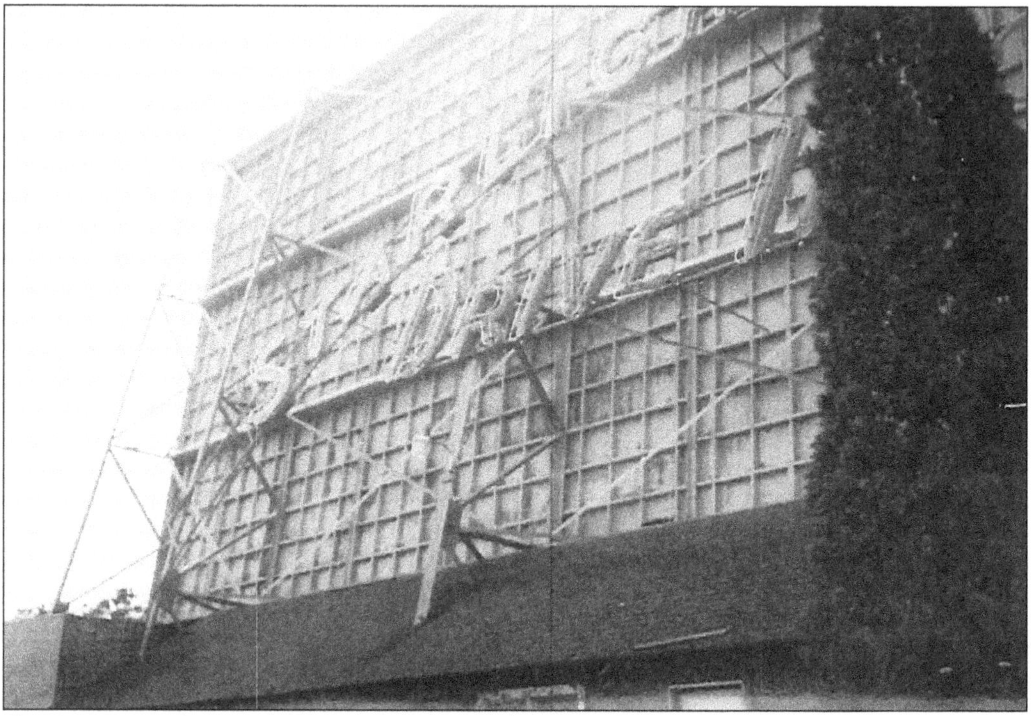

The Starlight Shines in Saugatuck. Located at 6100 Blue Star Highway, the Starlight (not to be confused with the Starlites in Addison, Benton Harbor, Lansing, Ludington, and so on) was opened in 1949 with a capacity of 300 cars. For most of its life, the Butterfield Theatres circuit operated it. (Courtesy of Goodrich Theaters.)

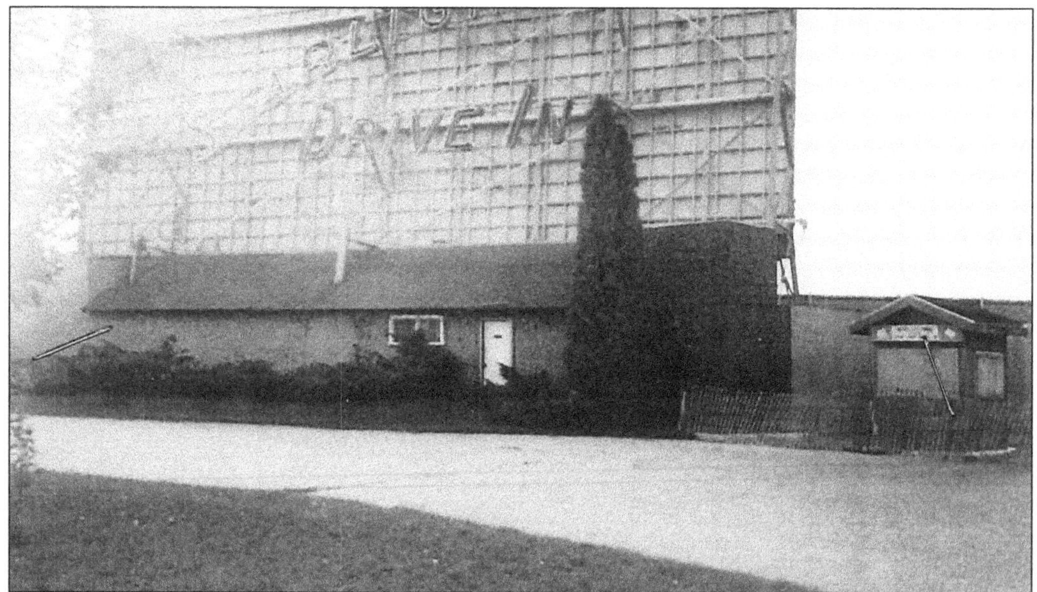

Screen and Driveway. Rather than an apartment, the screen base seems to have included the office and a storage area. The screen itself was interesting in that it revealed its structural underpinnings to the public without the customary outer skin to conceal them. It did, however, proudly proclaim its name across the screen's face. (Courtesy of Goodrich Theaters.)

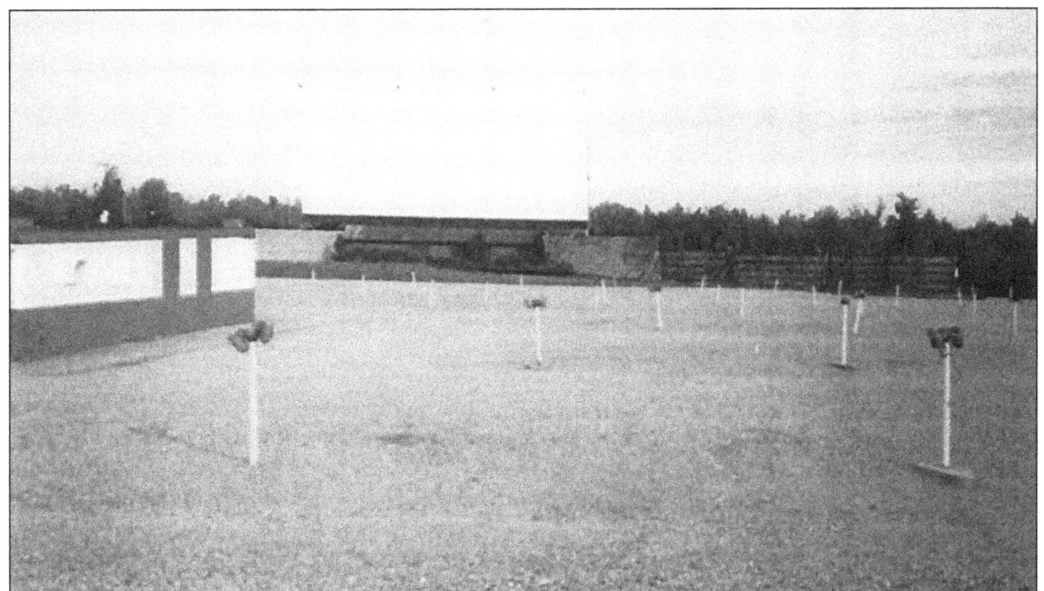

The Lot. The Starlight's modest lot is tidy and covered with gravel, setting it a step above the basic dirt (mud) lots of many other small theaters. The screen, as seen here, must have been modified or replaced, due to its wide aspect ratio. Although not exactly grand, the Starlight was a perfectly nice drive-in. (Courtesy of Goodrich Theaters.)

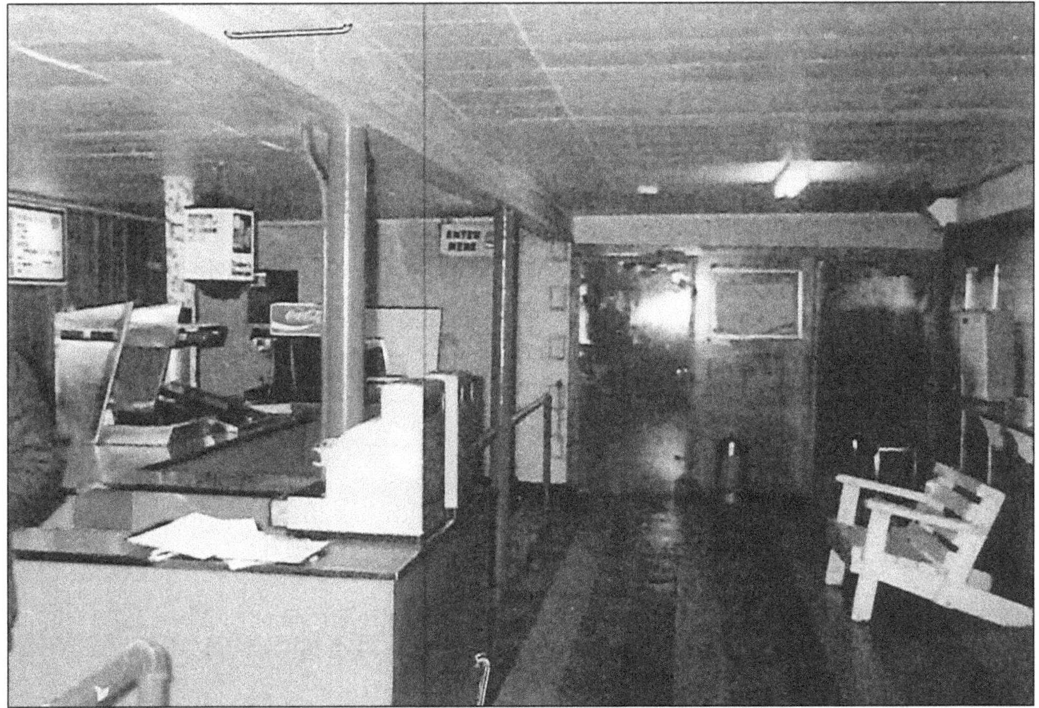

Concessions. Not too big, not too small, the Starlight's concession was just right for its size, with a surprising two cafeteria-style concession lines. Although not sporting the polished chrome railings of the larger theaters or the dazzling white counters, it still managed to be tidy and inviting. The Starlight closed around 1987. (Courtesy of Goodrich Theaters.)

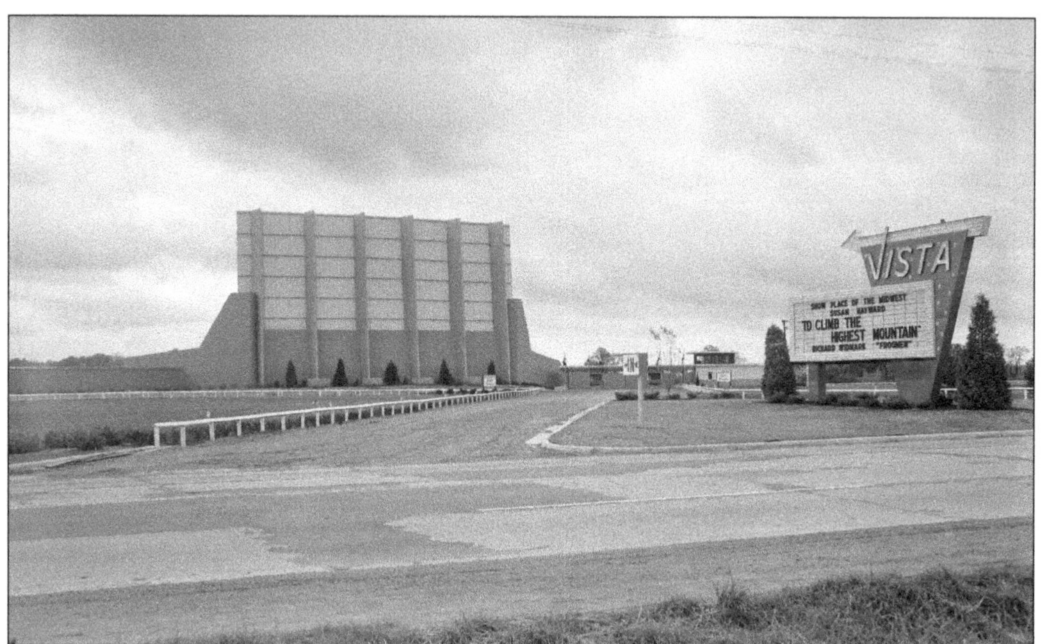

A Spectacular Vista. One of the handful of drive-ins to qualify as really deluxe was the Vista in Walker. Built in 1955, the Vista was located just outside of Grand Rapids, at 4500 Lake Michigan Drive, and boasted an amazing 1,300-car capacity. From the photograph, one can tell is was an attractive facility. (Courtesy of Grand Rapids Public Library.)

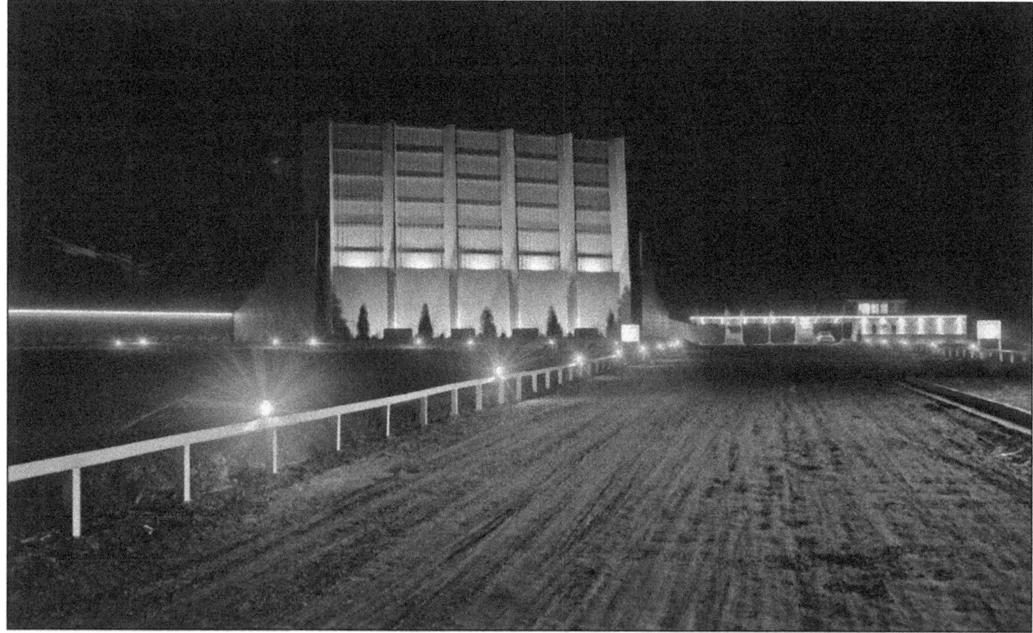

A Nighttime Vista. It was attractive by day and dazzling by night. The Vista, like the Denniston, was a Butterfield Theatre, and being constructed at the same time, it bore a family resemblance to it. Despite its magnificence, the Vista closed in 1978, only 23 years after it opened. After the site stood abandoned for years, a Meijer store was built on-site. (Courtesy of Grand Rapids Public Library.)

Seven

Up North

CHEBOYGAN DRIVE-IN AD. The northern parts of Michigan can be barren and cold, a virtual wilderness, and so the Cheboygan was a nice summer treat. It opened in 1952, on Highway 27, and held 300 cars. It was demolished around 1983.

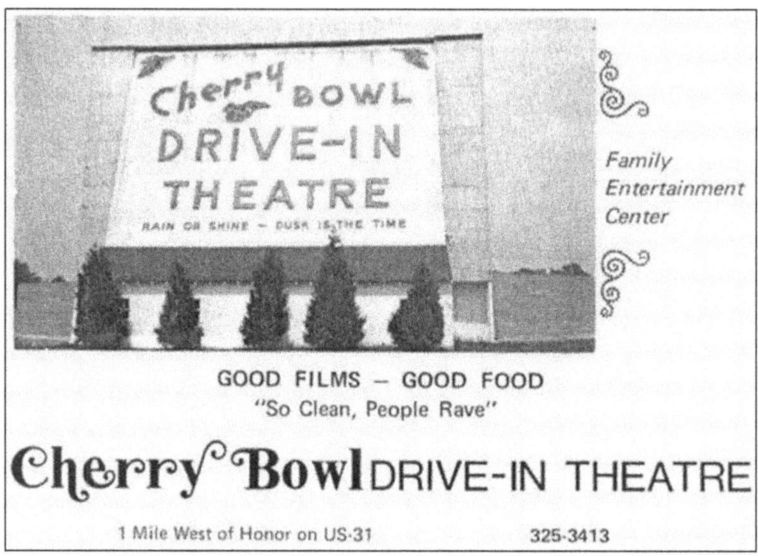

The Cherry Bowl! The charming Cherry Bowl Drive-In is located just outside of Traverse City, on US 23, near Honor. It proudly proclaims its 200-car capacity and that it is "So Clean, People Rave." One of the state's most charming drive-ins, the Cherry Bowl opened in 1953 and is still going.

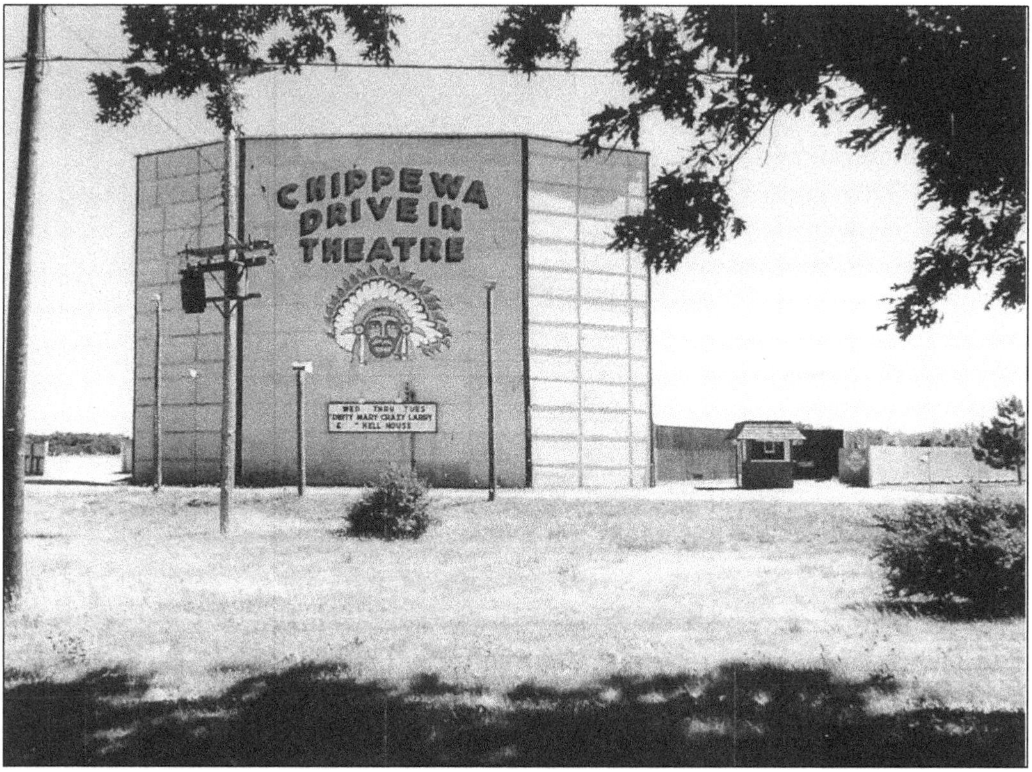

The Chippewa Drive-In, Manistee. The Chippewa was another Goodrich Theater and was located on US Route 31 outside of Manistee. Another modest country theater with a capacity of only 275 upon opening in 1950, it was, nonetheless, well appointed and charming. It was also one of several theaters to sport a Native American theme on its signage, which now is considered in dubious taste. (Courtesy of Goodrich Theaters.)

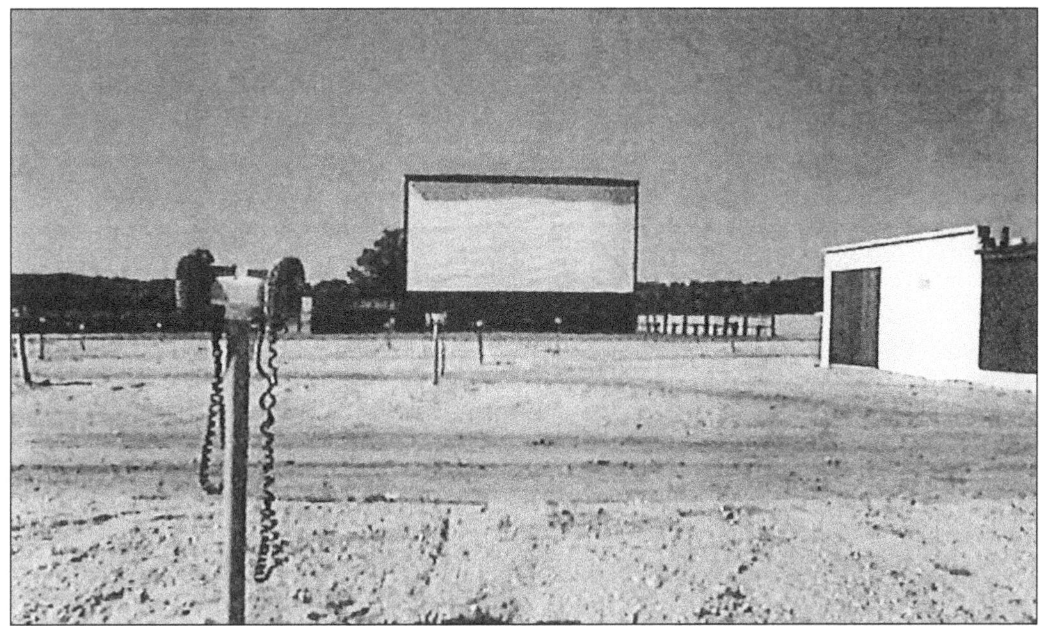

The Lot. The Chippewa's screen is the familiar wider version by the time this undated photograph was taken. The lot is tidy and well maintained, and like many of the rural theaters, the concession building can be effectively vandal-proofed for the winter season by closing sliding doors and shutters. (Courtesy of Goodrich Theaters.)

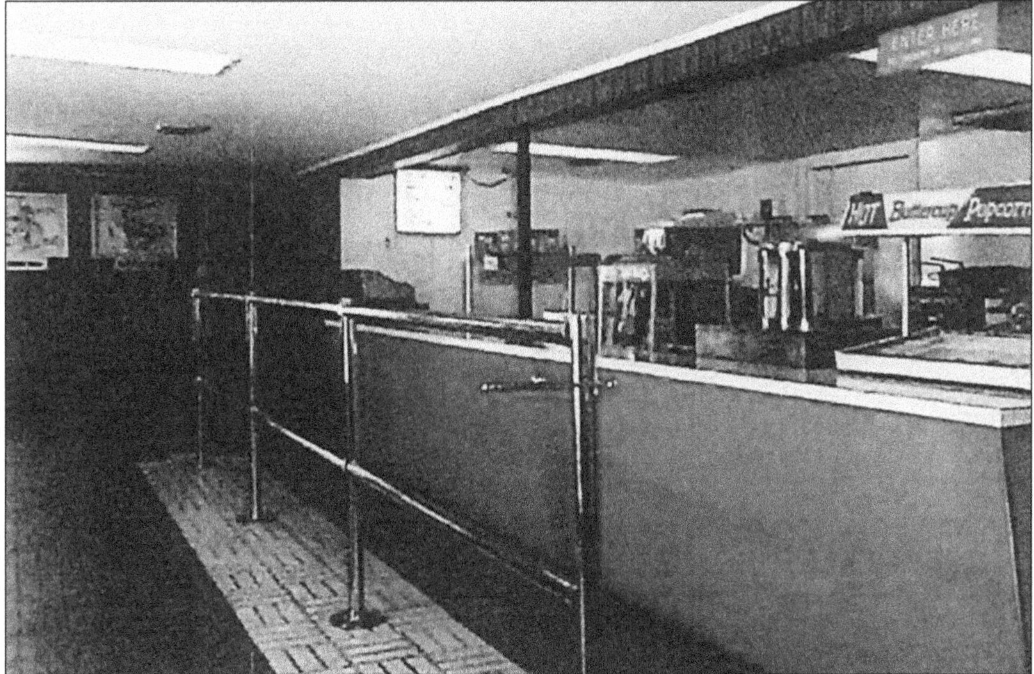

Concessions Again. Here is another concession stand with the chrome railing. Most of a drive-in's profits came from the sales of concessions and not the ticket price, which barely covered operational costs. During hard times, many theaters discouraged patrons from bringing their own food for this reason. (Courtesy of Goodrich Theaters.)

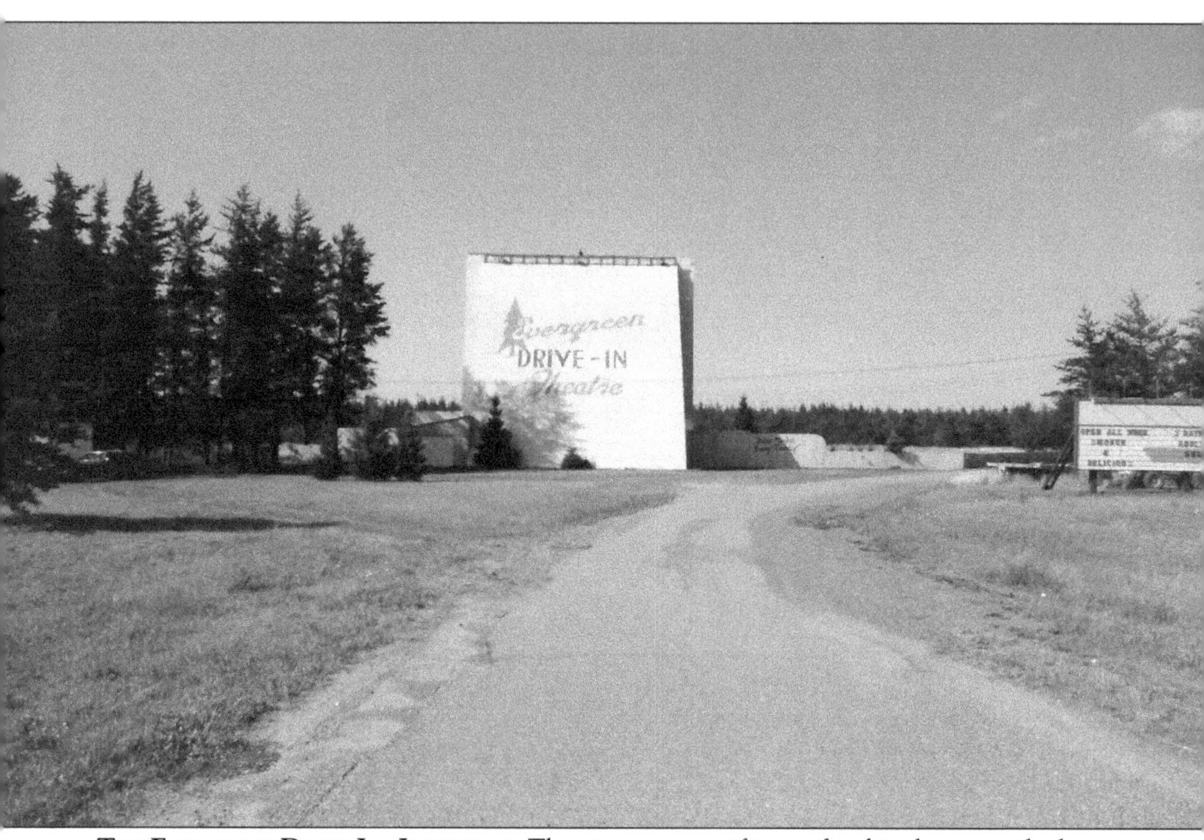

The Evergreen Drive-In, Ishpeming. The pine tree motif is apt for this theater tucked away in the wilds of the Upper Peninsula. The Evergreen, located on US Route 41, opened in 1950 and had a capacity of 200 cars. It operated for most of its life as a standard theater but eventually switched to X-rated. It closed in the mid-1980s.

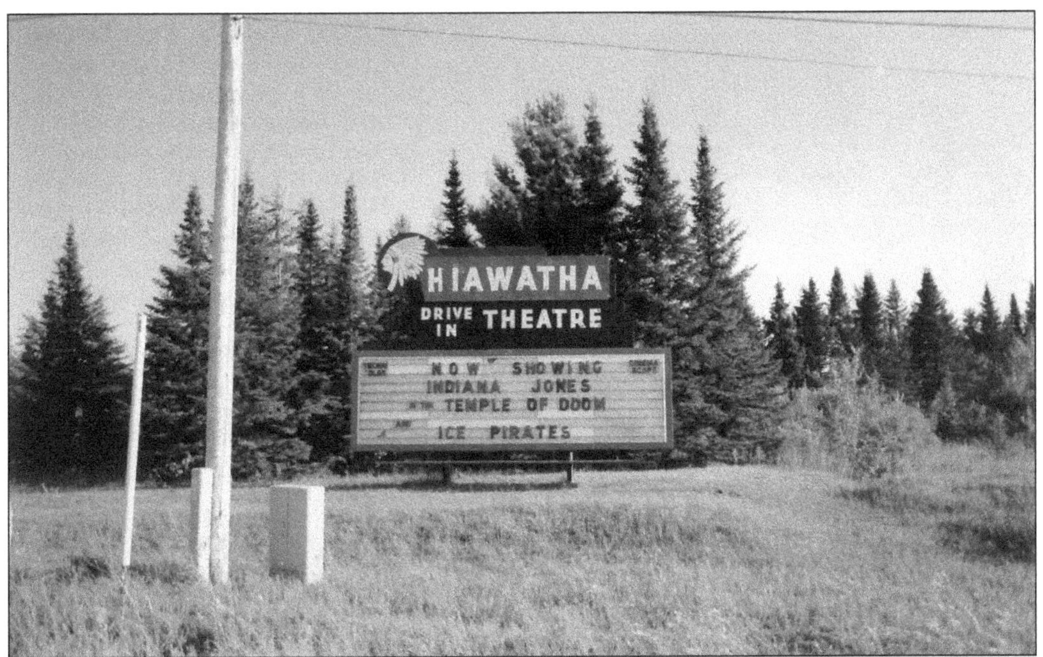

The Hiawatha, Chassell. Also up in the north woods was the Hiawatha. Another of the Indian-themed drive-ins, the Hiawatha was built in 1952 and had a 400-car capacity. Shielding the screen from neighbors was not typically a problem for northern drive-ins, as they were surrounded by pine forest and there were no neighbors.

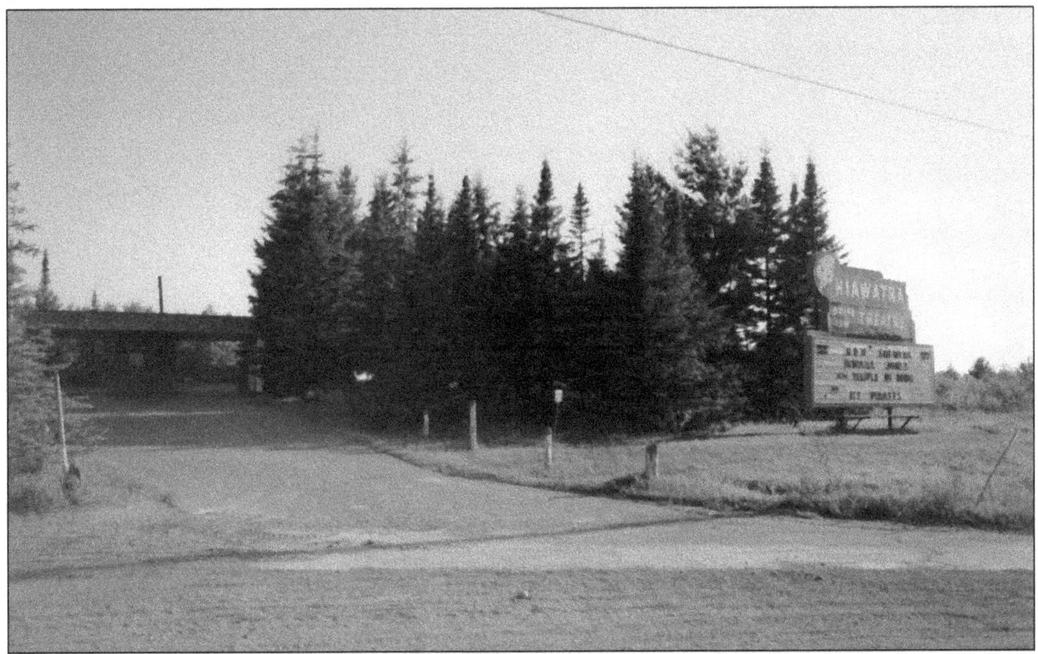

The Long Drive of the Hiawatha. Pictured here around 1984–1985, the Hiawatha was still doing fine, but it would close only a year or two later. The drive-in's property stood vacant for years afterward until it was eventually rezoned and plans were developed to create a residential subdivision on the site.

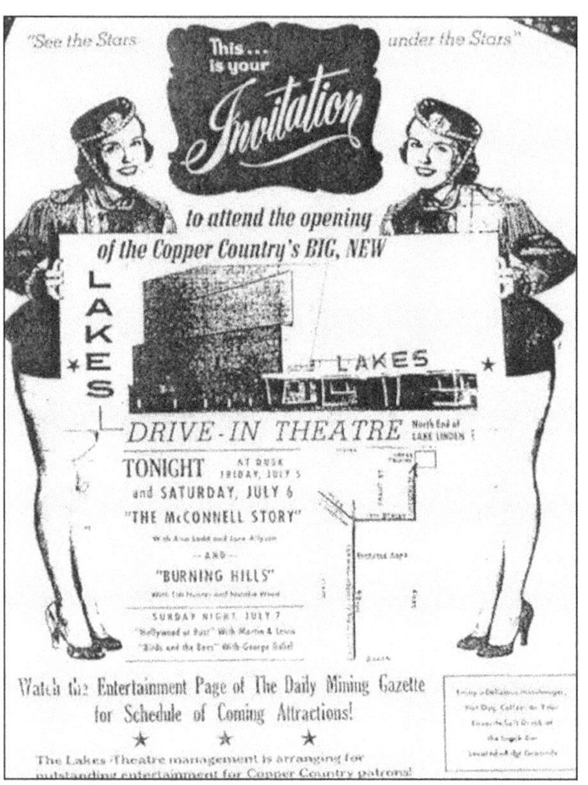

The Lakes Drive-In, Lake Linden. The Lakes was a surprisingly late theater for a small town, being built in 1957. The same people who ran the Delft indoor theater also ran the Lakes. It had a 350-car capacity and was located in a residential area. The screen, like many others, sustained damage in a storm in 1966 but was repaired. It closed in 1984.

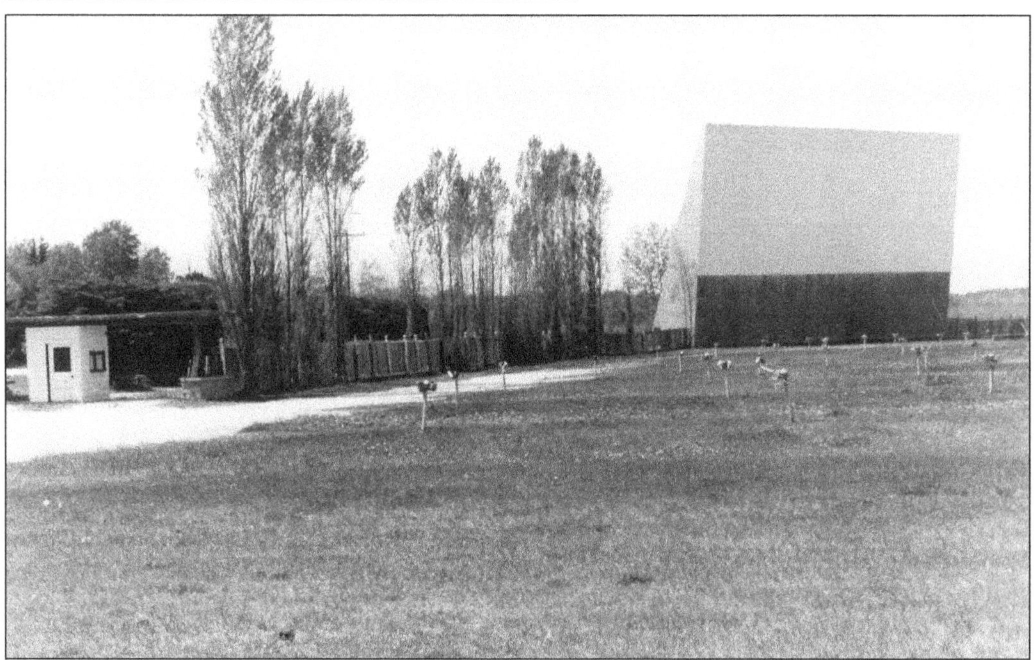

The Thunder Bay, Alpena. The Thunder Bay opened in 1955 with a capacity of 400. Although it had a fairly standard career as a theater, it was graced by the live concert appearance of Alice Cooper in 1980. This is more than a little surprising given the obvious small size of the lot. Even Alice was unable to save the theater, and it closed in 1988. (Courtesy of Curt Peterson.)

Eight

TOLEDO

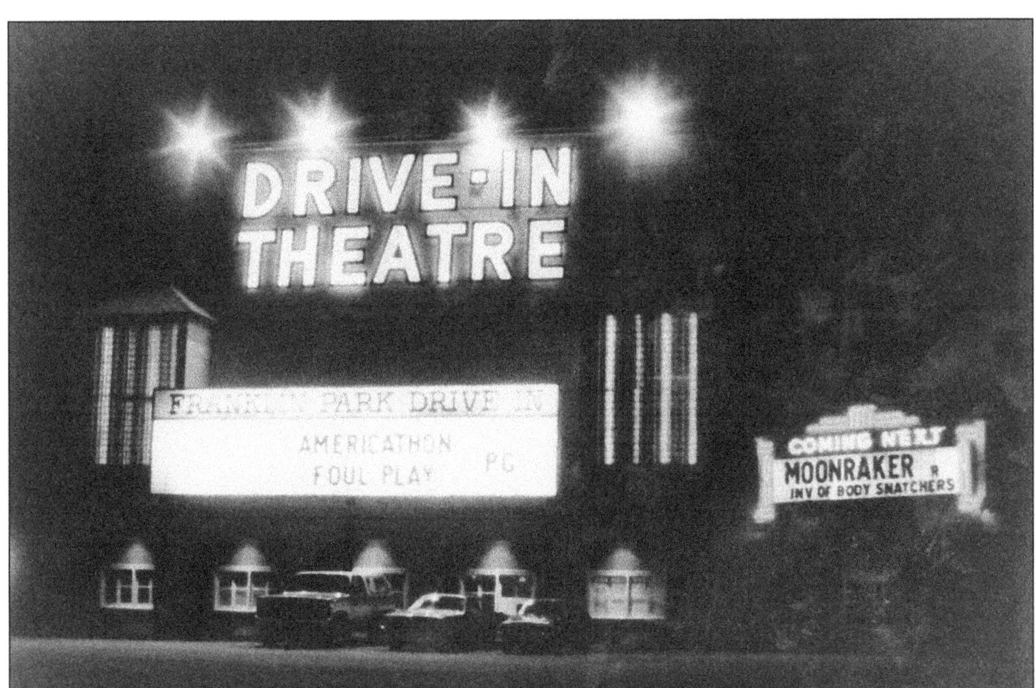

OUR NEIGHBORS DOWN SOUTH. But for the results of the well-known border war that severed Toledo from Michigan in the 1830s (but awarded Michigan the Upper Peninsula), Toledo's drive-ins would be Michigan's. Therefore, as a gesture of good will to Michiganders' cousins to the south, this book hereby presents Toledo's drive-ins, beginning with the beautiful, glowing, Franklin Park Drive-In. (Courtesy of Mike Veh.)

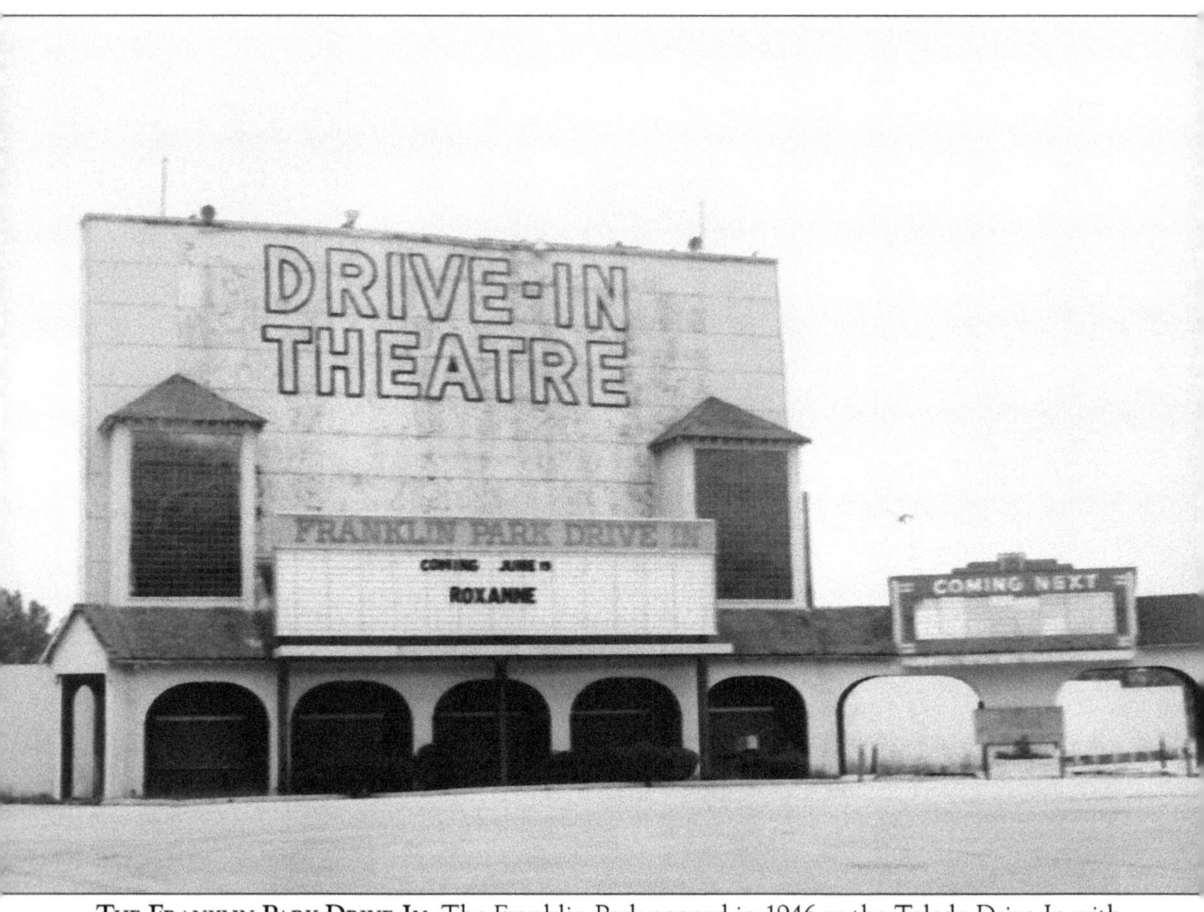

THE FRANKLIN PARK DRIVE-IN. The Franklin Park opened in 1946 as the Toledo Drive-In with a capacity of an astonishing 1,000 cars. The screen tower was an unusual variation of the 1940s archways-in-the-front style, with two glass-block-filled towers backlit with neon and flanking the central structure—these probably dated from the its widening.

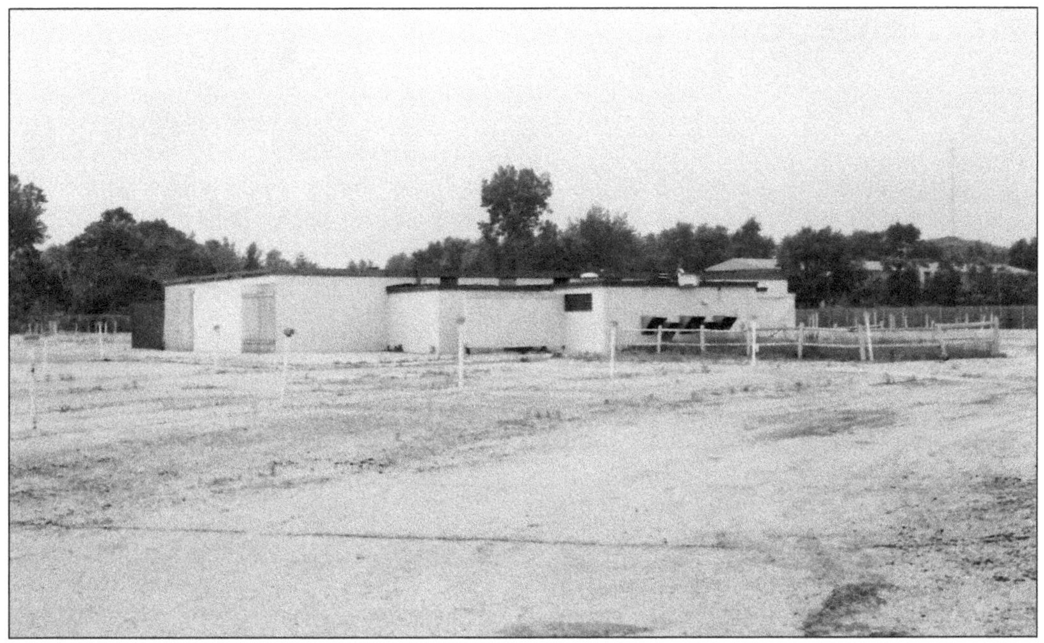

THE LOT. Major improvements were made in 1959, and the capacity was increased to 1,300. The theater, seen here in 1987, was popular even before the construction of the nearby Franklin Park Mall. When the theater was built, the now densely retail area was almost all farmland, except for the Franklin Dairy.

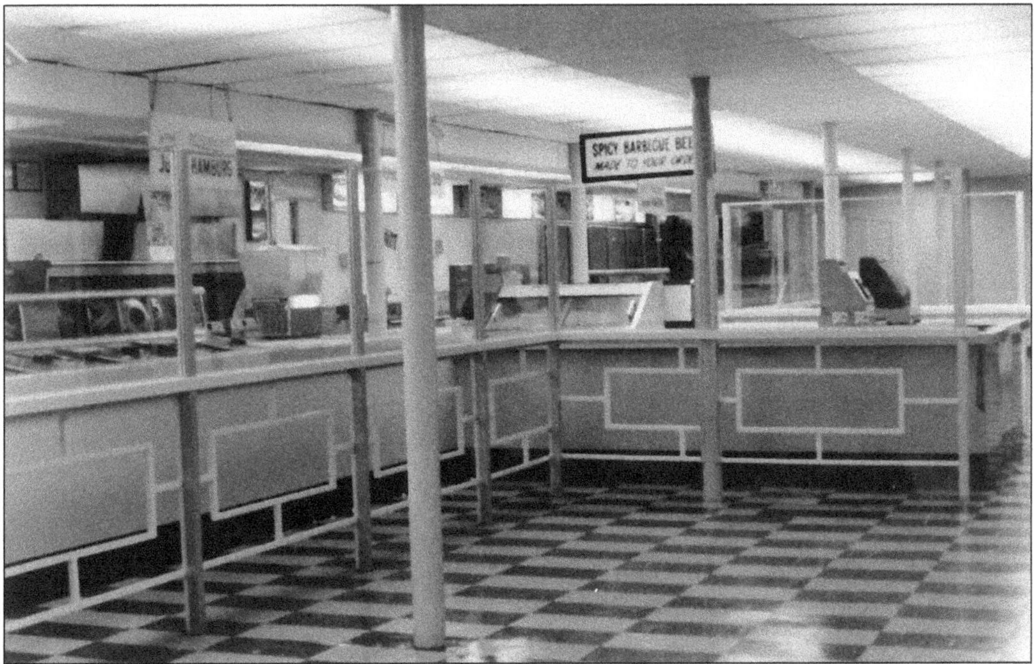

INSIDE THE CONCESSION STAND. The concession stand, as seen here in 1987, was a product of the 1959 improvements, thus the cafeteria configuration. Redstone Theaters operated the Franklin Park after 1963 and continued to until its closing in 1986. A Target store and strip mall now occupy the site.

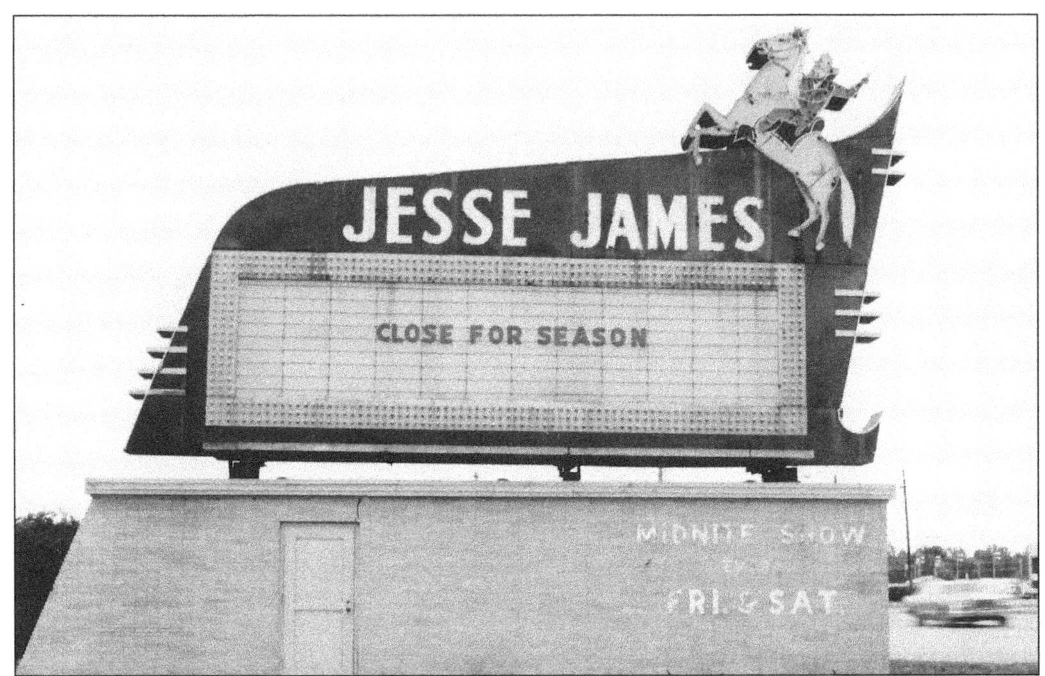

THE JESSE JAMES DRIVE-IN. The Jesse James was located at 521 South Reynolds Road and opened on June 4, 1953. It was a large modern theater with a capacity of 1,100 cars on 47 acres. It was named after co-owner Harold James, whose nickname was "Jesse," and it carried a Western motif.

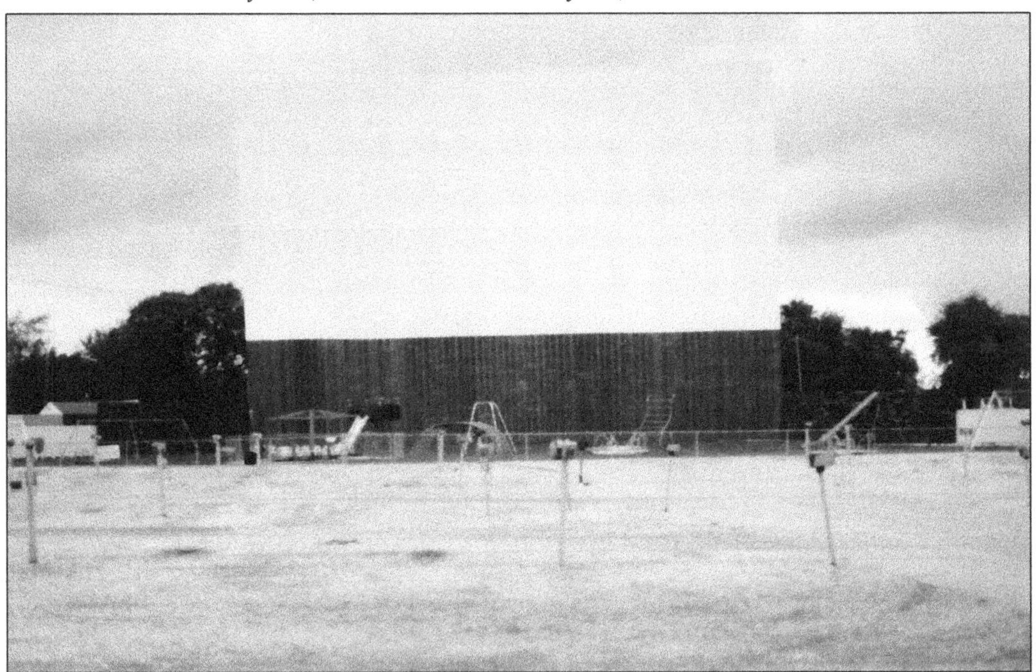

A LOT OF SCREEN. The Jesse James had a large 50-by-100-foot screen with a complete playground at its base and a gravel-covered lot. In addition to the usual opening night balloons and pony rides, the first 5,000 customers were entitled to a "free Alemite grease job." It is not recorded how many customers took advantage of this offer.

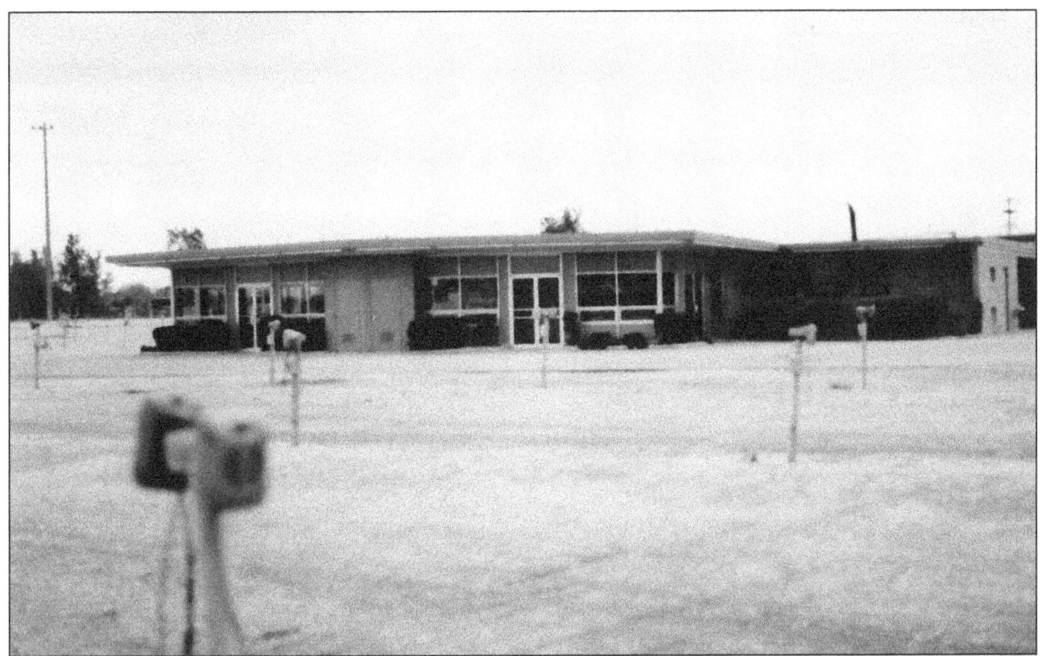

The Concession Building. Painted in red and blue, the snack bar had wide windows and glass doors to view the film or keep an eye on the countdown clock while buying tasty cheeseburgers, popcorn, or egg rolls. The speaker posts had red-lit caps, and a "moon light" kept the lot dimly lit to facilitate navigation.

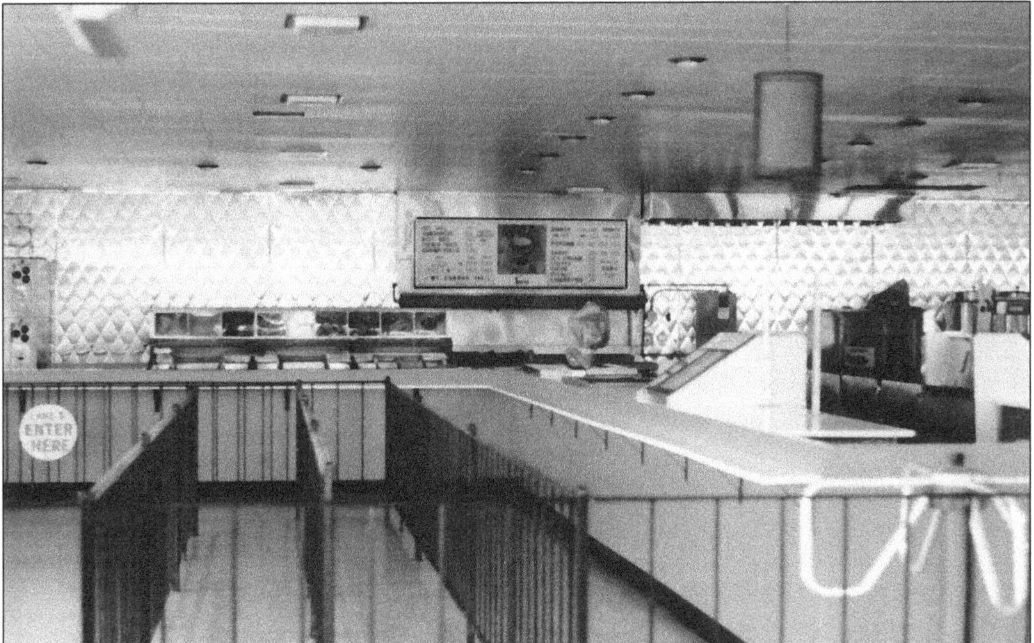

The Last Concessions. The Jesse James's concession stand was as nice as any in the city. Seen here after the season's end in 1979, it was ready to reopen but never did. Harold James, the last surviving co-owner, decided to close the theater and sold the property. A strip mall called the Jesse James Plaza was built on the site.

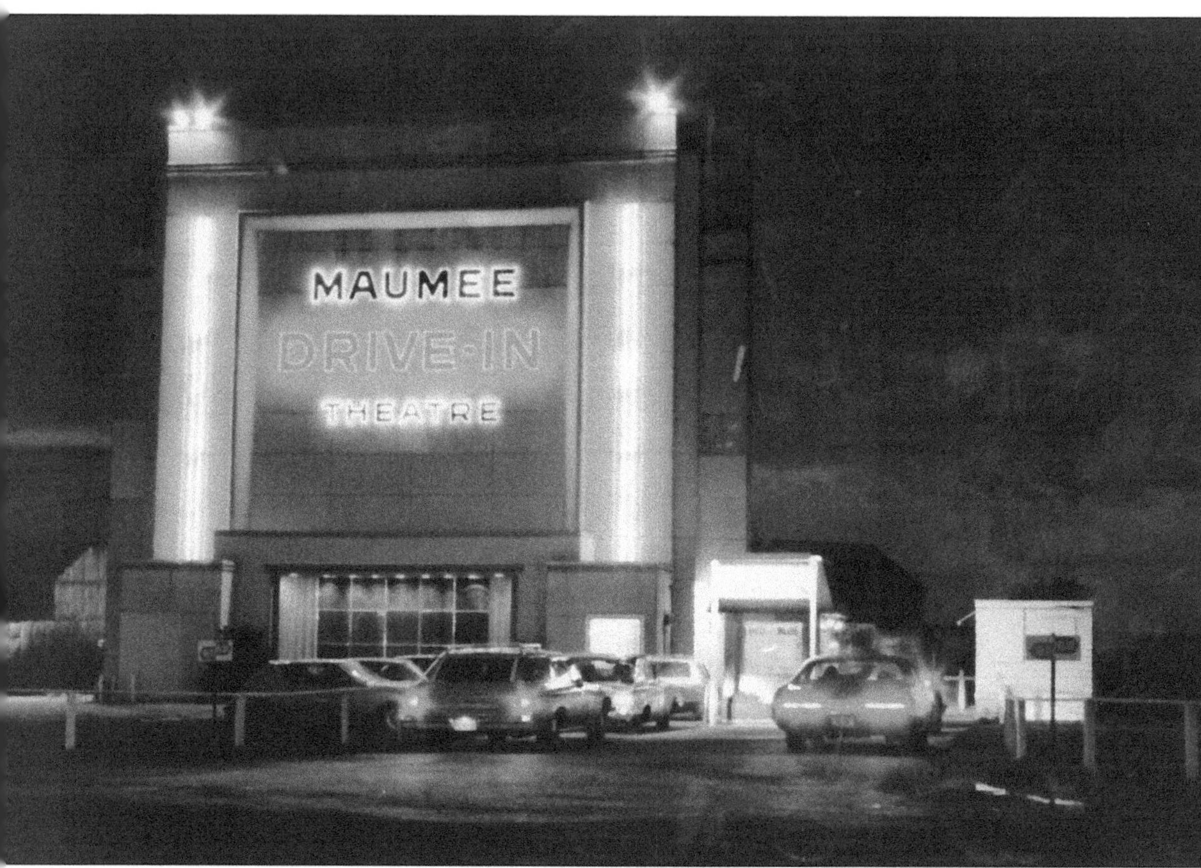

The Maumee Drive-In. Glowing with red and blue neon, the Maumee, also known as the Lake Erie Drive-In or the Drive-In Theater, opened in 1941, making it the oldest drive-in in the Toledo area. It was located at 1360 North Conant Street in Maumee, and had a capacity of 600 cars. The Maumee was the only local theater to be built with large speakers in the screen tower. (Courtesy of Mike Veh.)

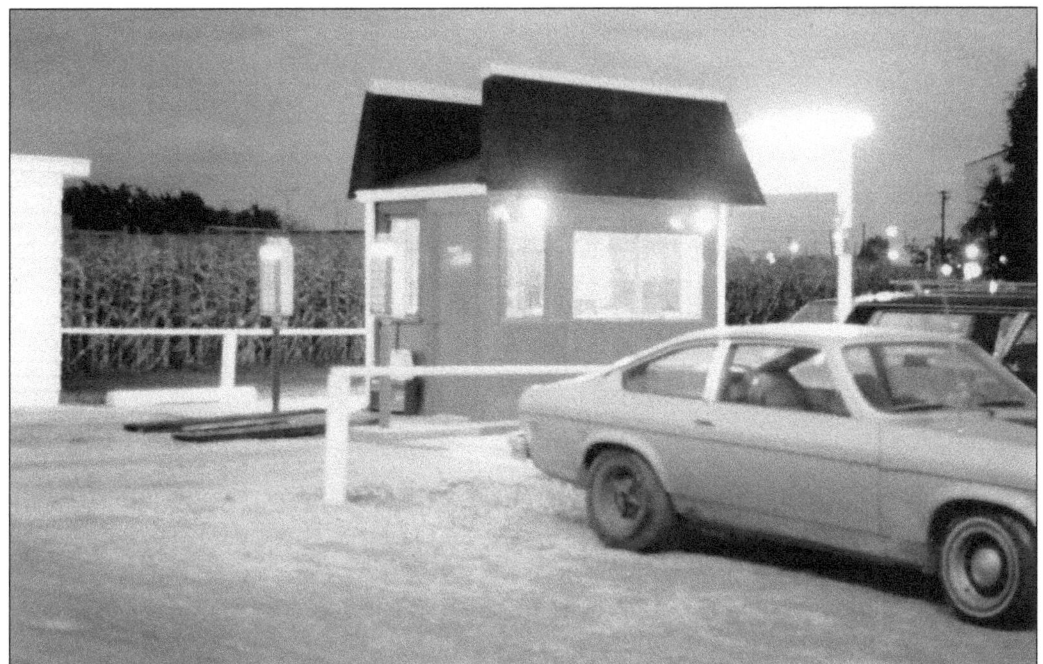

Box Office. The Maumee's tiny box office positively glows at dusk in this 1979 picture. In 1948, the large speakers were removed, and in-car speakers were installed, while the lot was increased to a 800-car capacity. In 1954, the screen was widened for scope pictures, and new projectors were installed. (Courtesy of Mike Veh.)

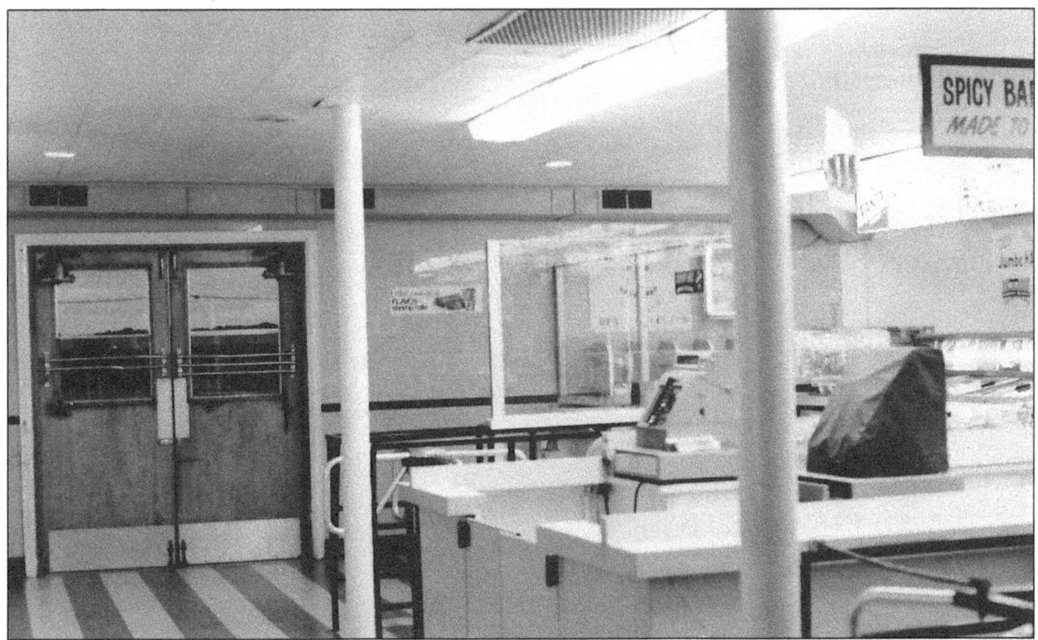

Striped Floors and Double Doors. The 40-by-40-foot concession building was built in 1949, at the same time the more modern steel-framed screen tower was constructed. In 1978, the Maumee was twinned and remained that way until Redstone, the operator, closed it along with the Franklin Park and Miracle Mile Drive-Ins in 1986. It was demolished in 1988.

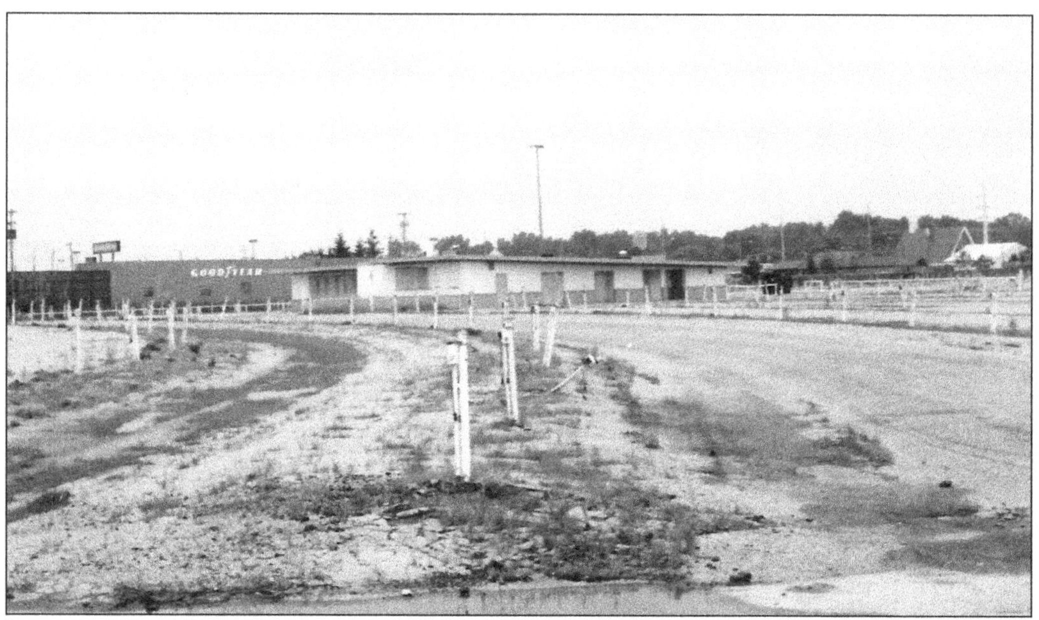

The Miracle Mile. The Miracle Mile was opened in 1954 with a capacity of 1,500 and was located at 4918 Jackman Road. It had state-of-the-art projection and sound, including the three-speaker in-car stereo and rentable plug-in electric heaters. The screen tower was 60 by 120 feet with a reputed 425-foot projector throw from the booth.

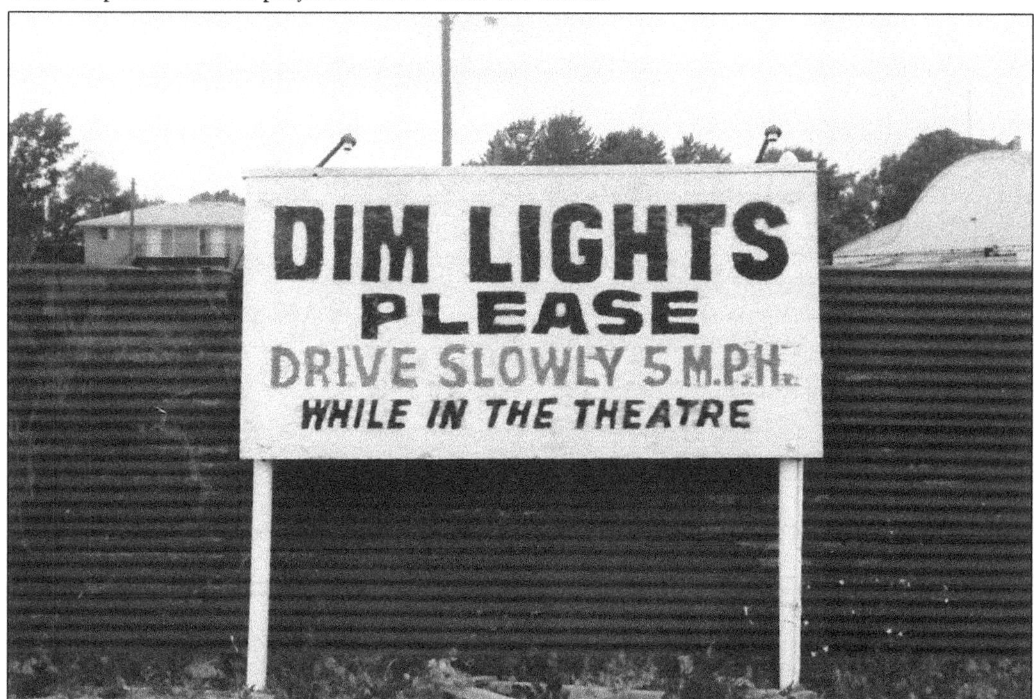

Sign of the Times. Signs such as this one graced most drive-ins, as did aisle lights, so-called moon lights, and the occasional row of spikes to prevent entry through the exit drive. The large, modern Miracle Mile contained all of these and more. At 1,500-plus cars, it was the largest drive-in in the Toledo area.

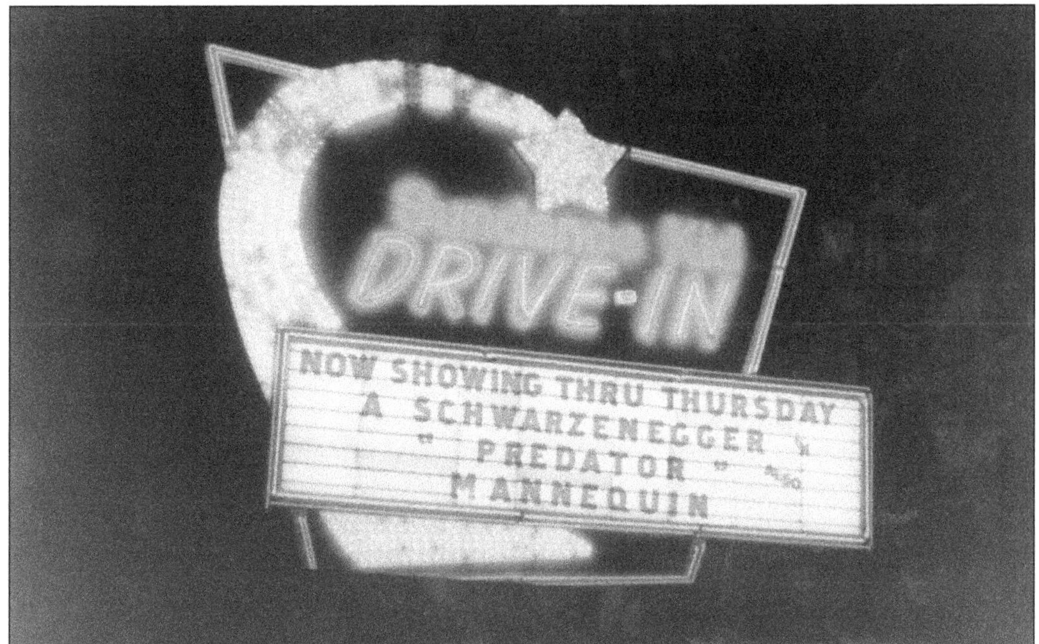

The Sundance Kid. The Sundance Kid, also known as the Parkside, at 4550 Navarre Avenue, outside of Toledo in Oregon, opened in 1949 with a capacity of around 500 cars. The attraction sign seen here is identical to the one from the former Starlite Drive-In, once located on the site of the Starlite Plaza on Monroe Street.

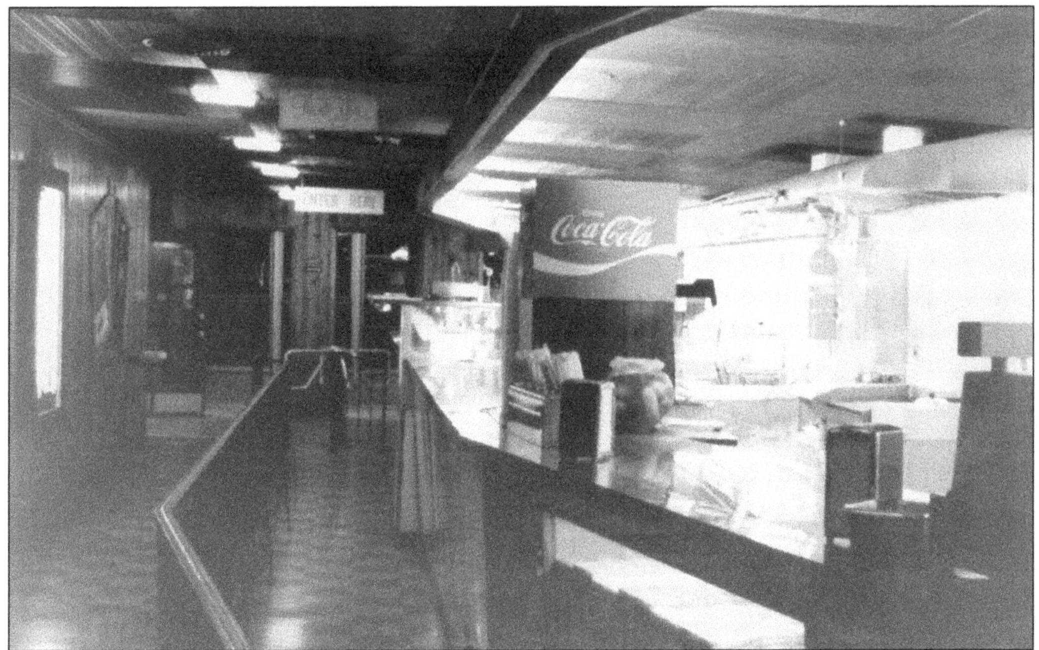

The Snack Bar. In 1979, a second screen was added, and in 1986, the Parkside was renamed the Sundance Kid, at the same time the Eastside Drive-In was renamed the Butch Cassidy by the new owner, who was formerly attached to the Jesse James. The Sundance Kid is Toledo's only remaining drive-in.

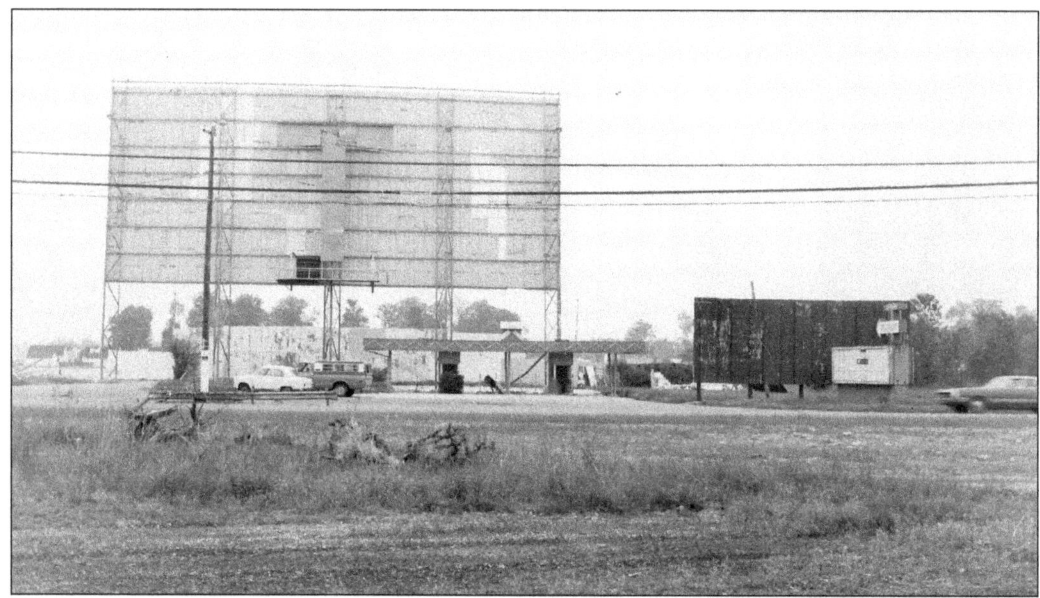

The Telegraph Drive-In. The Telegraph, named for its location just south of the state line on Telegraph Road, opened in 1946 with a capacity of nearly 700 cars. In 1958, a new Cinemascope screen was installed along with associated equipment. The original screen also contained speakers (until 1948). The Telegraph was adorned with a giant, red neon *T* on the screen back. (Courtesy of Bill Frisk.)

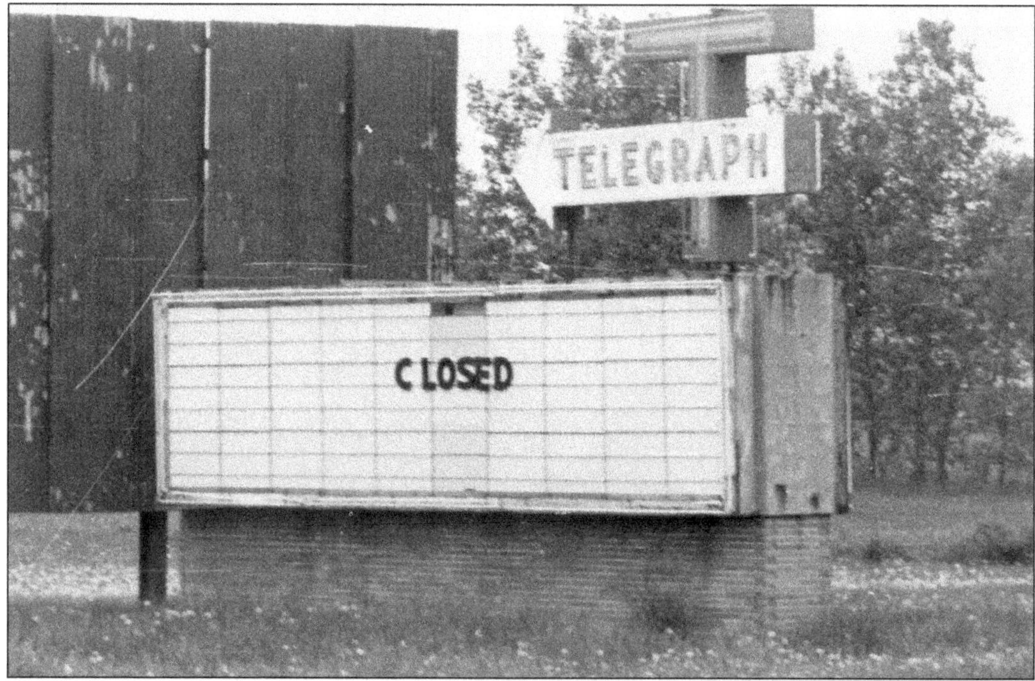

The Marquee. The Telegraph's attraction sign also had a neon *T* and the neon name Telegraph. The Telegraph operated until it was torn down in 1979. The attraction sign was sold to a church, which planned to lengthen the *T* into a cross; some of the box office neon was moved to a local bar; and a strip mall was constructed on the site. (Courtesy of Bill Frisk.)

Nine

The Picture Dims

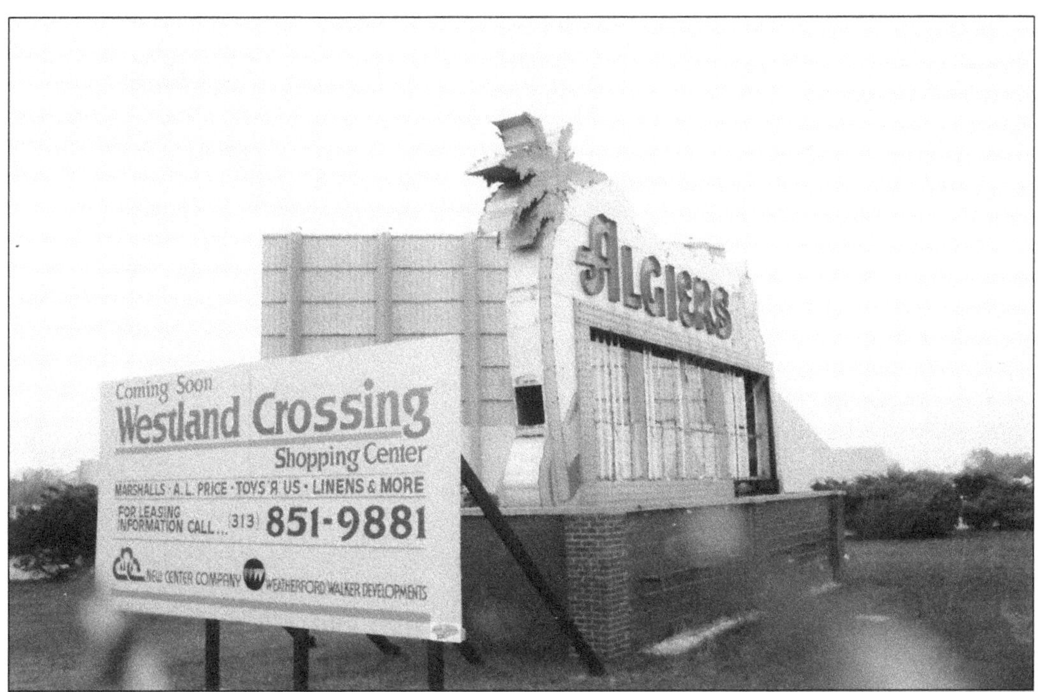

The Algiers Redux. As the astute reader may have noticed, by the 1980s, the drive-ins were an endangered species. A sad but typical example is the once great Algiers in Westland (see page 20), which was sold and slated for demolition by 1985. A ubiquitous and soulless big-box store and strip mall replaced it.

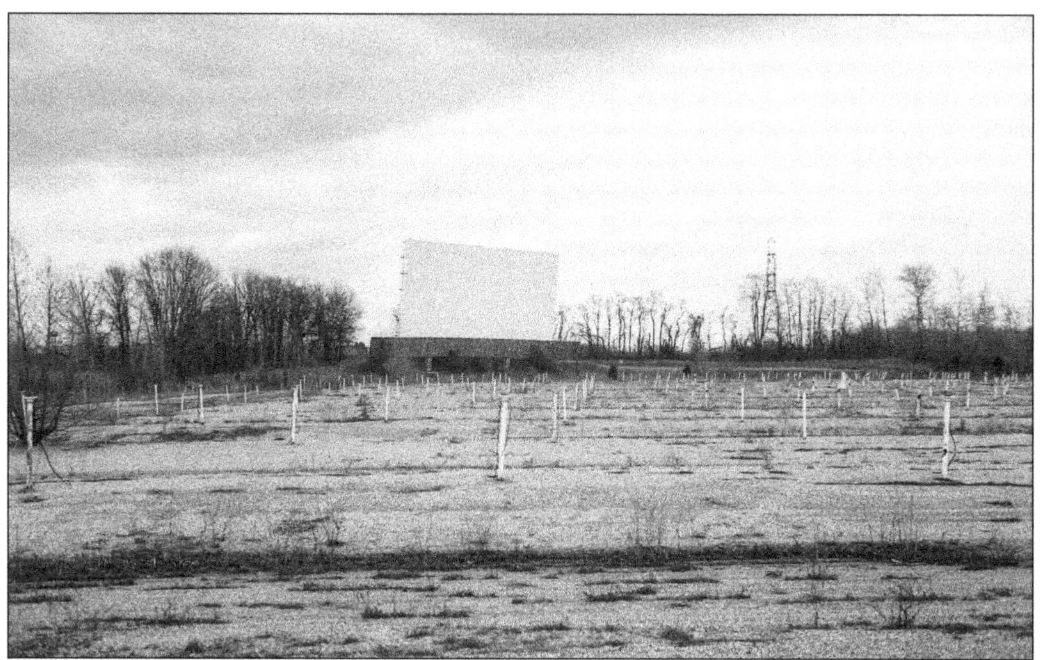

The Closed Cascade. One of the most magnificent theaters in the state, the Cascade Twin, outside of Grand Rapids (pages 81–82), closed in 1992 and stood for years as a sad, ghostly version of itself. Originally, it was mothballed so that it could be reopened if desired, but eventually, the elements and vandals took their toll. (Courtesy of Jeff Raterink.)

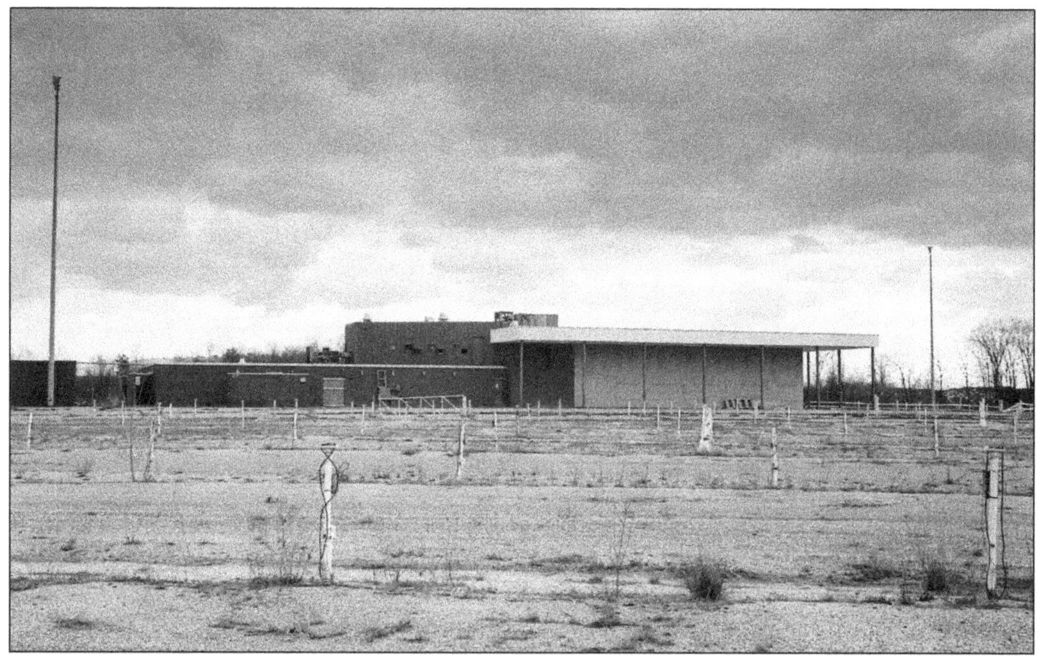

The Brooding Concession. The immaculate concession building, with its huge booth and sprawling eight-lane food service area squats here in the center of the vacant three-screen complex all but forgotten. Its floor-to-ceiling windows are boarded shut and will look out on blobs and surfers no more. (Courtesy of Jeff Raterink.)

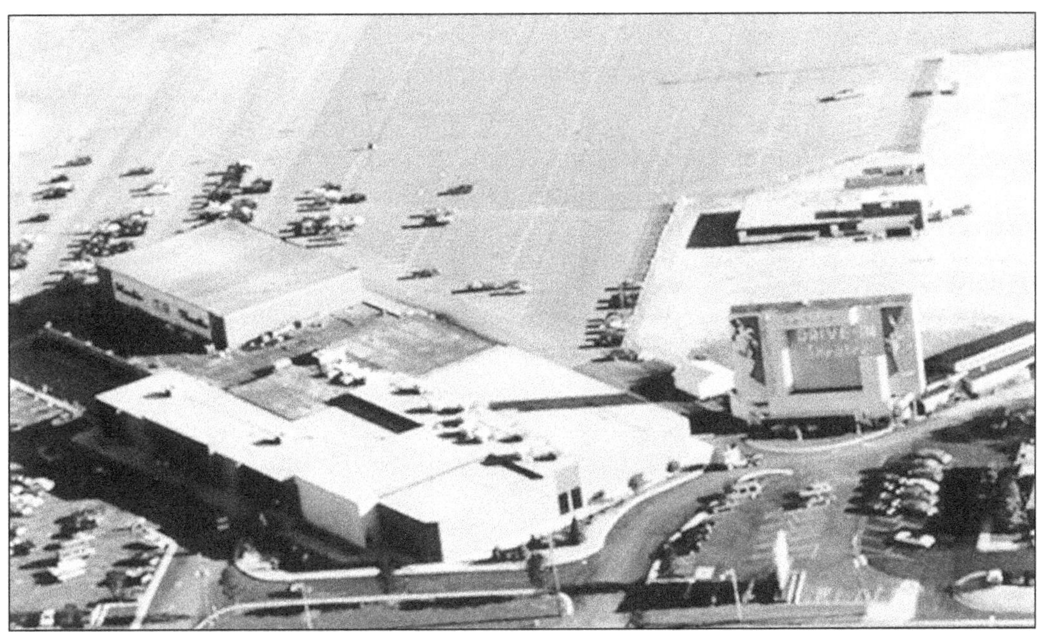

Tightening the Beltline. The Beltline Drive-In suffered a truly terrible fate, as the neighboring cinema's parking lot metastasized into the Beltline's lot. This aerial view tells the sad tale of a drive-in being whittled away slowly over time (see pages 77–80). Ironically, the same theater chain that owned the drive-in also owned the cinema. The drive-in was eventually demolished. (Courtesy of Jack Loeks Collection/Celebration Cinemas.)

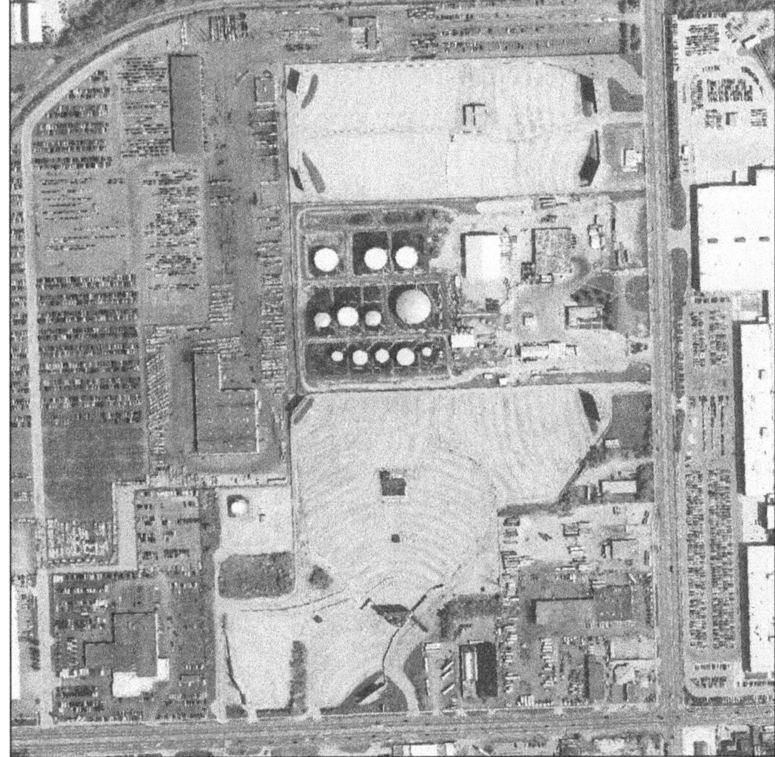

Madness Prevails. Almost the opposite of the above is the still operating Ford-Wyoming. To stay alive, the Ford-Wyoming kept subdividing the lot and adding screens until the nine-screen venue seen here prevailed. The original lot has been turned into a five-screen complex, and another four screens have been annexed to the north (see page 27). The annex was later closed, which left only today's five-screener. (Courtesy of Historicaerials.com.)

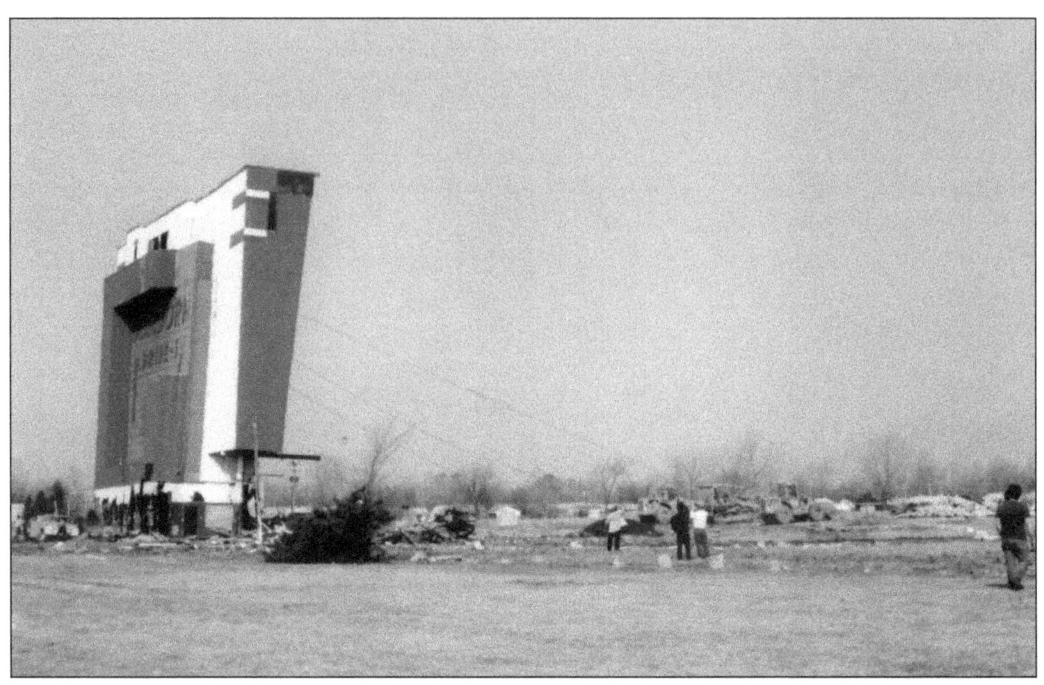

Dearborn Demo. The Dearborn Drive-In suffered a sad fate. After standing empty for some time, the property was sold and the theater had to come down. To do this, acetylene torches were used to weaken the structural steel at its base, and then cables attached to the top were fastened to bulldozers out in the lot.

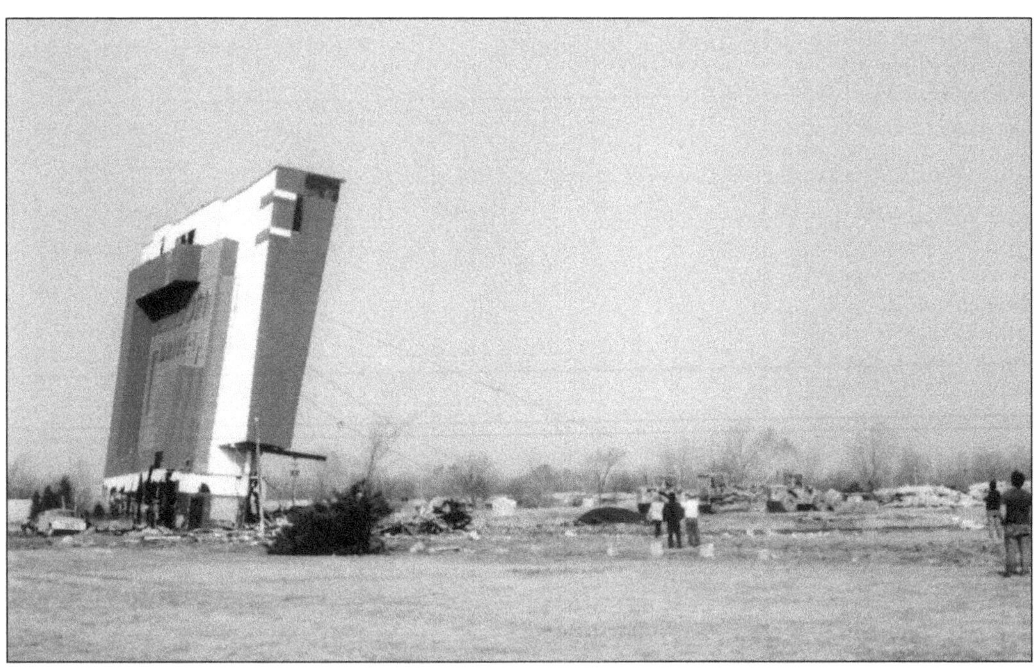

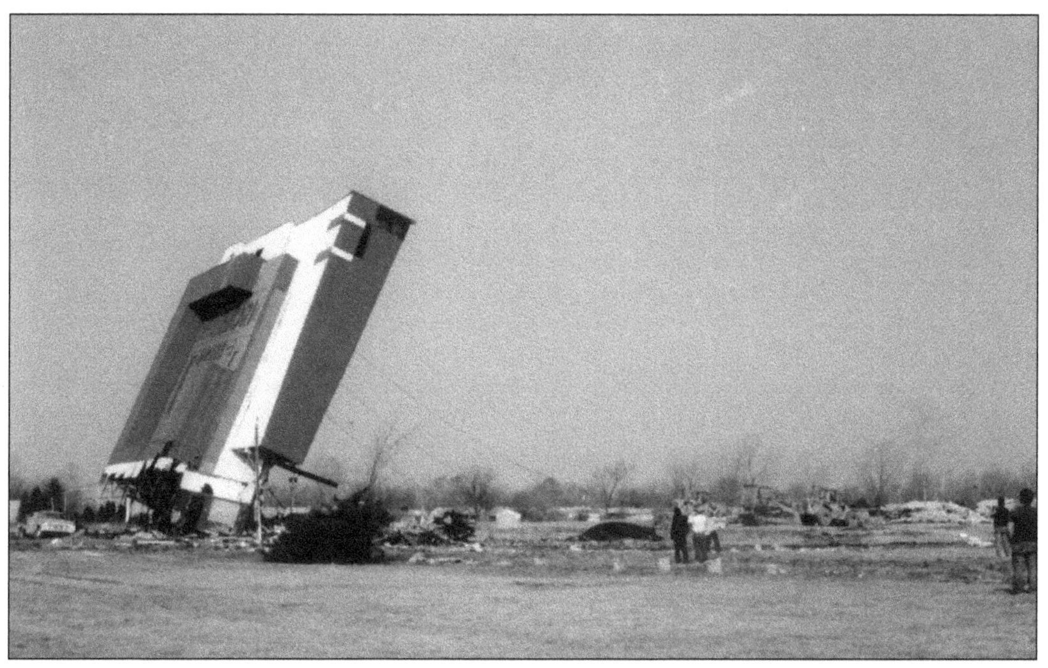

Going, Going, Gone. The bulldozers exert tension on the cables, and the screen is slowly pulled over. Despite its toppled condition, the structure remains remarkably intact, although enveloped in a cloud of dust. Contractors then cut the fallen tower to pieces and hauled away the sad remains. An empty lot suitable for a chain store is all that is left.

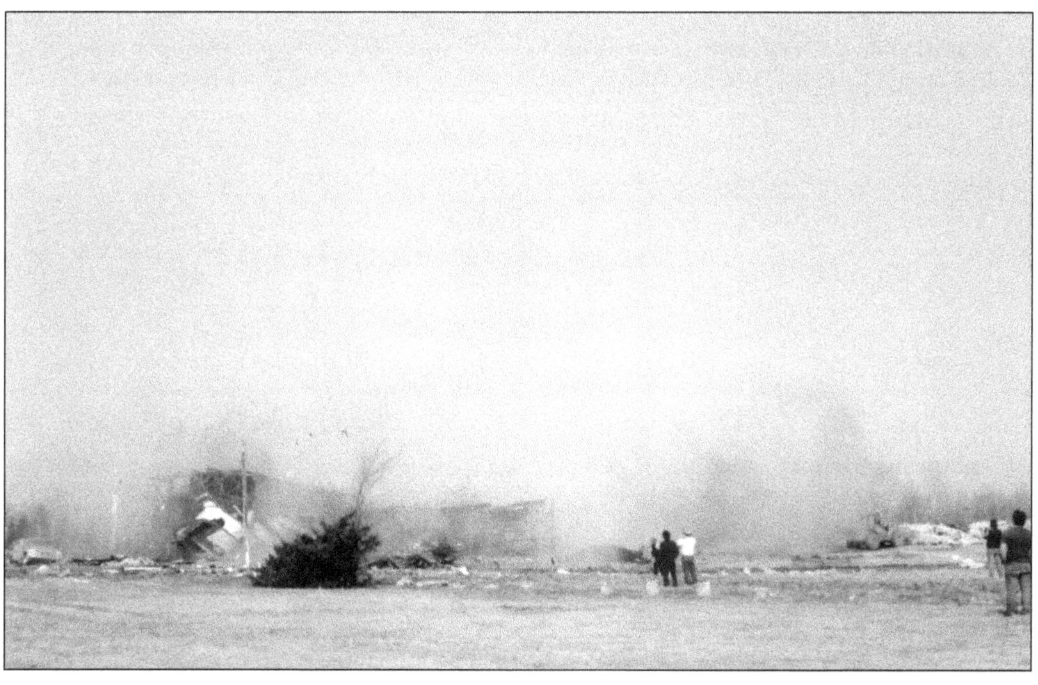

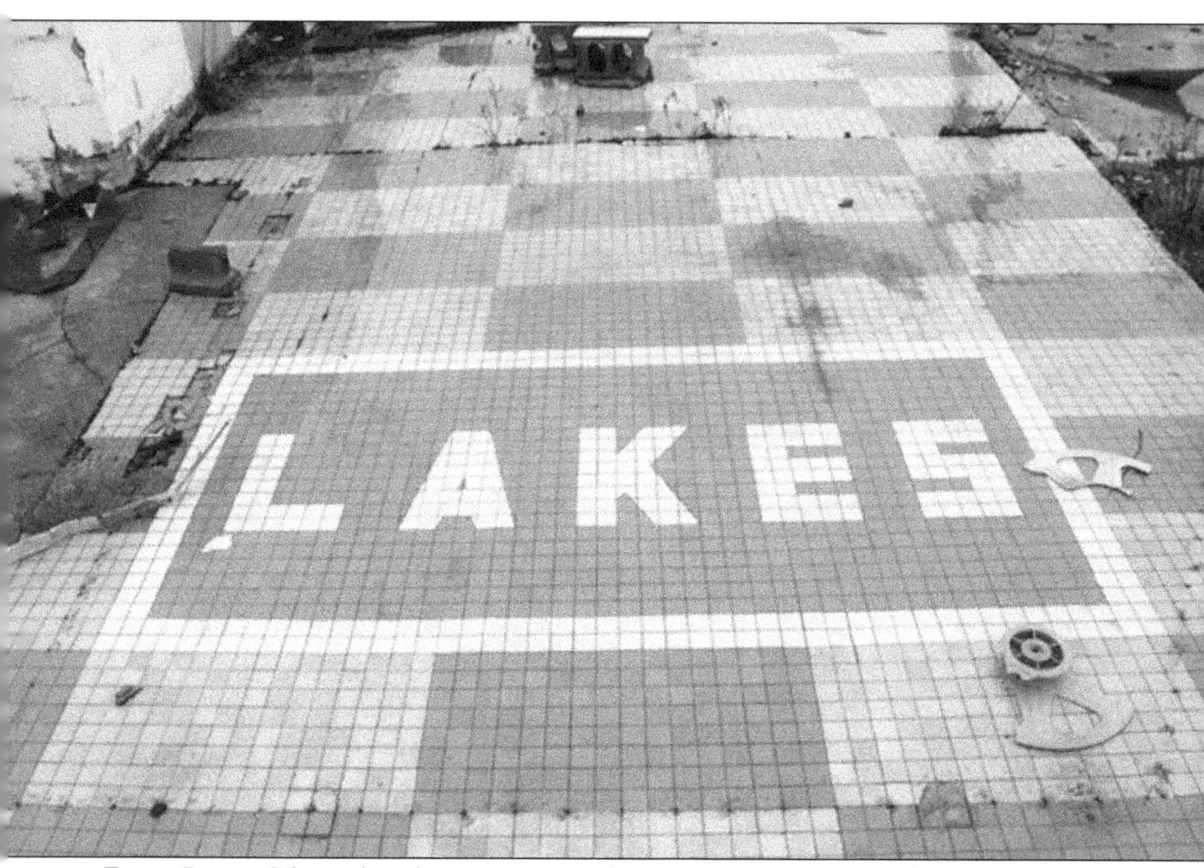

Empty Lakes. Often, when drive-ins are torn down but are not in areas where property values encourage new development, their remains linger on for years. Empty concession buildings, rusting projectors, and weathering screens are sometimes all that is left to suggest what was there. Such is the case with this building-less tile floor at the Lakes. (Courtesy of Gary Ritzenthaler.)

Ten

AFTER THE GOLDEN AGE

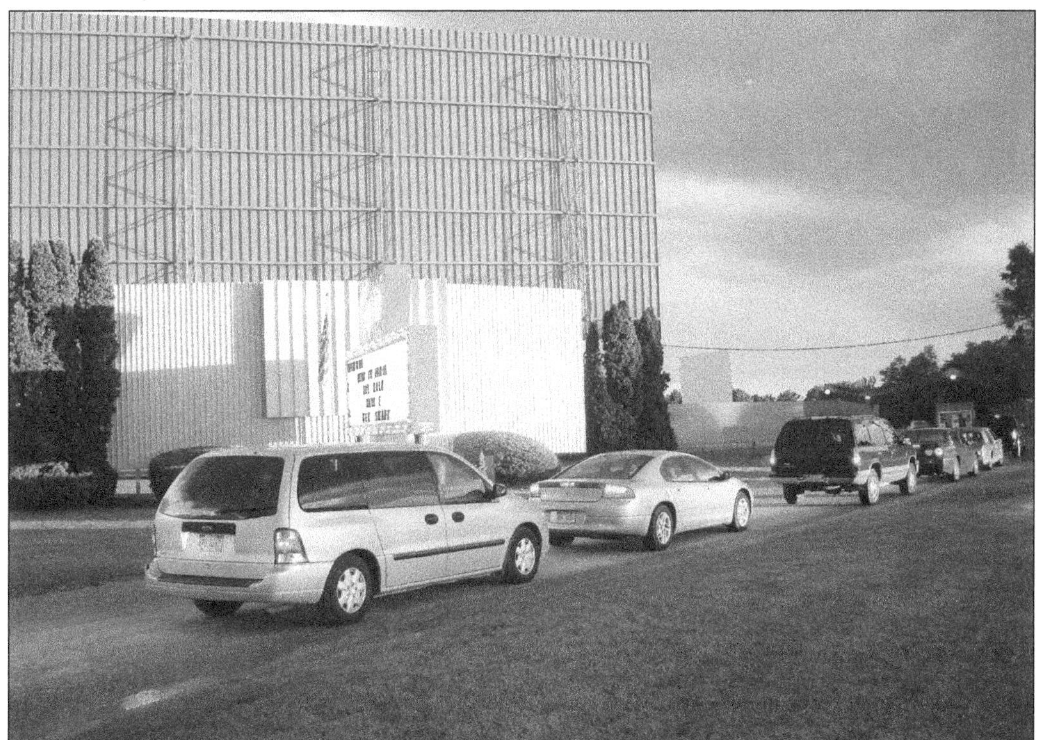

THE CAPRI. Although most drive-ins vanished by 1990, a few still remain. Preeminent among these is the Capri, in Coldwater. In 1964, the Magocs family built it, and they have operated it ever since. As seen in the picture, cars still line up to see first-run films every night during the temperate season. (Courtesy of Ron Gross.)

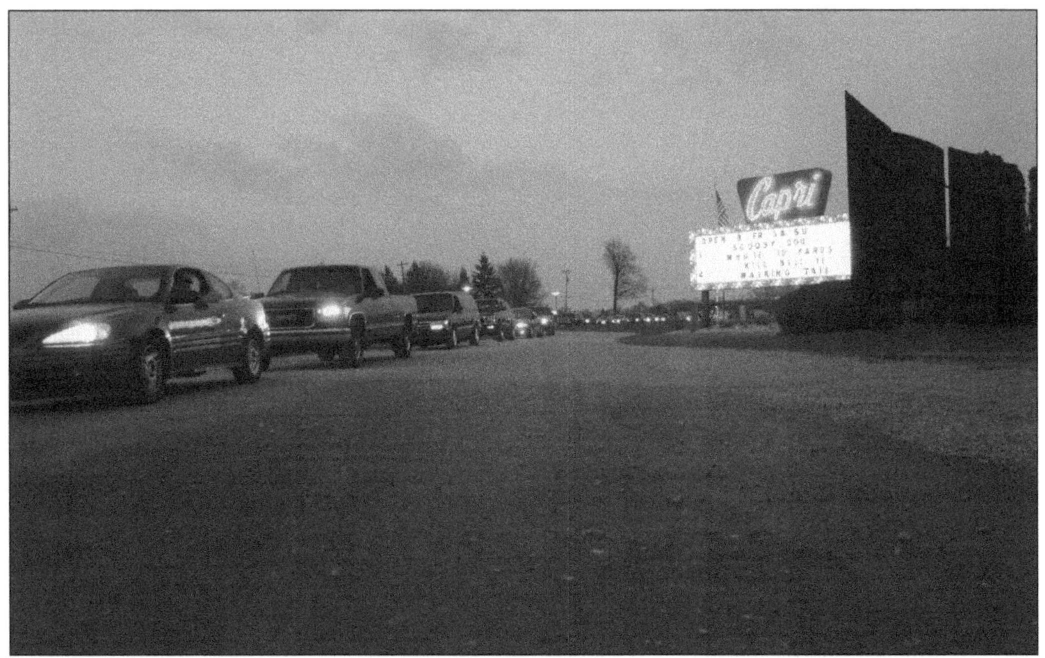

Lines of the Times. Michigan Avenue, west of Coldwater, is frequently backed up in the evening. Because the Capri was twinned from its originally 1,500-car capacity, four features are shown every night. The main screen, visible in front, has a slightly larger capacity than the second, which was erected in a rear corner of the lot. (Courtesy of Gary Ritzenthaler.)

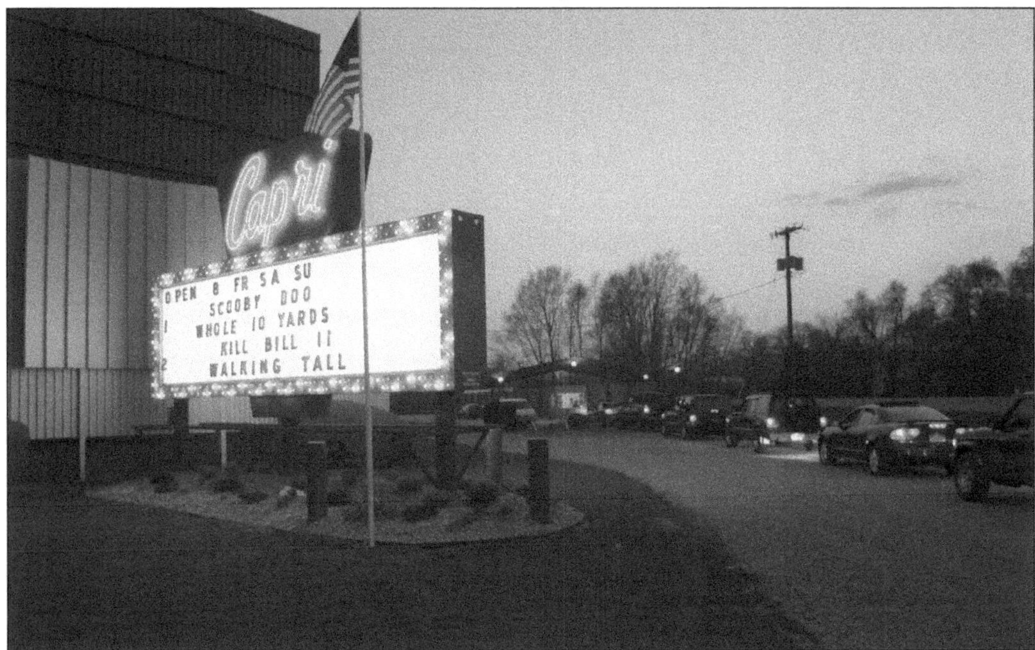

A Golden Hour. Here is another beautiful evening view of the Capri. Except for the age of the cars and the films advertised, it could well be the 1960s. The only concession to modernity is the removal of the in-car speakers in favor of FM radio sound. The Capri recently installed digital projection equipment, ensuring its continued operation. (Courtesy of Gary Ritzenthaler.)

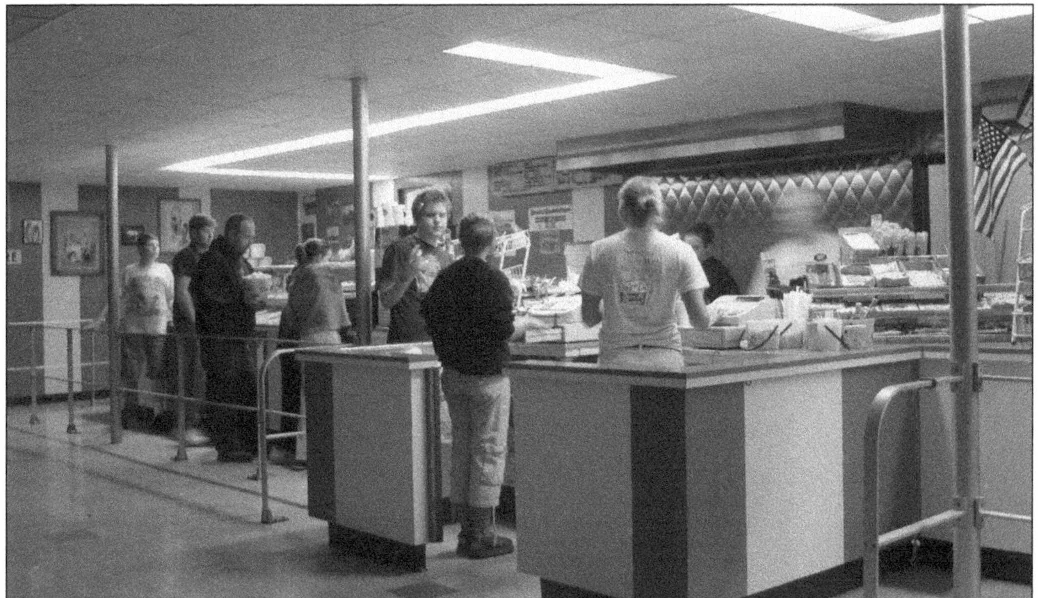

Food for Thought. The concession stand is also virtually unchanged from its original incarnation. Every night, one or both of the two cafeteria-style service counters is staffed, usually by a member of the Magocs family, and open for business. Again, except for the prices (cheeseburgers are no longer 50¢), it might be the 1960s. (Courtesy of Gary Ritzenthaler.)

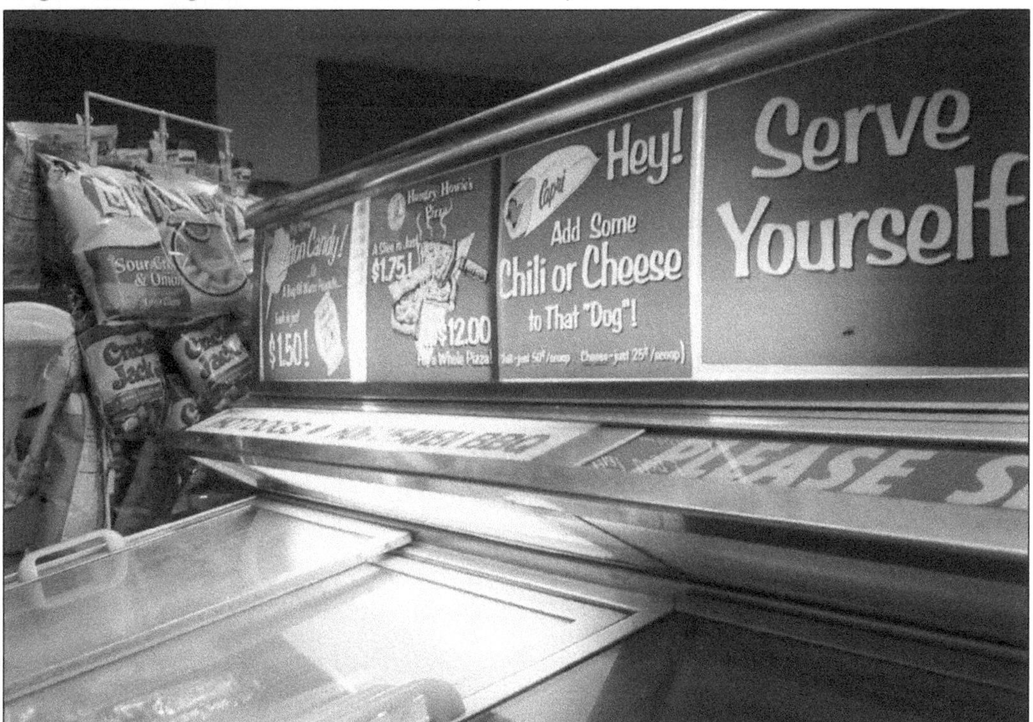

See the Capri. In the concession stand, there are warming cases that hold cheeseburgers and hot dogs and other tasty treats. They are encased in foil-paper envelopes, exactly as they were years ago. The popcorn is buttery, and the Coke is fizzy and cold. (Courtesy of Gary Ritzenthaler.)

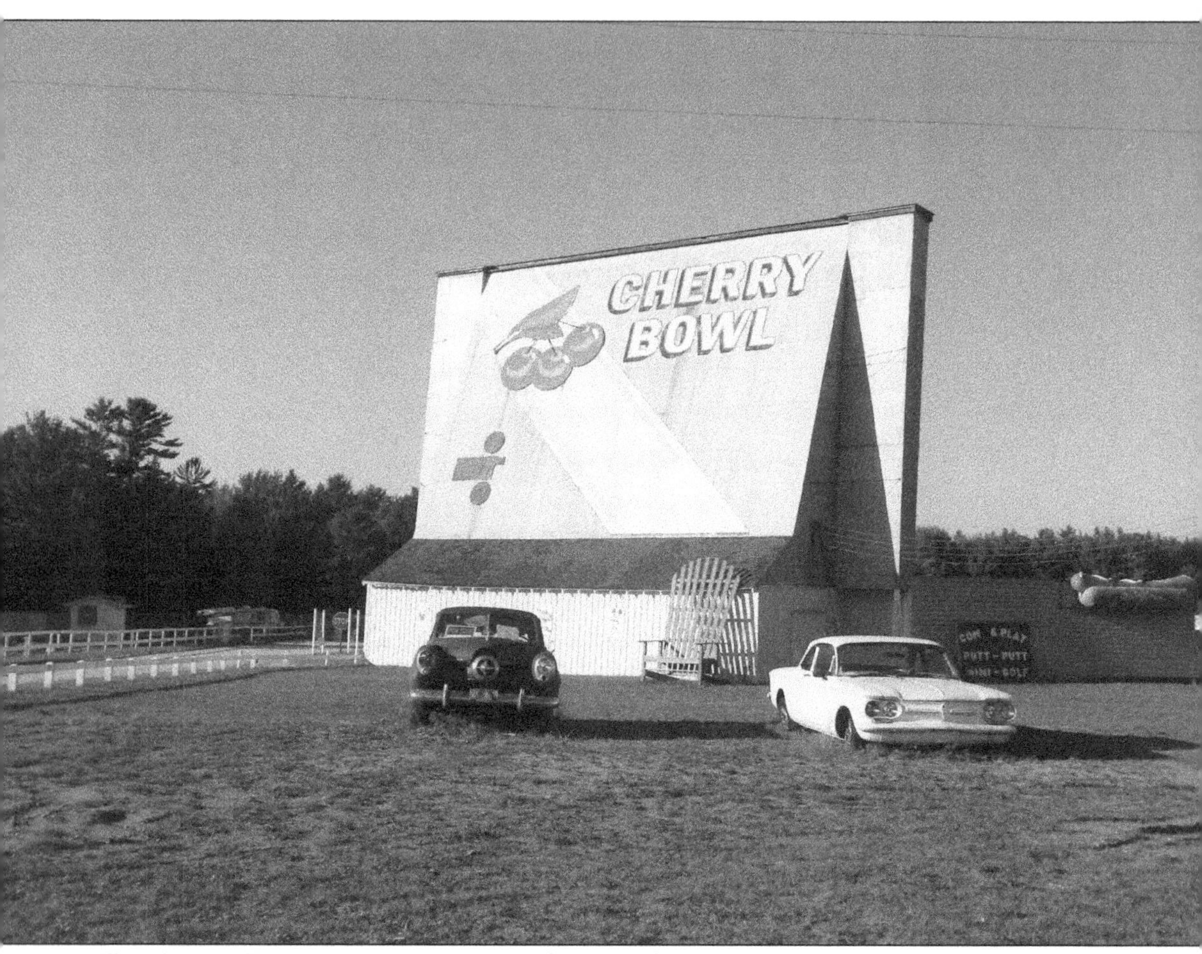

The Cherry Bowl. Near tiny Honor is the tiny Cherry Bowl, which is still popular and open every summer. Despite its 300-car capacity and its single screen, it is frequently filled. The recent conversion by the film industry from film to digital files put the Cherry Bowl's continued existence in jeopardy. (Courtesy of Ron Gross.)

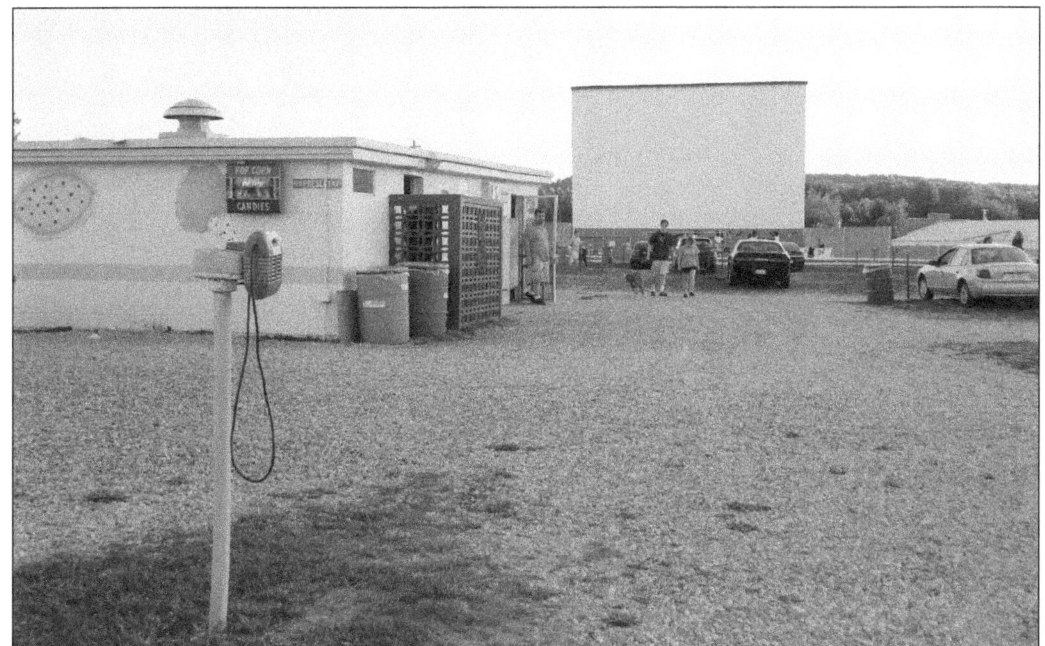

Little is a Lot. The tiny lot is filled with happy people when night falls. Families gather with lawn chairs and blankets; they stay in their cars or sprawl on their hoods or sit on their tailgates. Couples snuggle, kids in pajamas drowse, and others down the occasional beer. This is what going to the drive-in is all about.

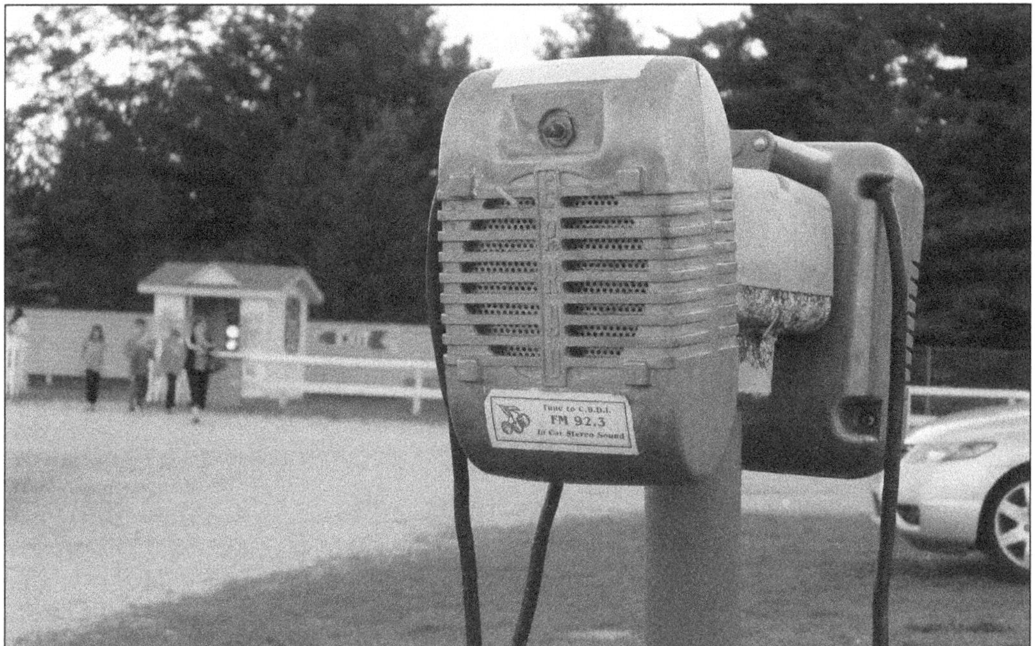

High-Tech. In 2013, the Cherry Bowl won a contest intended to bestow upon a poor but worthy drive-in a new digital projection system. The little Cherry Bowl's future is now all but assured well into the 21st century, so that future generations can enjoy popcorn and movies al fresco on those warm summer nights. (Courtesy of Ron Gross.)

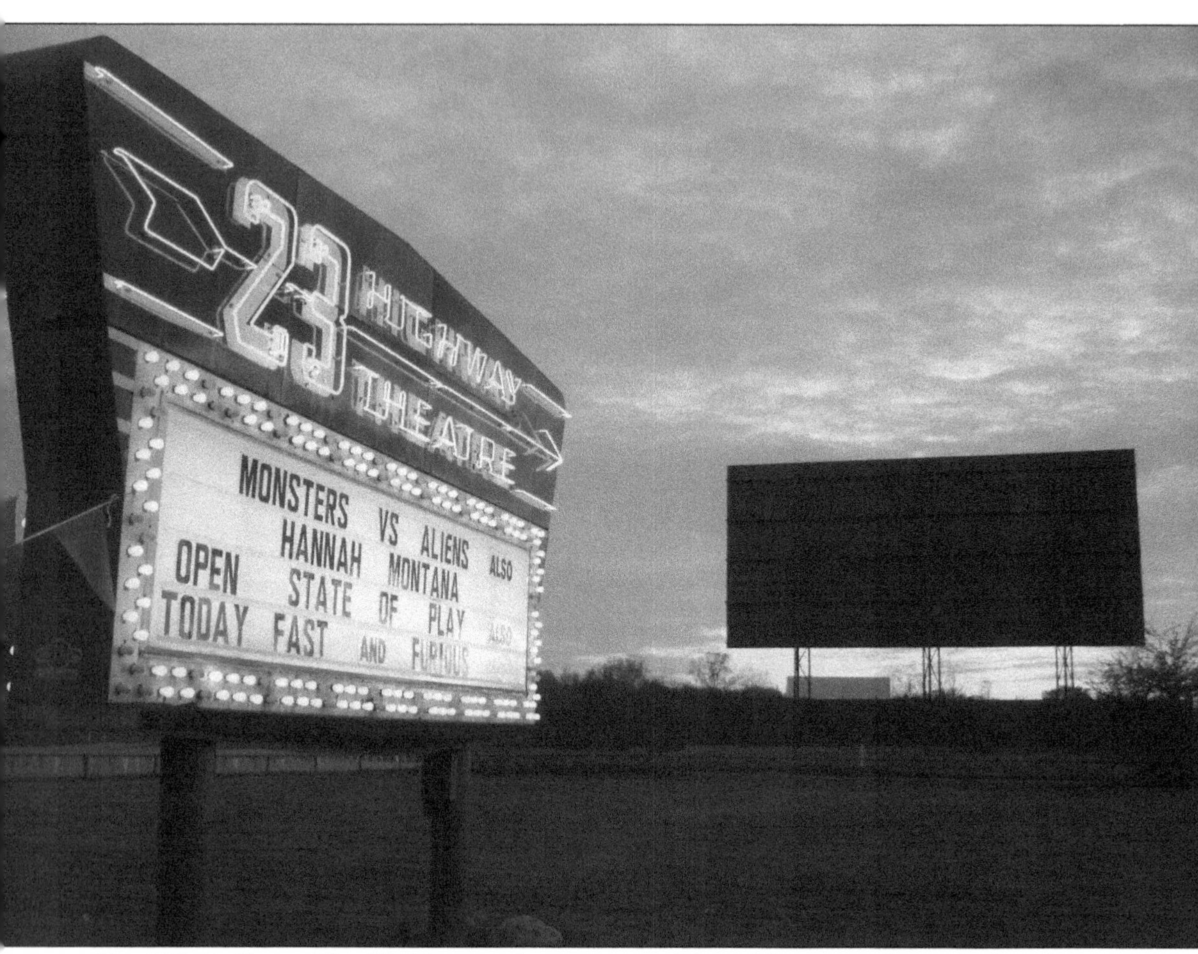

The US-23, Flint. The US-23 is another survivor of the golden age and was the last drive-in in the Flint area. Its original screen was destroyed by fire, but it was quickly replaced with a new one. It is less decorative, perhaps, but it does the job. The US-23 has a total of three screens today with all new digital projectors.

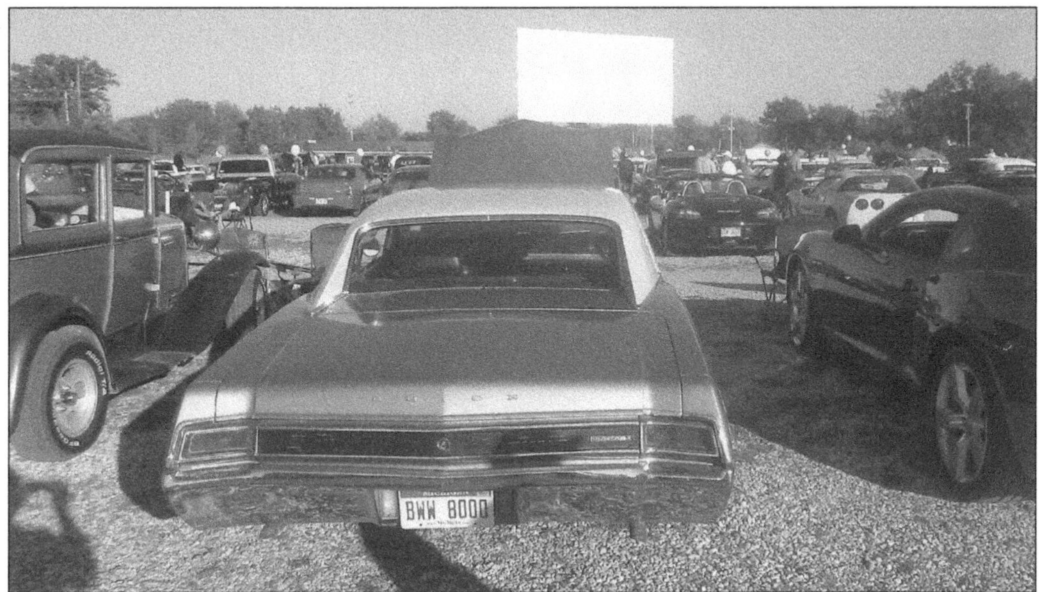

Cars of the Past. Frequently, drive-ins like the US-23, Cherry Bowl, and Capri hold special events such as classic car rallies, in recognition of their nostalgic roots. These events usually fill the lot and bring in additional visitors specifically for the cars. (Courtesy of Ron Gross.)

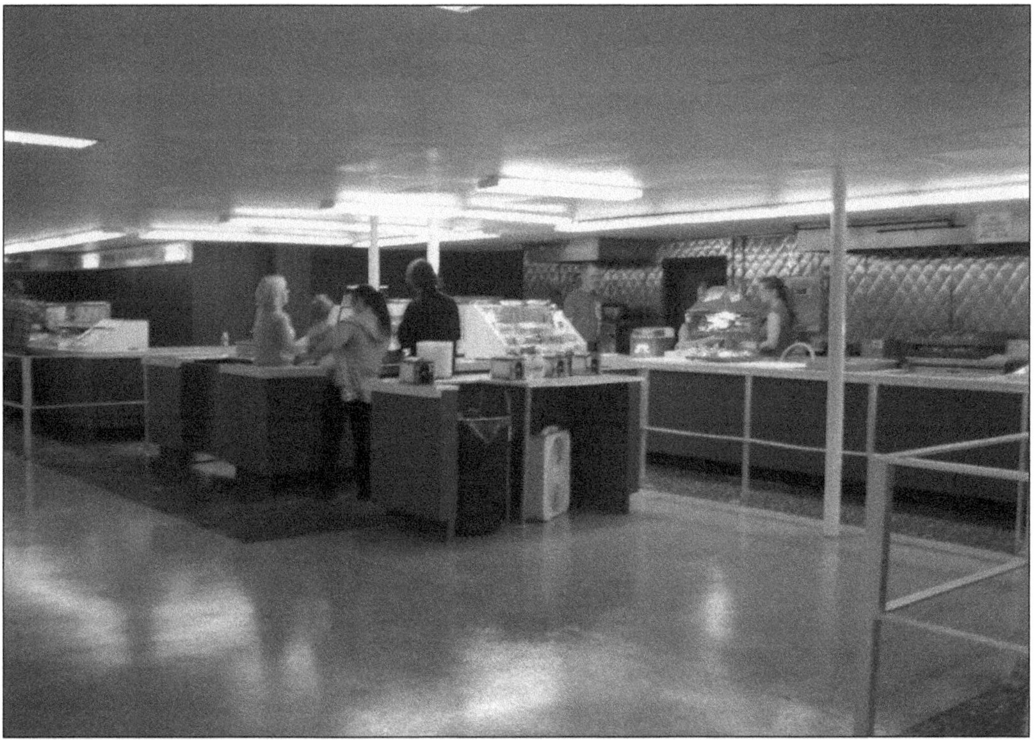

Another Concession. The concession stand at the US-23 is large and clean and still able to provide its many customers with lots of tasty treats. On warm summer nights, the residents of Flint can still enjoy comedies and car chases and spooky happenings from the comfort of their vehicles or lawn chairs or blankets. (Courtesy of Ron Gross.)

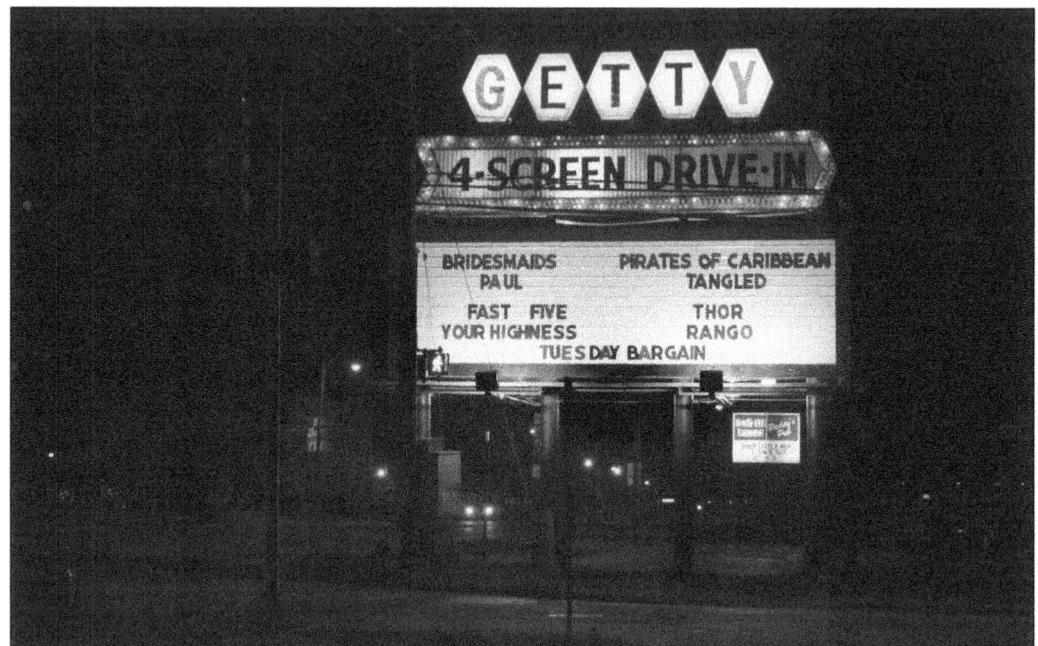

GETTY GOING. The Getty in Muskegon is still going strong, with its four screens alight every night during the summer. Unlike the days when the drive-ins were restricted to the showing of older films, the Getty shows a slate of first-run movies. It is a far cry from the days of the single-screen NK Drive-In. (Courtesy of Celebration Cinemas.)

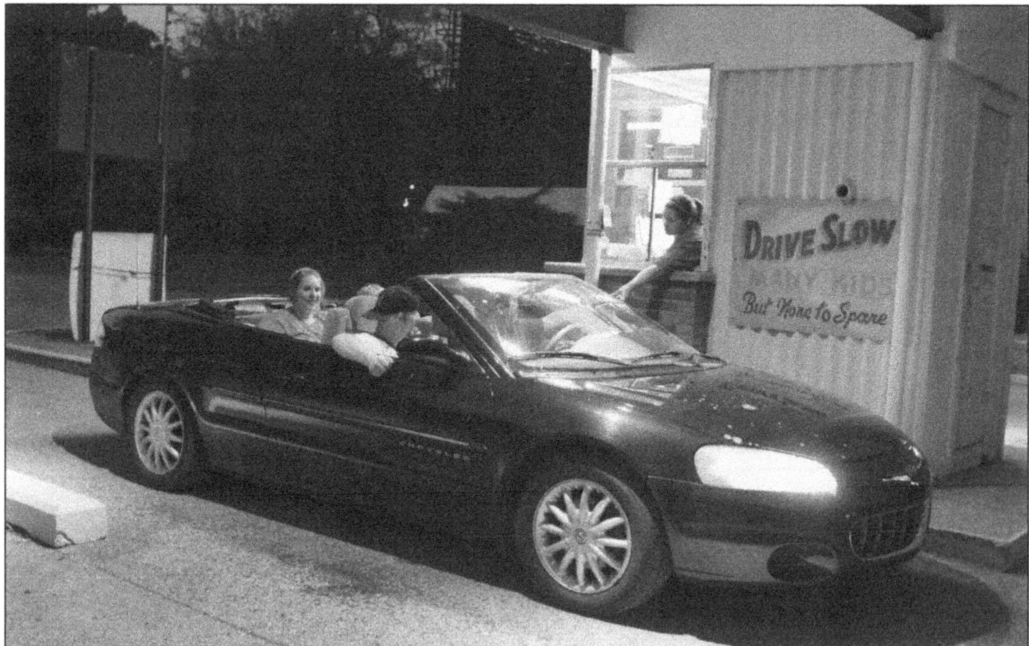

TICKETS ARE SOLD. Despite all sorts of other technological innovations, despite radio sound and higher resolution and brighter images, tickets are still sold by a person stepping out of a little booth and are exchanged for money by hand. It is part of the charm of the drive-in. Any automation of the process would just be wrong. (Courtesy of Celebration Cinemas.)

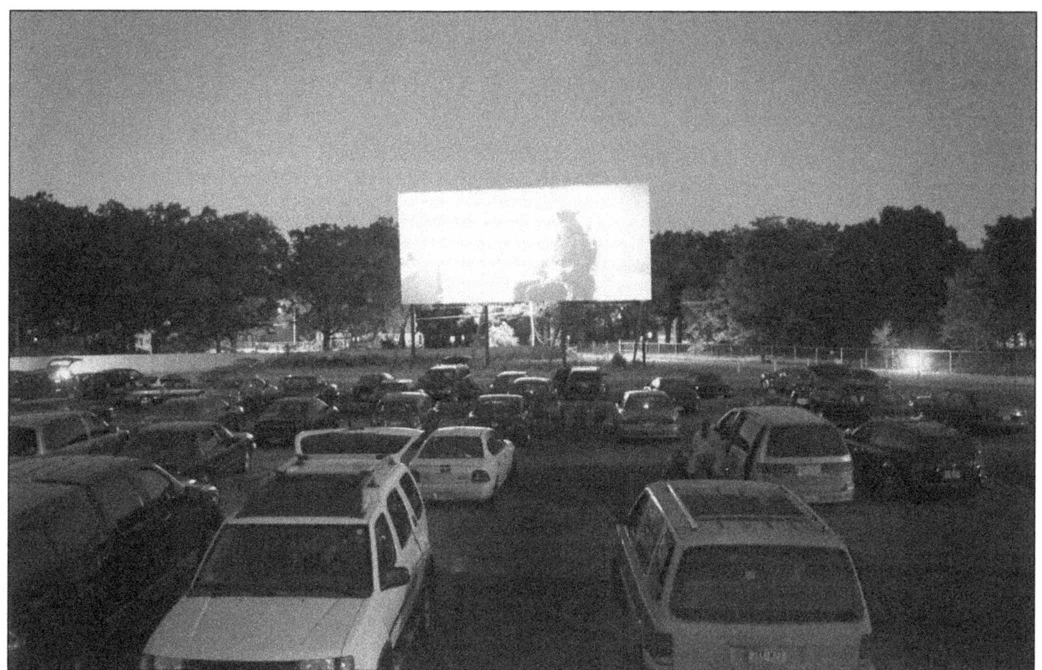

Picture This. Four screens and four brand-new sets of digital projection equipment are what will keep the Getty going into the 21st century. The Getty's owners decided that they would stay open for the foreseeable future, and it was necessary to upgrade—and so they did. (Courtesy of Celebration Cinemas.)

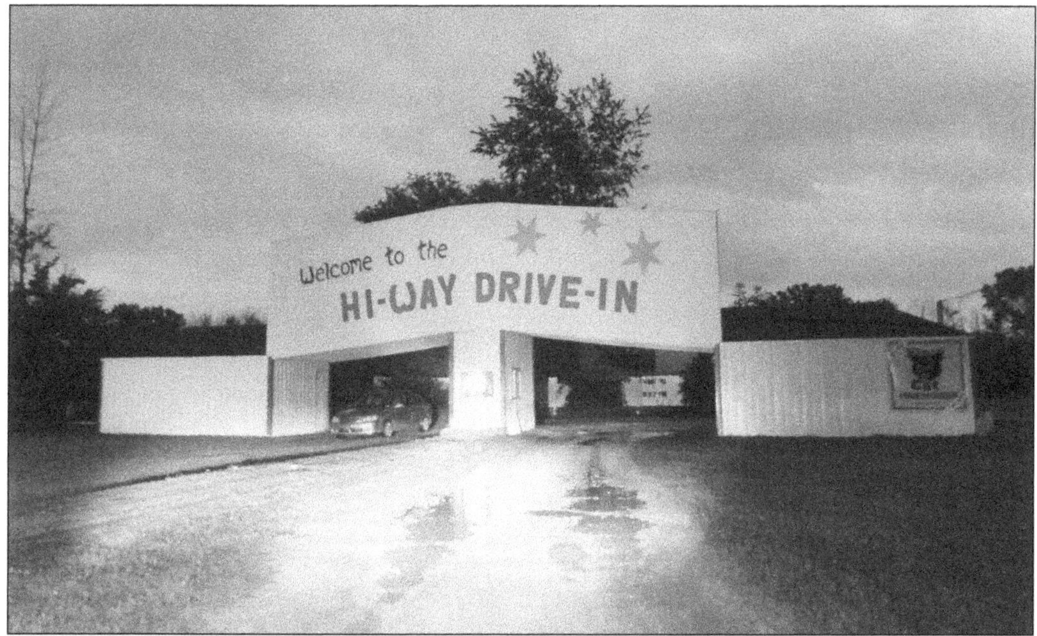

The Hi-Way Drive-In, Carsonville. The Hi-Way is not much different than when it opened. Although it was open for the 2013 summer season, the Hi-Way's future is far from certain. Still, the small country theaters do have less trouble with ambient light than the big city ones. Many city theaters had their pictures almost washed out in that way. (Courtesy of Ron Gross.)

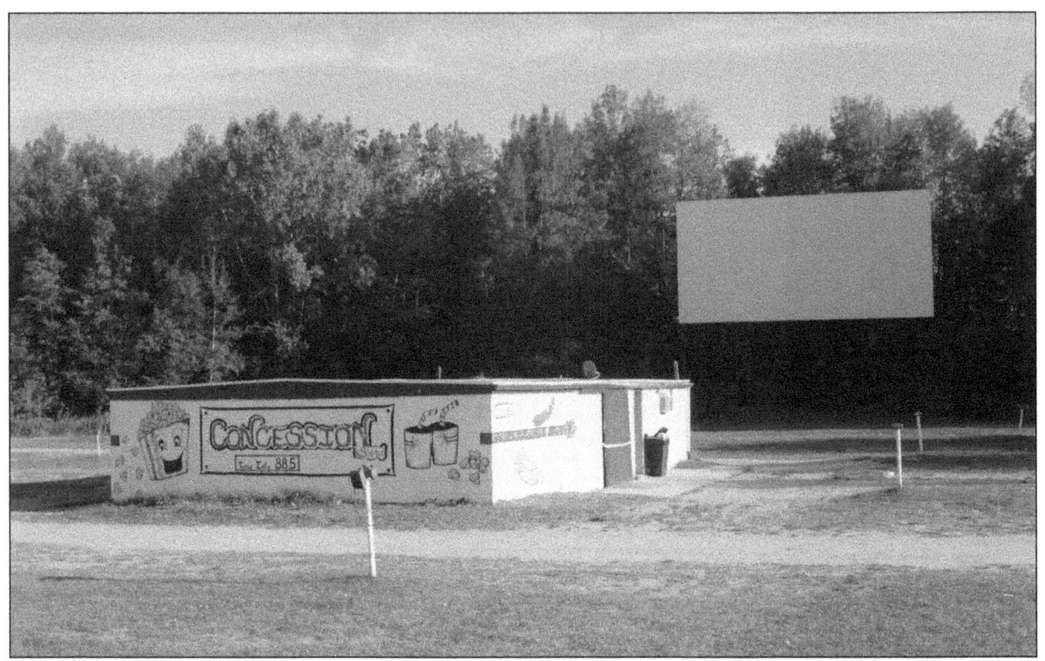

CONCESSION ART. The lot's small size is evident in this picture, as is the charming appearance of the concession-and-projection building. A 200-car drive-in this far out in the country without digital equipment would probably have a difficult time acquiring it. And without digital projection, a theater's future is not too bright. (Courtesy of Gary Ritzenthaler.)

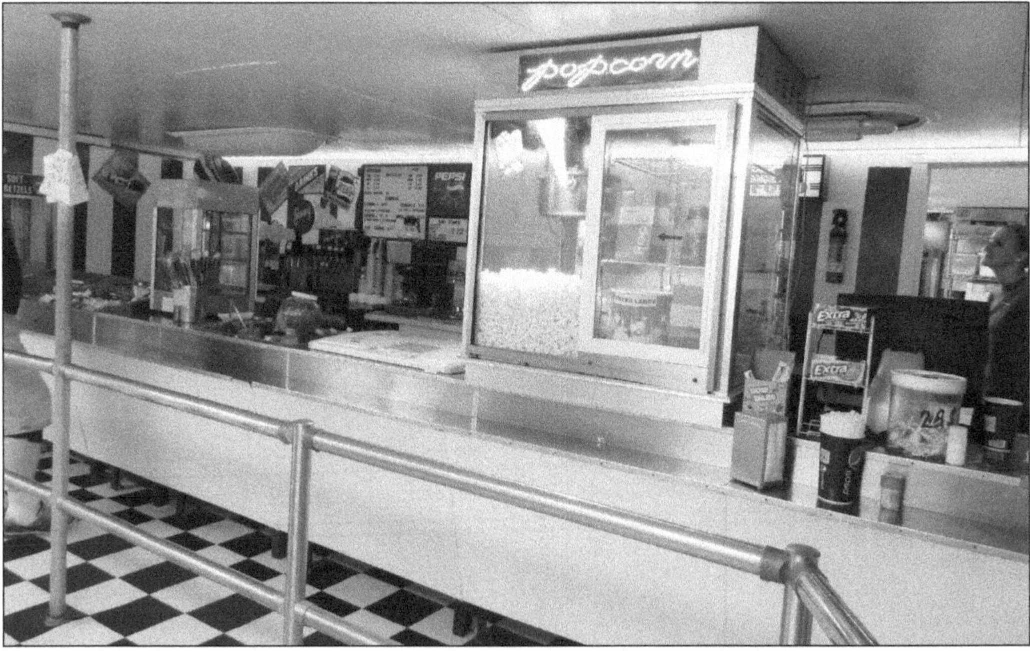

TOP OF THE POPS. Hot, buttered popcorn is still popped at the Hi-Way. In larger, mostly indoor theaters, only a small fraction of the popcorn is prepared on-site (enough for it to smell like popcorn), and the rest is purchased in large bags called "pillows" and mixed with the fresh popcorn—but not at the Hi-Way. (Courtesy of Ron Gross.)

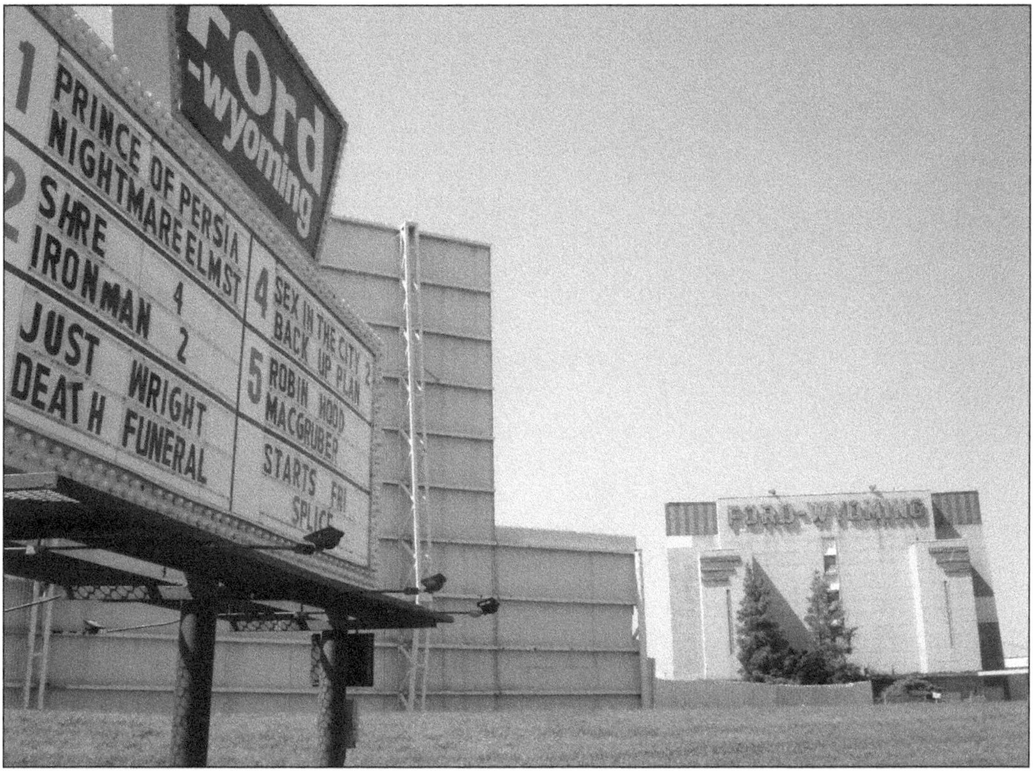

NOTHING KEEPS RUNNING LIKE THE FORD. The Ford-Wyoming (the Ford), in Dearborn, can claim two distinctions—that it is the last remaining drive-in in the Detroit area and that it has been the largest drive-in in the country. With a current complement of five screens, it is down from its peak of nine, but it is still an elaborate facility. (Courtesy of Ron Gross.)

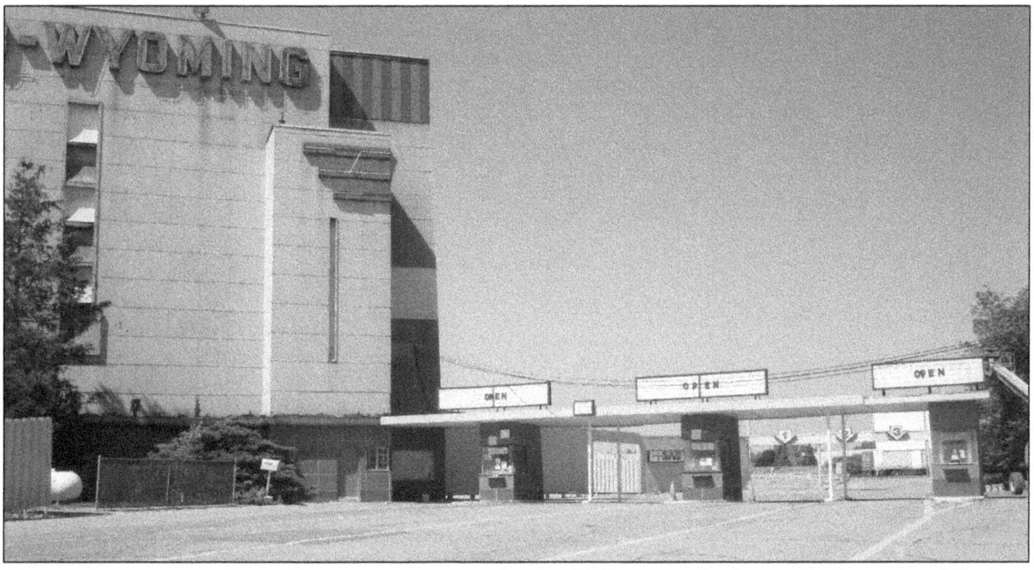

TICKET LANES. Seen from this vantage point, the Ford-Wyoming looks much the way it did when it was new. Sure, the screen is wider, and there is much more cinematic variety, but otherwise a motorist arriving in his 1950 Studebaker would be right at home. (Courtesy of Ron Gross.)

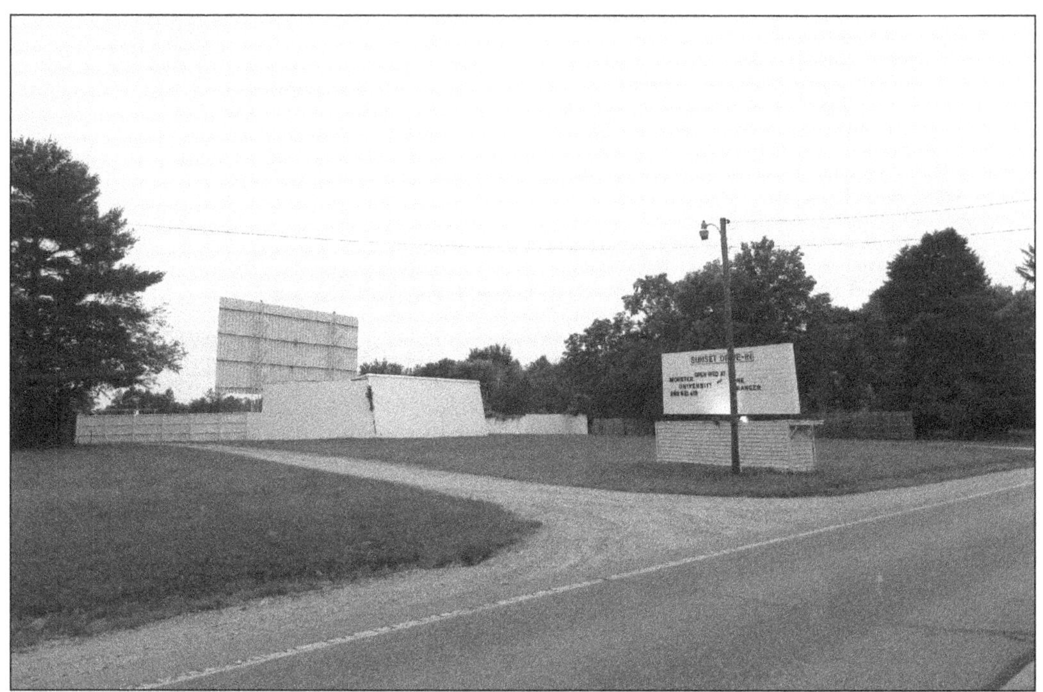

ANOTHER SUNSET. The Sunset Auto Theatre, in Hartford, opened with a 288-car capacity in 1948. It currently exemplifies the same small drive-in experience (except for the absence of speakers) as it always did, with its clean lot and tasty food at reasonable prices. (Courtesy of Ron Gross.)

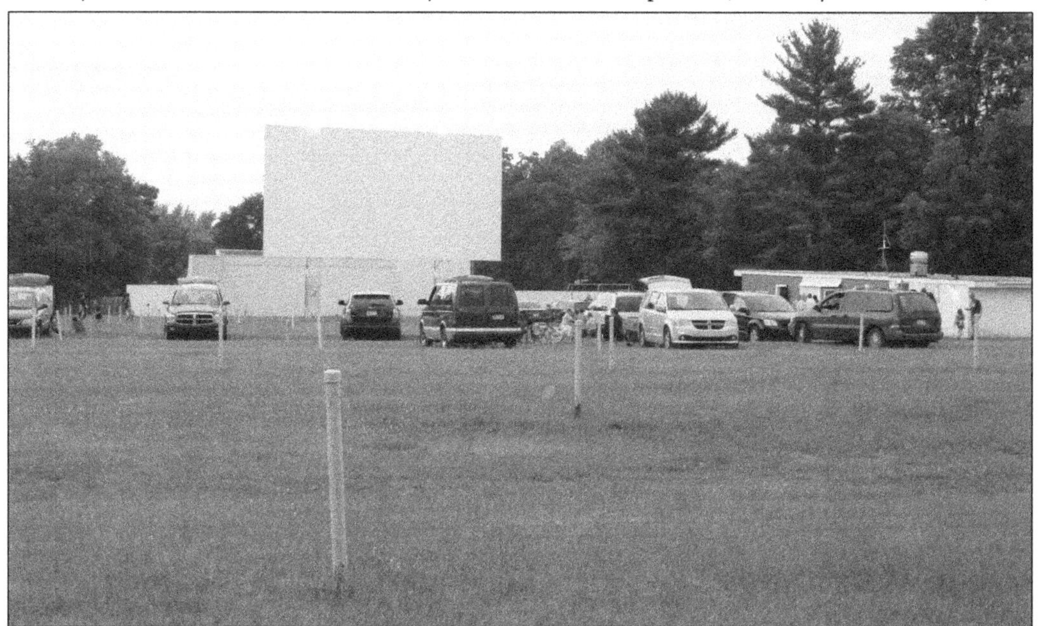

GRASSY LOT. As with most of the small drive-ins, the Sunset has a grass-covered lot. The amount of wear and tear is not sufficient to generate much mud, and the grass is pleasant to roll one's sleeping bag out upon. Note the early customers who have backed their SUVs up so they can watch from the rear; station wagons used to be the style of car to back into parking spaces. (Courtesy of Ron Gross.)

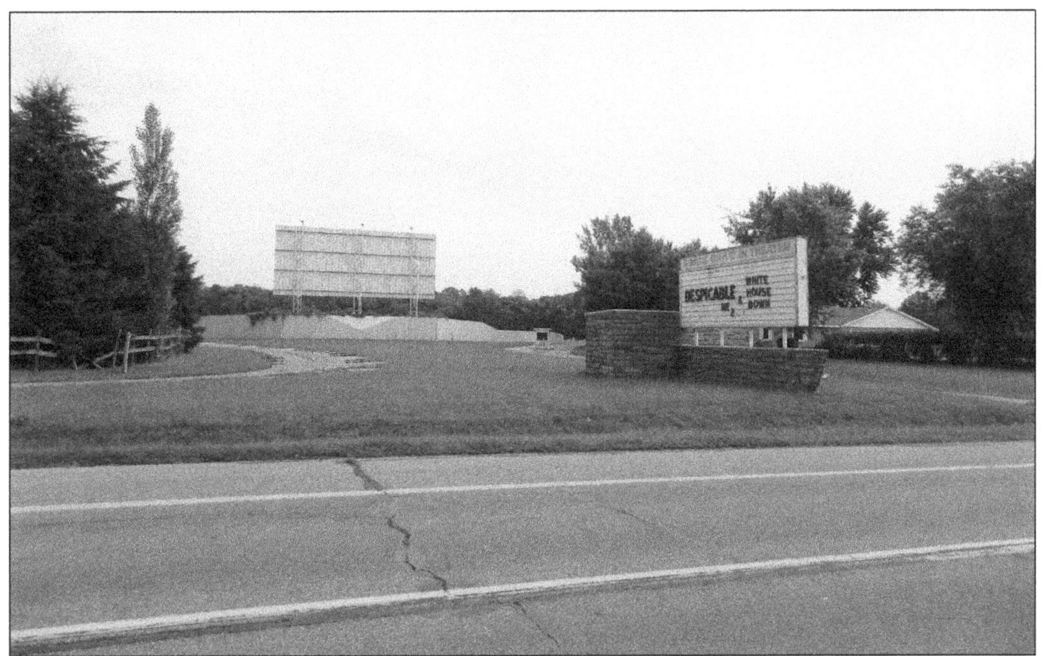

The 5-Mile Drive-In. The 5-Mile, in Dowagiac, was a late entrant to the drive-in game, dating from only the early 1960s, but because of this, it came with all the amenities a little theater could want. If there appears to be a resemblance between the 5-Mile and Sunset, it is because Neal and Glenda Edwards operate both of them. (Courtesy of Ron Gross.)

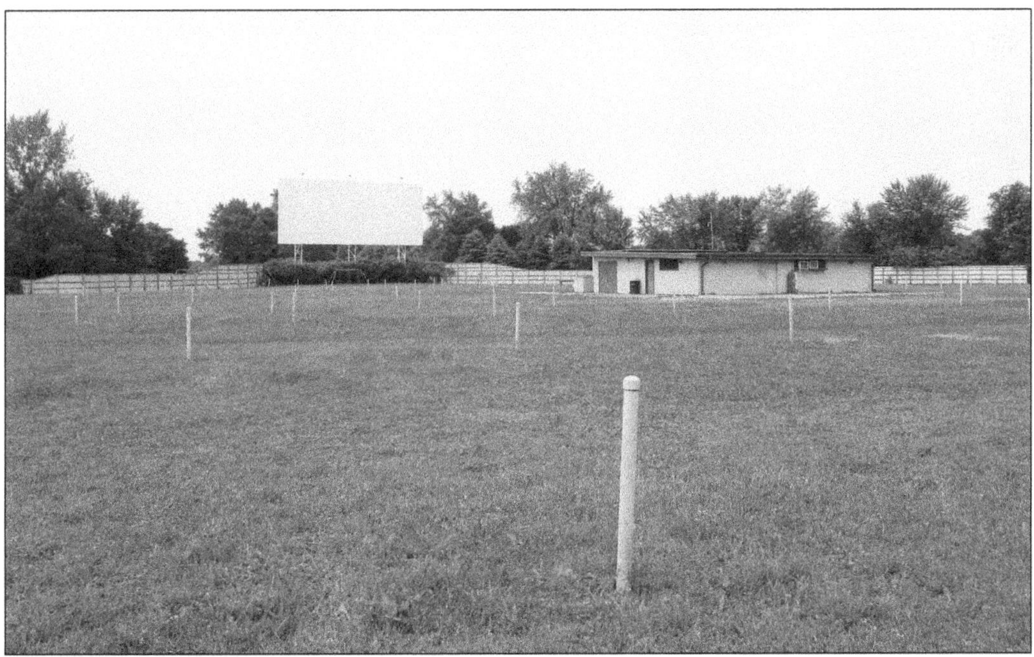

The 5-Mile Lot. Again, very similar to the Sunset, the lot (or "ramps" in drive-in jargon) of the 5-Mile is grassy and tidy. Note the attractive landscaping at the base of the screen. Both the Sunset and 5-Mile are on the endangered list because, as of this writing, they have not yet changed to digital projection. Only time will tell as to their fates. (Courtesy of Ron Gross.)

List of Drive-Ins

Location	Name	Capacity	Screen Number	Page(s)
Addison	Starlite	300	1	-
Adrian	Lenawee	300	1–2	-
Adrian	Sky	280	1	50, 51
Albion	Albion	290	1	-
Algonic	Seaway	700	1	-
Alpena	Alpena	275	1	-
Alpena	Thunder Bay	500	1	94
Ann Arbor	Scio	400	1	48, 49
Ann Arbor	University	1,033	1	2, 52, 53
Ann Arbor	Ypsi-Ann	500	1	54
Bad Axe	M-53	300	1	-
Baldwin	Pine Aire	265	1	-
Battle Creek	Auto	500	1	66–68
Battle Creek	West Point	600	1	-
Bay City	Starlite	650	1–2	60
Bay City	Tuscola	600	1	62
Bay Shore	Northland	282	1	-
Belleville	Willow	1,000	1	44
Benton Harbor	Starlight	450	1	-
Big Rapids	Drive-In	328	1	75, 76
Brighton	Lakes	500	1	47
Burnside	Burnside	400	1	59
Burton	Miracle Twin	915	2	-
Cadillac	Cadillac	300	1	-
Caro	Caro	500	1	57-59
Carsonville	Hiway	400	1	119, 120
Caseville	Blue Sky	250	1	56
Charlotte	Maple City	400	1	-
Chassel	Hiawatha	400	1	93
Cheboygan	Cheboygan	300	1	89
Clare	Northland	500	1	-
Coldwater	Coldwater	265	1	-
Coldwater	Capri	1,000	1–2	111–113
Corunna	Skyway	500	1	-
Dearborn	Dearborn	1,040	1	24, 108, 109
Dearborn	Ecorse	1,050	1–2	24, 25
Dearborn	Ford Wyoming	750	1–9	26, 27, 107
Dearborn	Jolly Roger	1,000	1	37, 38, 121
Detroit	Belair Twin	1,750	2–4	21–23
Detroit	Eastside	650	1	-
Detroit	Westside	700	1	43
Dowagiac	5-Mile North	452	1	123
East Tawas	Tawas	250	1	-
Escanaba	Hilltop	500	1	69
Escanaba	Kenmar	500	1	-
Farmington	Grand River	750	1–3	32, 33
Flint	South Dort	775	1	55
Flint	Northland	1,000	1	-

Flint	Flint	750	1	-
Flint	US-23	1,500	1–3	63, 64, 116, 117
Flint	Westside	500	1	55
Gaylord	Sky-Hi	318	1	-
Gladwin	Meredith	350	1	-
Grand Rapids	Beltline	250	1–3	77–80, 107
Grand Rapids	Cascade	2,500	2–3	81, 82, 106
Grand Rapids	Division	550	1	-
Grand Rapids	Drive-In	600	1	-
Grand Rapids	Plainfield	998	1	-
Grand Rapids	Vista	1,300	1	88
Greenville	Drive-In	350	1	-
Hartford	Sunset	288	1	122
Hastings	Drive-In	275	1	-
Hillsdale	Drive-In	175	1	-
Honor	Cherry Bowl	250	1	90, 114, 115
Houghton Lake	55-HI	250	1	-
Hubbard Lake	Sky-View	200	1	-
Hubbard Lake	Paul Bunyan	300	1	-
Ionia	Ionia	350	1	-
Iron Mountain	Tri-City	390	1	-
Ironwood	Ironwood	390	1	-
Ishpeming	Evergreen	200	1	92
Jackson	Belair	550	1	-
Jackson	Jackson	520	1	65
Kalamazoo	Douglas	680	1	83
Kalamazoo	Portage	400	1	-
Lake Linden	Lakes	350	1	94, 110
Lansing	M-78 Twin	1,000	2–3	-
Lansing	Northside	400	1	71, 72
Lansing	Crest	800	1	68
Lansing	Drive-In	400	1	69, 70
Lansing	Starlite	700	1	73–75
Lapeer	Sunset	527	1	61, 62
Linden	Silver	400	1	-
Madison Heights	Galaxy	1,400	1	30, 31
Manistee	Chippewa	276	1	90, 91
Manistique	Highway-2	350	1	-
Marlette	H&S	280	1	-
Marquette	Outdoor	450	1	-
Marysville	Marysville	550	1	-
Mendon	M-60	250	1	-
Midland	Sunset	470	1	-
Mio	Dai-Roy	300	1	-
Monroe	Denniston	1,000	1	45–46
Monroe	Dixie	300	1	46
Monroe	General Custer	300	1	46
Morenci	Skyline Auto Theatre	200	1	51
Mt. Clemens	Mt. Clemens	1,000	1	-
Munising	Superior	200	1	-
Muskegon	Auto	400	1	-
Muskegon	North	650	1	-

Muskegon	Getty	750	1–4	83, 84, 118, 119
Negaunee	Airport	500	1	-
Niles	Niles	870	1–2	84, 85
Petoskey	Northland	282	1	60
Pinconning	Bay	300	1	-
Plainwell	131	298	1	-
Pontiac	Blue Sky	700	1	56
Pontiac	Miracle Mile	1,540	1	40
Pontiac	Pontiac	720	1	41
Port Huron	Lakeshore	600	1	-
Redford	Town	1000	1	41
Rosebush	Sundown	380	1	-
Roseville	Gratiot	1,000	1–2	14, 33–35, 127
Royal Oak	Oak	1,000	1	-
Saginaw	Belair	700	1	-
Saginaw	Twilite	650	1	-
St. Johns	Family	350	1	-
St. Joseph	St. Joe	450	1	-
St. Louis	Sky Top	400	1	-
Sandusky	Hiway	400	1	-
Saugatuck	Starlight	300	1	86, 87
Sault Ste. Marie	Starlite	400	1	-
Scottville	Starlite	284	1	-
Spring Lake	M-104	500	1	-
Spring Lake	Ottawa	300	1	-
Spring Lake	Oasis	500	1	-
Stevensville	St. Joe Auto Theatre	450	1	-
Sturgis	Sturgis	280	1	-
Traverse City	Sundowner Twin	?	2	-
Traverse City	Traverse City	350	1	-
Trenton	Holiday	1,140	1	36
Troy	Troy	1,200	1	-
Van Dyke	Van Dyke	750	1-3	-
Walled Lake	Commerce	1,065	1	-
Walled Lake	Walalake	1,200	1	-
Walled Lake	Walled Lake	700	1	-
Waterford	Drive-In	600	1	-
Watertown	Star-Lite	280	1	-
Wayne	Algiers	1,000	1	20, 105
Wayne	Wayne	842	1–4	42
White Cloud	M-37	250	1	-
Wyandotte	Fort George	1,000	1	cover, 28, 29
Wyandotte	Michigan	1,000	1	38, 39
Toledo Area				
Maumee	Maumee	375	1–2	100, 101
Toledo	Eastside	375	1	-
Toledo	Franklin Park	500	1	95–97
Toledo	Jesse James	1,134	1	98, 99
Toledo	Miracle Mile	1,500	1–2	102
Toledo	Starlite	996	1	-
Toledo	Parkside	500	1–2	103
Toledo	Telegraph	500	1	104

Contact Information

5-Mile Drive-In
28190 State Route M-152
Dowagiac, MI 49047

Capri Drive-In
119 West Chicago Road
Coldwater, MI 49036

Cherry Bowl Drive-In
9812 Honor Highway
Honor, MI 49640

Ford-Wyoming Drive-In
10400 Ford Road
Dearborn, MI 48126
Getty Drive-In
920 East Summit Avenue
Muskegon, MI 49444

Hi-Way Drive-In
2778 East Sanilac Road
Carsonville, MI 48471

Sunset Auto Theatre
69017 Red Arrow Highway
Hartford, MI 49057

US-23 Drive-In
5200 Fenton Road
Flint, MI 48507

Harryskrdla.com

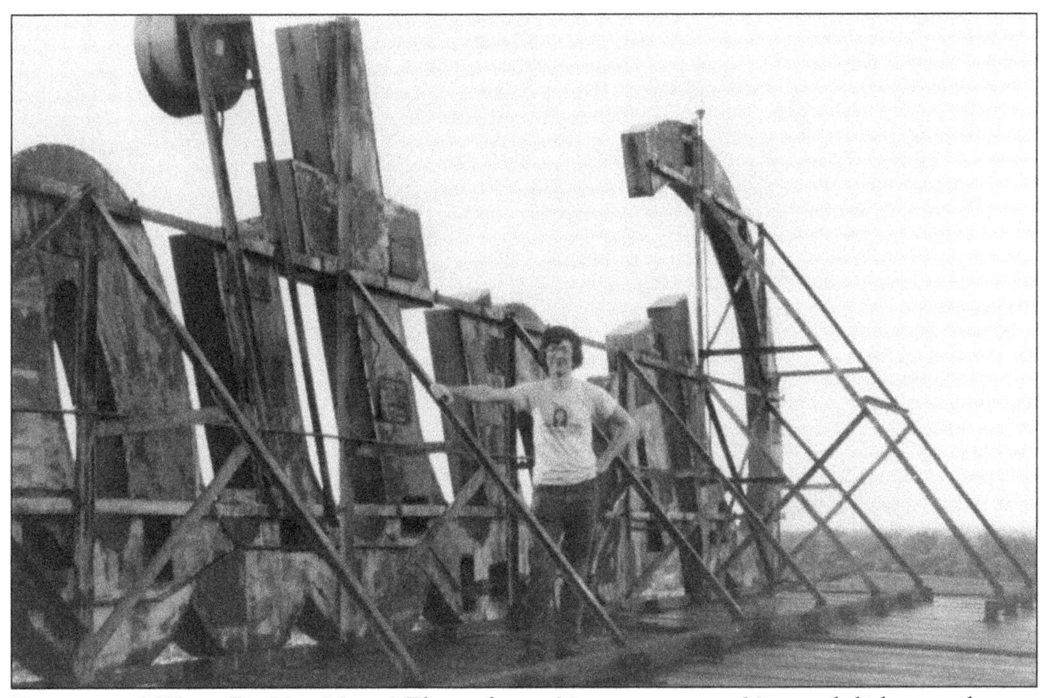

Dangerous? What Do You Mean? The author—30 years younger, 30 pounds lighter, and many shades of hair color darker—is seen here atop the Gratiot Drive-In's screen tower the day before its demolition in 1984. The top was reached by means of a long, unguarded ladder located near the long-disused waterfall pump inside the screen.

Visit us at
arcadiapublishing.com

www.ingramcontent.com/pod-product-compliance
Lightning Source LLC
LaVergne TN
LVHW060625110826
845147LV00015B/943

* 9 7 8 1 4 6 7 1 1 2 3 3 8 *